Women, Drugs

The Experiences of Women Drug Users in Prison

Margaret S Malloch is Senior Lecturer and Course Leader in Critical Criminology at the Centre for Studies in Crime and Social Justice at Edge Hill. She has conducted extensive research into women's experiences of imprisonment, prison systems in the UK, and responses to violence against women. She received a doctoral degree from Lancaster University in 1996 for her thesis entitled *Caring for Drug Users? The Experiences of Women Drug Users in Prison*. That research provided the impetus for this book.

Women, Drugs and Custody
The Experiences of Women Drug Users in Prison
Margaret S Malloch

Published 2000 by
WATERSIDE PRESS
Domum Road
Winchester SO23 9NN
United Kingdom

Telephone or Fax: 01962 855567
E-mail: watersidepress@compuserve.com
Online catalogue and bookstore: www.watersidepress.co.uk

Copyright: Margaret S Malloch. All rights reserved. No part of this book may be reproduced, stored in any retrieval system or transmitted in any form or by any means, including over the Internet, without prior permission.

ISBN 1 872 870 91 0

Catalogue-In-Publication Data: A catalogue record for this book can be obtained from the British Library

Printing and binding: Antony Rowe Ltd, Chippenham

Cover design: John Good Holbrook Ltd, Coventry. Artwork for front cover by Hannelie Grobler.

Women, Drugs and Custody

The Experiences of Women Drug Users in Prison

Margaret S Malloch

WATERSIDE PRESS

WINCHESTER

Acknowledgements

I am very grateful to everyone who participated in the research for *Women, Drugs and Custody*. Thanks go to all the prison governors who provided me with access, to the prison officers, medical and nursing staff, drugs workers and other staff and individuals who shared their views and experiences.

A number of people have helped me to complete this book by offering support, advice and encouragement. I would like to thank my friends and colleagues in the Centre for Studies in Crime and Social Justice, particularly Phil Scraton, Kathryn Chadwick, Karen Corteen and Elizabeth Stanley for the invaluable comments and constructive advice they provided as the research developed. Thanks also to Barbara Houghton, Eileen Berrington, Ann Jemphrey and Linda Moore. I am very grateful to Barbara Hudson for her advice, enthusiasm and encouragement. I value the continued support given to me by Anne and Donald Malloch and the ongoing encouragement provided by Alison and Donald.

Last, but by no means least, I would like to express my gratitude to all the women in prison who took part, and who were prepared to discuss very personal issues in the difficult surroundings of the prison in order to provide an insight into their experiences. I hope that this book will raise awareness of the reality of imprisonment for women, and particularly for women who use drugs, and will go some way towards making changes.

Margaret S Malloch

December 2000

Women, Drugs and Custody

CONTENTS

Acknowledgements *iv*

Chapter

1. Introduction *7*

2. The Imprisonment of Women *21*

3. The Social Construction of Drug Use *43*

4. Policies and Guidelines *64*

5. Disclosure and Withdrawal *76*

6. Illegal Drugs in Prison *102*

7. Resources in Prison *119*

8. Conclusion *140*

Bibliography *153*

Index *162*

CHAPTER 1

Introduction

In July 1994 three inspectors from HM Inspectorate of Prisons conducted an unannounced short inspection of HM Prison and Young Offender Institution Styal. Their concerns about the high level of drug taking in the prison led to a visit, one week later, by Dr Malcolm Faulk, the Inspectorate's specialist in healthcare. His ensuing report resulted in significant media attention when he suggested that the use of illegal drugs in Styal was so considerable that women were being introduced to drugs for the first time in the prison. It was possible, he said, for a woman to 'enter a shoplifter and leave an addict' (HM Chief Inspector of Prisons, 1995).

The Inspectorate report stated that prisoners and staff believed that drugs were freely available in Styal. At the same time, they noted that resources available to prisoners to help them withdraw from drugs and remain drug free were limited. These concerns have been repeated in most subsequent reports by the Inspectorates (HM Chief Inspector of Prisons and HM Inspectorate of Prisons for Scotland) into individual prisons in Scotland and in England and Wales. The report by HM Chief Inspector of Prisons into conditions on the women's wing of HMP Risley (1996) also attracted considerable media coverage when it was suggested that prisoners were carrying out forcible internal searches of other prisoners in search of illegal drugs (*The Observer*, 8 September 1996).

Following more general concerns about conditions in women's prisons, the Chief Inspector of Prisons produced a thematic report, *Women in Prison* (1997), which addressed the specific problems faced by women prisoners. In Scotland, following the deaths of seven young women[1] in HM Institution Cornton Vale, the Scottish Office commissioned a report from the Social Work Services and Prisons Inspectorates for Scotland to review community disposals and the use of custody for women offenders in Scotland, *Women Offenders—A Safer Way* (1998). Both reports continued to highlight the severe problems associated with drug use in women's prisons and to raise concerns that a high proportion of the prisoners were regular drug users. Other studies (Carlen, 1998; Devlin, 1998) have also highlighted this issue.

This book provides an analysis of the way in which the 'drugs problem'[2] is defined in prisons and the impact it has on the lives of prisoners and of staff. It is based on in-depth research carried out over the past ten years in Scotland and England, providing detailed accounts from prisoners and staff which discuss the impact drugs have on regimes and individuals. Policy developments and initiatives aimed at tackling the supply and demand for drugs are examined within the prison context.

BACKGROUND TO THE PROJECT

The number of drug users has increased significantly in all penal establishments over the last few years and the number of women believed to have been drug dependent prior to imprisonment has escalated. The problem of drug use in prisons and the high incidence of drug users in the prison population has been officially recognised (HM Prison Service, 1987; 1991; ACMD, 1988; 1989; 1993; 1996; Scottish Affairs Committee, 1994; Ministerial Drugs Task Force, 1994; Home Office, 1995; 1998). Official documents acknowledge that many prisoners are regular drug users. Individuals may be brought into contact with the criminal justice system either directly as a result of their misuse of controlled drugs or because their misuse of controlled drugs caused or contributed to their offences (ACMD, 1991; 1996; Scottish Affairs Committee, 1994).

The existing research in this area has been carried out by psychologists or drugs workers and mainly on male prisoners (Turnbull, 1992; Turnbull *et al.*, 1994; Shewan *et al.*, 1994; Keene, 1997; Mason *et al.*, 1997). In contrast, this book examines the response of HM Prison Service of England and Wales (HMPS) and the Scottish Prison Service (SPS) to drug users through an examination of policy guidelines and their implementation, focusing on women in prison. Analysis of current policy documents and interviews with prison staff illustrate the priorities and emphasis of current practice and the extent to which this meets with the expectations and capabilities of discipline and medical officers. The book focuses specifically on the application of policies and practices in relation to women prisoners. Uniquely, it provides accounts of female prisoners' expectations and their appraisals of policies and practices as they impact on their lives within prison regimes.

The research for the book was aimed at investigating the experiences of women who used drugs illegally and, more specifically, the way that they experienced the 'moment' of imprisonment (Carlen, 1983). In particular, it examined and evaluated the emphasis given by official reports on making the most of the opportunity presented by imprisonment to help drug users break or modify their habit. This provided a context within which to consider the variety of new initiatives which were proposed in reports produced by the Scottish Affairs Committee (1994); the Ministerial Drugs Task Force (1994) and in the Government White Paper, *Tackling Drugs Together* (HMSO, 1995). Government reports such as these have had a significant impact on prison policies and strategies. By drawing on the areas of concern identified as significant by the Prison Services (HMPS, 1991; 1995; 1998; SPS, 1994) the research focused on three key topics:

- disclosure of drug use on entry to prison;
- the use of illegal drugs within the prison system; and
- resources for drug users in prison.

(i) Disclosure of drug use on entry to prison

If an individual has been charged with a drug offence or if indicative information is provided from previous records it is likely that they will be assumed to be a drug user. In most other cases, however, the authorities are dependent on the prisoner's willingness to disclose information to them or for it to be noted during a medical examination. The book considers the obstacles and incentives informing the process of self-disclosure as it is perceived by prisoners. While the provision of medical assistance and the possibility of receiving support may encourage prisoners to disclose their drug use, other factors serve to prevent or reduce this likelihood. Drug use is illegal and women who have been criminalised may be reluctant to increase the stigma already experienced. Carceral institutions are unlikely to foster an environment in which confidentiality and trust are prominent. Rumours and suspicion are rife and, consequently, many prisoners fear the outcomes of being identified as a drug user, such as closer surveillance and stricter treatment. *Chapter 5* considers the issues concerning disclosure and the methods used within the prison system to identify drug users or to encourage self-disclosure.

(ii) The use of illegal drugs within the prison system

The presence of illicit drugs within the prison system has increasingly become recognised as significant and one which has serious consequences, particularly in relation to health (with the risk of infection and/or overdose) and to security (raising control and discipline concerns). *Chapter 6* discusses the recognition and definition of this problem and analyses the measures taken to prevent access to drugs and their use in prisons. It considers:

- the effectiveness of these measures as prisoners and staff experience them;
- their impact on the day-to-day running of the prison regime; and
- the problems presented by the use of drugs from the perspectives of both staff and prisoners.

(iii) Resources for drug users in prison

In an attempt to counteract the demand for illegal drugs in prison, the Prison Services have argued that drug users should be given opportunities to reduce or end their use of drugs during the period of their imprisonment. These should take the form of education, counselling and support, providing drug users with the potential for 'rehabilitation'. The book assesses the reality of such proposals through an examination of the available services and resources, noting the difficulties and contradictions pertaining to the development of therapeutic services within a carceral system. The commitment to therapeutic provision illustrates that the authorities are concerned to make resources available. However, the lack of resources *in real terms*, restricts therapeutic opportunities to a few prisoners. Additionally, the resources that *are* available may not appeal to, or be appropriate in meeting the needs of, prisoners who have access to them. Consequently, those drug users deemed to have been 'unsuccessful' in meeting the designated requirements/outcomes, or to have failed to present a sufficiently altered outlook (in terms of reform/rehabilitation), become easily labelled as 'untreatable' (Pitch, 1995). As Collison (1993: 389) notes:

> Once identified drug users become bodies to be dealt with by the criminal justice system, there is a presumption that they must either want to give up drugs or wilfully refuse to do so.

Thus both punishment and rehabilitation operate conditionally. *Chapter 7* considers the practical implications of making resources available for drug users and examines the views of prisoners and prison staff on their relevance and adequacy.

METHODOLOGY

The research project for the book set out to explore the effects of the prison regime on drug users by obtaining their views and experiences (see also Cohen and Taylor, 1977; Carlen, 1983; Gelsthorpe, 1990; Scraton *et al.*, 1991; Carlen, 1998; Devlin, 1998). Its objective was to present the views of women drug users in their own words and, more specifically, to illustrate the effects that the prison system has on the lives of individuals. Central to this is an examination of the everyday realities and experiences faced by women in prison and the resources made available within the regimes.

The research is contextualised within the framework of 'critical' criminology, emphasising the determining contexts of class, gender and neo-colonialism, and it considers the political management of 'crime' and 'social problems' by comparing the accounts of individuals within the prison system with 'official' discourses. This provides an analysis of the interconnections between structure and agency (Giddens, 1979; 1984). The dominant discourse (particularly official definitions of 'problems') is contrasted and critiqued through recognition of alternative discourses. It aims to establish the link between 'the personal troubles of milieu and the public issues of social structure' (Wright Mills, 1959: 14).

The influence of images and ideologies

By using experiential accounts and developing a critical feminist theoretical perspective, this book raises a number of key themes and issues. Firstly, it examines the influence of images and ideologies that inform the social construction and political management of particular groups and individuals. These operate at an economic level (determined by class location) and a political level (emphasised by political distinction, such as 'black', or 'women'). These determinants are underpinned by ideologies based on dominant ideological constructions of a 'rough'-'respectable' continuum against which women 'offenders' and/or drug users are judged. Processes of marginalisation and subsequent criminalisation operate through relations of class, 'race' and gender, and I believe these structural relationships determine who is subject to imprisonment. By examining the experiences of women drug users in prison, it is possible to examine the operation of specific discourses around women and 'deviant' behaviour and the impact of these processes on and within penal regimes.

Female drug users in prison form a 'hard core' of women who have failed, or have been failed by, community alternatives. In terms of the 'metaphor of bifurcation' (Pitch, 1995: 20), this group has been defined as the untreatable, judged as rejecting educational and therapeutic opportunities in the community. Consequently, they are pushed towards punitive and repressive responses. This dichotomy continues in prison where resources may be limited, but prisoners who fail to respond are also labelled as 'untreatable'. Stereotypical and negative images of criminal and/or deviant women, frequently considered more depraved and inherently evil than their male counterparts, prevail. This has as much to do with perceptions of non-conformity to social constructs of femininity as with law-breaking (see Smart, 1976; 1989; 1992; Carlen, 1983; 1985; 1998; Heidensohn, 1985; 1996; Kennedy, 1992; Lloyd, 1995; Devlin, 1998). The perceived 'deviance' of women drug users is exacerbated not only through drugs but also via their hedonistic associations which are considered inappropriate, particularly for women, mediated by class and 'race'.

Further, the disease model of drug use and drug users, which identifies drug using women as infected and polluted, combines with the depiction of crime and its potential for transmission and together they create a complex synthesis. Drug using women are portrayed as being at the intersections of medical and legal discourses. These ideological considerations influence the operation of the penal system as it affects women. This book examines the extent to which this occurs.

Punishment as a central concept in women's imprisonment
Secondly, the book provides an analysis of women's imprisonment which considers punishment as a central concept, despite the rhetoric of therapy and feminisation which regularly obscures this (see Carlen, 1983; 1998; Mandaraka-Sheppard, 1986; Howe, 1994; Malloch, 1999). Such analysis requires that the imprisonment of women be structurally located within patriarchal society, where men maintain a monopoly on political, social and economic power. Within this context, structures and social arrangements operate to institutionalise male domination, the 'male hierarchical ordering of society' (Einstein, 1979: 17). This makes use of formal and informal means: by individual men as husbands, fathers or partners; by institutional means such as economic control; and through the institutional power of the law, the courts, the police and the prison system.

Such processes are reflected and transmitted in the operation of legal discourse and the construction of penal regimes for women. Images of deviance and criminality operate in a specific way for women, as do measures of control. Within prisons this determines the emphasis given to the prioritisation of policies geared towards containment and control or, conversely, to reform or rehabilitation. Recent policy objectives concerning services for drug users in prison have highlighted the need to offer rehabilitation and educational opportunities to counter the demand for drugs. At the same time, increased security measures and punishments have been employed to tackle the supply of drugs.

This dichotomy is examined as inherently contradictory. Previous studies have illustrated the fundamental tension between treatment and punishment (or care and control) within the penal system (Scraton and Chadwick, 1986; 1987; Sim, 1990; 1994; Scraton, Sim and Skidmore, 1991; Ruggerio et al., 1995; Carlen, 1998). In a system geared towards containment and punishment, the operation of rehabilitative measures will always be limited. This book extends the contentions of these earlier studies by examining this contradiction and its relevance to an understanding of drug users and their treatment in prison.

The effects of factors influencing the allocation of resources
Thirdly, the emphasis given to the limitation of resources within prison (a deliberate emphasis based on notions of 'less-eligibility', discussed in *Chapter 4*) further enhances their prioritisation. When resources are limited, the use to which they are put will be determined by a number of considerations. This study examines the economic and ideological effects of the tensions and factors that influence the allocation of limited resources. It is suggested that discipline and control, as the main objectives of the prison system, are likely to receive greater prioritisation, in terms of security provisions than will rehabilitation or improved conditions for prisoners. Such considerations are influenced by ideological depictions of 'deserving' and 'undeserving', those worthy of 'treatment' and those for whom 'treatment' is deemed inappropriate. They are part of the process that determines who is sent to prison and how regimes operate within prisons.

Official discourse presents a legitimising basis for state operations, and the rhetoric of rehabilitation forms a part of this. The concept of rehabilitation goes some way towards alleviating the legitimacy dilemma for the penal system. Rehabilitation is aimed at modifying and changing behaviour, reintegrating individuals into society, redeeming them from their past behaviour and inculcating the expected social norms (although these are not necessarily homogenous). Rehabilitation operates to alter individuals, not their circumstances. Individuals are held responsible for their behaviour, while at the same time, a 'morality' is imposed which reinforces the assumption that 'offending' behaviour is morally incompatible with existing rules and regulations. Structural problems remain unchallenged and alternative discourses are opposed as untenable.

Thus, rehabilitation proffers a mechanism for the normalising process which is targeted at those individuals within the penal system. Using the assertions of Sim (1990), Castel (1991), Collison (1993), Hudson (1993) and Pitch (1995), the book illustrates the bifurcation of policies which profess to rehabilitate. The existence of rehabilitative programmes creates the impression that something is being done, no matter how limited or limiting. It also enables the distinction to be made between those who respond to treatment and those who 'fail'.

Institutionalised ideologies and official discourse
Fourthly, within a context of security, discipline and regulation, the effects of limited resources are obscured by the official discourses which define them. These discourses are informed fundamentally by wider ideological constructs and are examined in later chapters. Official discourse denotes the institutionalisation of particular images and ideologies as they are socially constructed. This plays a major role in the political management of individuals marginalised by relations of production, reproduction and neo-colonialism. As Scraton (1990: 29) notes:

> Official discourses, sustained in their prominence by power–knowledge relations, are developed and maintained through the primary determining contexts directly relevant to any given society.

Institutionalised ideologies thus come to define the formal and informal responses of state agencies. By focusing on the experiences of drug users in prison this study examines how social constructs and ideologies, derived from the structural relationships of advanced capitalist society, come to create and inform negative reputations concerning individuals and groups (Scraton and Chadwick, 1987; Scraton, 1987; Scraton, Sim and Skidmore, 1991; Sim, 1990). It is suggested that these images inform official discourse and have repercussions for social policies and professional practices. This is of significance in the formal and informal hierarchies of the prison system where occupational culture and institutional power form the basis of organizational activities. The implementation of policies and guidelines by prison staff is examined within this context. As Scraton (1990: 14) notes:

> While state officials possess and use professional discretion in the administration of their duties, they remain constrained by their training, their role and their institutional parameters. As part of the interactive processes which comprise agency, they draw their legitimacy, status and *raison d'être* from the social structure and its attendant institutions of social control and political management.

Official discourse is mediated at different levels. The day-to-day operations of the prison function at an interpersonal - as well as structural - level and it is through this process that opportunities for resistance arise. Prison staff who are required to implement prison policies have discretionary power and are able to determine the practices which accrue from official guidelines. Their own perceptions and opinions are likely to influence the approach they adopt towards prisoners. Prisoners, too, will attempt to subvert the operational practices of the prison regime and to resist the stereotypes and images which are used to define them.

By providing detailed accounts of the experiences of both prisoners and staff, this book examines the influences which determine operational practice, the ways in which institutional guidelines are subverted or negated when they do not correspond to the standpoints of the operators (prison staff). Specifically, the experiences of prisoners illustrate the impact of policies and their discretionary implementation. This also highlights the ways in which prisoners resist the normalising processes of the prison system.

A critical, feminist approach

The research for the book employed a methodology which reflects a commitment to feminist politics and critical theory. Identifying a distinctive 'feminist methodology' is notoriously difficult but clearly a commitment to feminism can be incorporated into the selection of research methods and into the research process (Stanley, 1990). Defining the methodology within a feminist framework brings its own problems. As Skeggs (1992: 15) notes: 'When women do research on women they are usually labelled feminist, both by the researcher and the readers of the research. There is no male equivalent to the feminist researcher'.

This book aims to provide *different* information by using a critical feminist approach. Although the methods used are essentially qualitative, and not exclusive to feminist theory, as Stanley and Wise (1993) indicate, what is fundamental for feminist research is the presence of a feminist consciousness for the researcher, informing the nature of the relationship between the researcher and the women being researched. The parameters of the research, then, need to be informed and defined by feminist theory.

Four key themes can be identified as constituents of feminist research (see Gelsthorpe, 1990; Hammersley, 1992; Stanley and Wise, 1990; 1993). They include the topic itself, which should involve some recognition of gender and its subsequent power relations. According to Stanley and Wise (1993) this does not mean the research needs to be limited to the study of women alone, but that it should highlight the position of women or some aspect of women's oppression (Kelly, 1990; Skeggs, 1992).

Secondly, the methods employed should enable the researcher to gain insight into the experience of the individual respondent while attempting to link this to wider structural relationships, making 'cases' into 'issues' (Sivanandan, 1990). Ultimately it is a priority to *collectivise* individual experiences in an attempt to initiate change. Ramazanoglu (1992: 210) notes: 'There is no alternative to political commitment in feminist or any other ways of knowing. Since knowing is a political process, so knowledge is intrinsically political'.

Thirdly, for feminist researchers the relationship between the researcher and the researched should be as non-hierarchical as possible. Finch (1984) discusses the ease with which female researchers can establish 'rapport' with women respondents (see also Oakley, 1981) when conducting less structured interviews. Often, researchers discover they are able to encourage a respondent to talk about themselves free of more usual inhibitions. As Gelsthorpe (1990) notes in relation to her own research in a male prison, female researchers soon become seen as 'counsellors' with many staff and prisoners feeling the need to talk to an outsider.

The fourth key theme, as Stanley (1990: 12) notes: 'should locate the feminist researcher firmly within the activities of her research as an essential feature of what is "feminist" about it'. Similarly, overidentification is not problematic for the feminist or critical researcher in the way that it has been for traditional research. As already indicated, it is important to achieve a level of empathy (for want of a better word) with the research subject. Indeed, feminist researchers argue that women's experience *as women* means they will identify with many aspects of the lives of the women being researched (Finch, 1984; Oakley, 1981). At the same time, 'false universalism' - ignoring the differential impacts of class, race, sexuality and (dis)ability - must be avoided.

'DOING' THE RESEARCH

The research for the book began in 1993 and has been continually updated to monitor changes which have taken place up to 2000. The study is based on in-depth interviews with 80 women prisoners and 40 members of discipline staff (both male and female). Ten nursing officers were also interviewed as were a number of prison governors and senior staff. Policy-makers at HMPS and SPS headquarters also participated. Respondents are taken from five women's prisons in Scotland and England (four closed and one open institution). Some prisoners were known to the authorities as drug users, others were not.

Official reports, guidelines, statistical data, related research, government documents, and newspaper and journal articles were analysed. Some were obtained generally, other material was collected from HMPS or through the Prison Service College at Wakefield. Drug dependency units and drug agencies were visited; health workers, outreach workers and drug counsellors were interviewed both formally and informally to monitor changes and developments in practice.

Through contact with drug workers it was possible to meet women drug users who were attempting to become or remain drug free, some of whom were in rehabilitation units. A small number of female exprisoners who had used drugs in the past were also contacted and interviewed. Many of the respondents argued that the resources available for women were woefully inadequate, subsumed under services much more effectively targeted towards men. All respondents agreed that women face the same problems associated with drug use as men experience - and more besides, due to the very fact that they are women.

Interviews with prison staff, specifically discipline and medical officers, provide accounts which illustrate the difficulties faced by staff working in this field. More specifically, they provide unequivocal evidence of the effects of prevalent ideologies and social constructs as they apply to female prisoners and female drug users. These accounts also illustrate how deeply-held beliefs and assumptions inform the daily routines and practices of prisons.

All research projects create problems and dilemmas for the researcher, demanding adaptability and improvisation. Research into state institutions often causes unique difficulties. Generally, 'official' definitions and solutions are prioritised in reports and documentation by state agencies and institutions, and the views of those affected by them—in this case prisoners—are frequently negotiated out of the picture.

Access

In prison research gaining access to the 'view from below' is frequently problematic. Even when it is possible to obtain the views of people in prison, the secrecy and obstructiveness of many institutional regimes means even the most appropriate methodology may be limited or annulled. Throughout the research project, gaining access continues to be an ongoing process, often strengthened by the gatekeepers' expectations of what they might gain through co-operation. Further, given the prevalence of official definitions and controls over research findings, the use to which the research may be put requires careful consideration and reflection (Carlen, 1994).

As Skeggs (1992: 14) notes, access cannot be obtained without some form of confrontation with the 'nuances of power'. There are difficulties which will arise when attempting to carry out critical research into state institutions. There are further problems to be negotiated when carrying out studies into sensitive, potentially political issues such as illegal drug use. Nevertheless, it is surprising how accessible certain institutions and individuals can actually be. In the case of this study, a proposal outlining the research project and its aims and objectives was sent to the Home Office Research Unit requesting access to as many women's prisons as possible. This was met with a lengthy silence.[3] While awaiting a reply from the Home Office, individual prison governors were contacted. The aims and objectives of the research were outlined and access was requested to interview prisoners and staff. This proved more fruitful, although the responses were somewhat varied. Some governors wrote back stating that they had too many research projects already taking place, the impression being that there were as many researchers in some prisons as there were prisoners.

Frequently, however, access was provided because there was an interested worker within the prison who was trying to develop services, and who was keen to illustrate what was being done for drug users. Once access had been obtained to a few prisons it became easier to gain access elsewhere as the project gained credibility and provided an opportunity for comparison. Generally, access was secured through personal communication supported by a telephone conversation. This was followed by an introductory visit to the prison prior to the research being carried out.

The research was aided by the much publicised initiative of the 'new openness' of penal institutions, a point also identified by Devlin (1998). Additionally, the issues associated with drug use were being increasingly recognised as problematic within prisons and individual governors were interested in the contribution of research to the debate. Being a female researcher with no official backing was beneficial and, perhaps, afforded greater access, with many people going out of their way to be helpful, given the assumed unthreatening position of the researcher.

After contacting individual prisons, significant access was eventually obtained to five prisons in Scotland and England (four closed prisons and one open prison). A number of other prisons offered access for a single visit. In several institutions, access was afforded with a condition that the prison was not named and those in it were not identified. As a result, the names of all institutions have been removed and each prison has been denoted by a number.

The prisons
In their anonymised form, the prisons involved in the project can be summarily described as follows:

- **HMP One** is an open prison and a young offender institution. It is rurally situated and holds women (aged 15 and over) who have been sentenced for periods of custody ranging from short-term up to life imprisonment. At the time of the research the prison's Certified Normal Accommodation (CNA) was 262.
- **HMP Two** is a closed adult prison and young offender institution located in a rural setting but within travelling distance of a small city. It holds all categories of prisoners, sentenced and remanded. At the time of the research its CNA was 219.
- **HMP Three** is a closed adult prison and young offender institution situated 12 miles from a major city. It has recently been adapted to accommodate remand prisoners, but had a CNA of 211 when most of the interviews were carried out there.
- **HMP Four** is a remand and local prison for women in a rural setting. Its CNA was 152.
- **HMP Five** is a local prison for women centrally located in a major city. It also serves as a national resource for prisoners with psychiatric illness. Its CNA was 532.

Although the role and the regimes of each prison were specific to the individual institution[4] there were many similarities in terms of training, educational facilities and the availability of personal officer schemes. Training was similar in all prisons, generally including sewing machine work, assembly tasks, office skills, hair and beauty skills, painting and decorating. Work experience placements were available in the community for selected prisoners as were home-leaves (see Carlen, 1998; Devlin, 1998 for more detailed accounts of the daily operation of women's prisons).

Each prison was different in regime and physical organization and this meant that the methodological approach taken varied to some extent, particularly when contacting respondents. There are specific problems in carrying out research in prisons, not least the extent to which prison officers have to be relied upon and the need to 'fit in' seeing prisoners during the hours when they are not locked up (see also Smith, 1989). It was not uncommon to be taken onto a wing and left there only to discover there were no prisoners around. Nor was it unusual to be left in rooms or on wings waiting to be escorted elsewhere. This was frustrating and wasted a considerable amount of time. In one prison this problem was alleviated after a few days when a set of keys was provided, enabling relative freedom of movement.

The participants
Obtaining participants was somewhat problematic. In some prisons, the staff asked for volunteers to participate, particularly women who were 'known' drug users. While many came forward on this basis, it soon became clear that many other women did not disclose their drug use in prison for a variety of reasons. By making it clear that anyone who wished to participate in the research could do so, it was possible to speak with women who had gone through withdrawals with no medical supervision or who had maintained their drug habit within the prison. Many people had something to say on this issue. Often when a woman had been interviewed, she would suggest someone else or would encourage other women to take part: the 'snowball' effect. Several women asked specifically to participate; some were users, others were not but had concerns about the extent of drug use in the prison and often had experienced the intimidation that went along with it.

One problem identified in carrying out the research in prison was that the issue of 'informed consent' was often unclear. Where officers had asked women to participate or when women had been approached on the wings, it was not clear how confident women were in their ability to refuse. Nevertheless, each participant was told the purpose and objectives of the research and confidentiality was guaranteed. All participants appeared willing to provide information and discuss the issues they felt to be significant.

Many women were providing information that could leave them feeling very vulnerable because of the security issues it raised - especially when they talked about their use of drugs in prison. They only had the researcher's word that it would not lead to them being identified. As Kelly (1990) notes, it is important to be aware and attempt to assess the impact of the research on the respondents. This is often difficult within a prison regime and it highlights the need for sensitivity. Researchers need to be aware of the potential consequences for the prisoner if confidential information becomes public knowledge within this environment. Trust needs to be developed and guarantees of anonymity have to be made and kept. A 'dual' power structure operates in prison research and is manifested through the relationship between the researcher and the research respondents, and between the researcher and the context of the total institution.

Interviews with prisoners often became emotional when they were recounting their own experiences. Attempts to support emotionally upset respondents were often unsatisfactory when there were precise time limits. Often, women stated that they had 'lost everything' through their drug use and/or imprisonment. They recounted experiences where partners had died from drug-related disease or overdose, children had been taken into care, and family and friends had given up on them. For many women, the guilt and despair they felt was compounded by the isolation of imprisonment. Any response in those circumstances seemed totally inadequate. However, women reported that participation in the research enabled them to discuss issues in a way that they could not do with others within the prison system due to fears around confidentiality and security. It appears that researchers were regularly asked for advice, information and not infrequently found themselves offering support to a respondent. This presented problems when trying to fulfil multiple and different functions (as researcher and counsellor). However, helpful information was passed on to prisoners wherever necessary and details of more appropriate resources distributed where possible. Shared experience - another tenet of feminist research - was also difficult when experiences of prison were considered. Nevertheless most women were keen to talk and a rapport was easily established which related to more general interests, shared experiences and concerns.

Drawing conclusions
Although semi-structured interviews and accounts which provide an individual's experience may each be assumed to be unique, there are very real similarities in the experiences of the women interviewed, thus making it possible to establish common features reflecting their situation in prison. The accounts provided by the respondents indicate that many issues affect them in broadly similar ways, as will be discussed in the following chapters. This highlights the need to look to the structural issues and factors of the prison regimes and/or the nature of drug use rather than to the individual person.

Inherent in qualitative research is the problem of how the researcher interprets the responses provided (see Gould *et al.*, 1974: xix). To an extent, the conclusions drawn depend on the type of questions asked. However, in a semi-structured interview more in-depth information is often obtained by allowing the respondents to define the issues they view as the most important. As Moore (1977: 96) notes, interpreting the data provided is not always straightforward and depends on '... that elusive factor of empathy, of being able to see the world through the eyes of specific others'. The extent to which this is achieved is consequent on the 'rapport' established between the researcher and the respondents.

One potential obstacle was that the interviews necessitated spending time in the company of both prisoners and prison officers, which could have led prisoners to perceive the researcher as working with prison staff. In reality, however, these concerns did not appear to hinder the research to any significant degree and prisoners provided detailed and personal information.

In carrying out research into closed institutions there is, in many ways, a power differential underlined by the fact that the researcher can leave the prison after the interviews while the women cannot. This is recognised by Van Maanen (1991: 41) who points out the fundamental distinction between the researcher and the respondent's understanding of the 'social world'.

Although the data obtained presents a partial account of individuals' experiences within the prison system, the depth, quality and quantity of interviews carried out presents an important opportunity to evaluate the effect of the penal system on women's lives as drug users. Accounts from both staff and prisoners present very different experiences of institutional life and exhibit the various perspectives held by different groups within one setting. By using a critical and feminist methodological approach a significant amount of experiential information could be obtained to highlight this distinction.

The disparity which exists between official strategy objectives and their implementation in practice becomes clear when the experiences of staff and prisoners are taken into account. The chapters which follow examine this discrepancy by outlining official definitions of the problems associated with drug use in prisons and potential solutions. The data presented illustrate how policy and its implementation affect the experiences of those involved in the day-to-day operation of the prison system.

ENDNOTES for *Chapter 1*

[1] Which rose to eight when another young woman took her own life on 3 July 1998.

[2] For the purposes of this study, 'drug use' relates to the non-medical use of drugs intended to be used as part of a course of medical treatment, or the use of illicit drugs which have no generally accepted medical purpose.

[3] When the Home Office Research Unit eventually responded one year later, (having allegedly misplaced the file for this project and the request for access) the bulk of the interviews had been carried out and their authorisation only afforded access to one further institution.

[4] Although many of the resources are available in all institutions the operation of regimes varies significantly. The penal system operates a progression system which exists within individual prisons and throughout the penal system. Following sentence, this progression system will begin for each prisoner. Conditions and opportunities will improve for the prisoner (in terms of living accommodation and opportunities for work and education) on the basis that the prisoner complies with the rules and requirements of the institution. For long-term prisoners this will generally involve movement between prisons (i.e. from closed accommodation to an open prison) and the opportunity to work in the community and have home leave. However, the existence of a progressionary regime and an incentive-based system means that disincentives will also apply. Thus non-co-operation or indiscipline will mean that privileges are not made available to the individual, or they can be removed.

CHAPTER 2

The Imprisonment of Women

In order to understand and analyse women's imprisonment, and the experiences of women drug users in prison, it is crucial to examine the broader issues which relate to the political, social, ideological and economic contexts of gender relations. Modern research (Carlen, 1983; 1998; Devlin, 1998) illustrates that women's experiences of custody and the operation of penal regimes for women differ significantly from those of men. By examining the historical development of the prison system as it emerged for women lawbreakers, it is possible to uncover the ideological assumptions and expectations which underpin women's experiences of the contemporary prison system. This chapter examines the context of the prison, illustrating the specific characteristics of the system as applied to women.

REGULATION AND CONTROL

The distinctive regimes that have emerged in women's prisons are directly related to the ways in which techniques of surveillance, both penal and non-penal, have always been systematically applied to women. Orthodox economic accounts of imprisonment fail to provide any explanation for this. This point is made by Howe (1994) who notes that Foucault's masculinist view of the expanding forms of surveillance omits to consider that women have always been subject to intrusive forms of regulation and control.[1]

The context of the regulation and control of women has to be located within an examination of patriarchy and patriarchal relations, for it is these which determine women's social, political and economic status. Kelly and Radford (1987: 238) define patriarchy as 'a systematic set of social relationships through which men maintain power over women and children'.

Patriarchy itself is diverse. Its effects will differ since women are clearly not a single homogenous group and are distinguished through relations of class, race/ethnicity, sexuality and (dis)ability. Nevertheless, it is possible to examine women's experiences of the hierarchical structures of gender relations. Chadwick and Little (1987: 271) note:

> Through the transmission and perpetuation of common-sense images and ideologies women learn the role, the place and the acceptable forms of behaviour to which they must adhere in order to gain status, respectability and protection. The strength of ideology is that it becomes internalised and, therefore, manifested in and through the daily lives of the people it categorises.

Hutter and Williams (1989) examine some of the forms the social control of women can take and the subsequent effects on women at various stages of their lives. In particular, they are concerned with the way in which an image of the 'normal' woman is constructed. They argue that by looking at the explicit controls over women who are seen as 'deviant', it becomes possible to clarify the concept of 'normal behaviour'. It also illuminates the extent and nature of the covert controls used to persuade *all* women to fit their behaviour into this 'normal' construction.[2] This becomes evident when the emphasis of historical and contemporary prison regimes for women is examined.

This process is further enacted through the administration of law and the operation of the legal system. Brophy and Smart (1985) point out that although the experiences of individuals within the criminal justice system will vary, the general experience of women indicates the differential effect of the law.

> Experience tells us . . . that while statutes might not differentiate or discriminate between women and men, legal practice certainly does. Experience also tells us that the idea of a complete legal equality and even equal treatment is not a sufficient goal for feminists where, structurally women are in a disadvantaged place vis-à-vis men. (Brophy and Smart, 1985: 3)

The criminal justice system and legal processes, despite claims of neutrality and equality, affect men and women differently and unequally, reflecting and reinforcing elements of male dominance rooted in patriarchal relations. In a society where one gender group is treated as the 'norm' it will follow that equality will be sexually specific and legal directions will have differential effects. The law will thus affect and be affected by patriarchal relations, in the realms of both production and reproduction. As McCann (in Brophy and Smart, 1985: 117) argues, 'As part of the state apparatus the courts may be seen to operate to support the status quo, and in so doing to endorse and reinforce the divisions upon which the status quo is based'.

As long as men continue to dominate the official apparatus, it will be men who will define and administer 'justice'. Scraton and Chadwick (1986: 132) state:

> The ideological construction of masculinity and femininity, well-established institutionally in policies and practices of discrimination on the grounds of gender, carries major consequences for women who become involved with the criminal justice system.

These consequences affect women in three major areas. Firstly, women are treated unequally in relation to men; secondly, they are treated differently as victims and thirdly, they receive different treatment as offenders. All are dependent on the ideological assumptions which operate with regard to women (Smart, 1976; 1989; Heidensohn, 1996). The effects of any over-arching ideology become ingrained in modes of thought and language and are shared by both men and women.[3] For feminists then, there is a need to examine the present sites of intervention for criminology (policing, the courts and the prisons), and consider how gender is constituted in these sites. As Cain (1990b: 10) points out:

> Only by starting from outside, with the social construction of gender, or with women's experiences of their total lives, or with the structure of the domestic space, can we begin to make sense of what is going on.

For many feminists the female body features significantly as the target for various discourses of control for women both within penal theory and in the study of the operation of social controls in the lives of women. Howe (1994: 216) notes the need to locate women within a structural context imbued with power relations:

> One such power site where women undoubtedly exist is that of the prison. Another is the so-called private prison in which many women live their lives. Analyses of the social control of women reveal that discipline and punishment as well as power relations cross over institutional boundaries, impacting on the female body within and without the prison walls.

An examination of the body in terms of intersections of power enables a comparison of the methods by which various forms of control operate in relation to women. Consideration can be given to the ways in which controls function at an external level, imposed through institutional regimes, and an internal level, imposed as part of the discourse from dominant ideologies, to affect women's lives.[4]

Bartky (1990), McNay (1992) and Howe (1994) criticise Foucault for his neglect of the 'gendered character of many disciplinary techniques' (McNay, 1992: 11). As McNay argues, an analysis of the oppression of women needs to take into account the concept of the body as 'it is upon the biological difference between the male and female bodies that the edifice of gender inequality is built and legitimised' (McNay, 1992: 17).

As Howe (1994) notes, Foucault's view of the expanding 'penetration' of forms of surveillance omits to note that women have always been subject to intrusive forms of regulation and control:

> For women have always been controlled and disciplined, if not in the state-controlled ways anticipated by the Foucauldian social control theorists at least by other state control systems, notably social security, and, more broadly, within 'civil' society. (Howe, 1994: 115)

It would appear, therefore, that many of the controls which the penal system serves to enact are already present in the lives of women (Malloch, 1999). This highlights the fundamental necessity of analysing patriarchal social relations in terms of the imprisonment of women and in the wider penal sphere. It is crucial that systems of *punishment* are analysed in relation to the prison system and how they operate in relation to men *and* women. As Howe (1994: 40) states:

> ... in most political economies of punishment, prisoners - the people who bear the brunt of all the punishment structures - are lost from view. Second

and related, these accounts have remained profoundly masculinist: they not only ignore the fact that prisons hold women, they also remain oblivious to feminist challenges to Marxist categories of analysis.

An understanding of the political economy of imprisonment is useful in many ways in order to analyse the imprisonment of women and the way prison operates in terms of class. However, it is necessary to consider the operation of further determining contexts through a recognition of patriarchy. This is not to deny the interaction of class, race and gender. As Carlen (1985: 10) notes:

> Women who break the law come from all kinds of backgrounds, though, as with male lawbreakers, those women who land up in prison are much more likely to have come from the lower socio-economic groups than from the higher ones. Once their crimes become known however, all women lawbreakers have to confront the myths which permeate both the criminal justice system and the prisons.

The majority of historical and theoretical accounts of imprisonment fail to theorise adequately the experiences of women, either by omitting them from the analysis or by their assumed incorporation into ungendered accounts, presenting the experience of men as the 'norm'. As many feminist theorists have illustrated, theoretical accounts which are partial but claim to be universal are fundamentally flawed. Revisionist accounts usefully theorised the relationship between relations of production, marginalisation and punishment. However, they failed to incorporate an analysis of the relations of *reproduction*, thus undermining the totality of their argument. While processes of marginalisation affected a particular social class in terms of the relations of production, they acted *specifically* in terms of their effects on women. The ever-present surveillance of women's lives was omitted from most analyses of penality.

> The challenge, then, is to continue the project of exposing and enlarging our vision of what constitutes discriminatory penal practices, while remaining cognisant of the theoretical and political significance of critical feminist analyses of the private prisons of docile yet rebellious bodies, drugged and tranquillised bodies, famished self-policing bodies in which many women live their lives, 'free' from penal control. (Howe, 1994: 206-7)

Women have been subjected to a whole range of different ideological precepts which influence the development of regimes and practices. What is fundamental is the way in which men within a patriarchal system have defined these constructions. It is precisely these ideological constructs which affect women both inside and outside the penal system, although women[5] do continually try to resist this.

THE DEVELOPMENT OF THE PRISON

From the well-documented accounts of the development of the modern-day prison it can be seen that punishment by incarceration did not always occupy its present position as the most serious penalty available in the hierarchy of punishment (see Fitzgerald, 1977; Foucault, 1977; Ignatieff, 1978; Melossi and Pavarini, 1981; Morgan, 1992).

Ignatieff (1978: 28) charts the development of the prison from its inception, arguing that it was 'more a place of confinement for debtors and those passing through the mills of justice than a place of punishment'. Foucault (1977) identifies the 1770s as the period when punishment was transformed. Prior to 1775, he argues, punishment was ritualised and public with 'serious' offenders being executed or transported,[6] employers able to chastise their workers without recourse to external bodies, and prison used as punishment for summary offences.

Institutional confinement, as it initially developed, took three major forms: the debtors' prison, the jail and the house of correction. Foucault (1977) points out that the expansion of places of confinement, notably asylums, developed from the old leper colonies as a means of containing the ill and the deranged. Institutional confinement was also widely used for the containment of the growing numbers of propertyless individuals who were subject to a variety of corporal punishments such as the stocks, branding, whipping and ultimately execution. These measures were generally applied to populations displaced by the advent of industrialisation and the end of the feudal system, notably vagrants and 'masterless' men. Between 1400 and 1700 the increasing numbers of landless people were perceived as a pressing danger to the state and the established order. Having no designated master, they were considered to be vagabonds and their status was a criminal one (Beier, 1985).

During the 1500s the establishment of the Bridewells provided a mechanism intended to reform the dispossessed and deviant through work.[7] Beier (1985) notes that the purpose of the Bridewell was to transform the 'vagabond's' character. They operated as houses of correction but were also intended to be punitive with discipline established through whipping, confinement, hard labour and cuts in food allowances. Regimentation was enacted through routine, dress and diet. However these institutions were widely corrupt and a recognised failure in solving the problems of vagrancy. By the early seventeenth century they were dealing overwhelmingly with offenders, although some continued to employ the poor, and there was growing confusion over the roles of the houses of correction and the workhouse.[8]

The developing legal system

The changing social structures occurring during this period, the erosion of the 'old order' of the feudal system and the advent of industrial capitalism, were accompanied by attempts to establish and legitimise the development of the state to sanctify and maintain the new economic order (Quinney, 1980). New laws were created and attempts to regulate this new social order were pursued, centring on the dominant sphere of the market (Melossi and Pavarini, 1981; Melossi, 1990).

To maintain social order during a period of major transformation, it was necessary for the state to establish and consolidate its right to control. To do this it required hegemony and legitimacy (Gramsci, 1971). The legitimacy of the social structure had to be demonstrated by the apparent lack of widespread social dissent. Force and consent had to be balanced to ensure that when force was applied by the state it appeared to be done with the consent of the majority. Ideology was as important as material forces were in producing or resisting change. Dominance was not achieved simply by ideology as such, 'but by the institutions and practices which derive from it' (Ransome, 1992: 118-9). This was important in the realm of the law. To gain consent the law had to be respected and to achieve a higher level of control it required *moral* consent from all social classes, particularly the labouring classes. However, as Scraton (1990) has pointed out, social relations of production, reproduction and colonialism inform a particular hegemonic form which in turn becomes installed in institutional policies and practices. He notes: 'It is through the process of institutionalisation that relations of domination and subjugation gain their legitimacy and achieve structural significance' (Scraton, 1990: 30). So while concessions may have been made to the lower social classes, structural hierarchies were preserved and reproduced through this mechanism.

The use of capital punishment for minor offences, particularly for the new property offences now codified in legislation, contributed to the growing social unrest of this period. 'Humanity' thus became introduced to the distribution of punishment (Foucault, 1977). This required not only that the humanity of the offender was recognised, but that the enactment of punishment was seen to be legitimate and reasonable. The notion of 'humanity' in this sense derives from the general theory of contract where individuals accept the laws of society and therefore the law itself. Punishment is therefore justified as a mechanism which operates in defence of society and not simply the retribution of the sovereign. As a result, Foucault (1977) argues that power was regulated and punishment was to be enacted on the soul rather than the body. Imprisonment became established as an intermediate form of punishment for offences for which transportation or execution were considered overly harsh. By 1750 prison was used for offences against private property (game taking etc.) and industrial indiscipline (Ignatieff, 1978; Melossi and Pavarini, 1981).

Changing philosophies also surrounded such developments. With some 'punishments' (execution and perhaps transportation) there was no possibility or hope of achieving any reintegration into society, while for other penalties (banishment, imprisonment) reintegration was a likely outcome. When a certain amount of punishment had been administered, the recipient was allegedly allowed to re-enter society on an equal basis. Rehabilitation served a similar purpose, having theoretically reformed the individual. With changing ideas about the potential for rehabilitation and more importantly reform (the rebuttal of the notion of 'original sin'), those sanctions which had the ability to transform became increasingly adopted.

With the growing use of imprisonment, the chaotic conditions prevalent in institutions at this time became a target for the reformist movements of the 1800s, closely linked to developing notions of hygiene and its importance. Interpretations of the motives behind the reform movements vary, with Foucault (1977) considering reform as a veil for increased control, while Ignatieff (1978) explores the belief in salvation propagated by the early reformers who viewed hygiene as an avenue for 'changing' the poor.[9]

The influence of the development of medicine

The development of medicine as a profession led to a transformation in ideas whereby it was possible to witness 'the language of social and moral condemnation veiled as the language of medicine' (Ignatieff, 1978: 60; see also Sim, 1990). Mort (1987) argues that medicine did not simply develop the scientific legitimacy for a class-based offensive against the poor. He believes that it was the attempt by the medical profession to stake their claim for expertise which 'became critical to forms of social regulation' (Mort, 1987: 23) and particularly to the regulation of the working-class at the time of developing industrial capitalism. The spread of disease had also become a target for the reformists within this context with notions of 'contagion' taking on a particularly problematic and widespread nature.

As Mort (1987) notes, while the causes of disease were unknown, various authorities believed that disease was spread by the urban poor, and was a direct result of their physical and moral habits. The experience of the workhouses had illustrated that disease could spread from the 'immoral' and poverty-stricken to the sober and industrious. Mort (1987: 16) notes:

> The proposed solution was twofold: to isolate the human sources of infection, subjecting them to a regime of compulsory inspection and detention, combined with propaganda to educate the poor into a regime of cleanliness and morality.

Measures to regulate and control disease were linked to measures to reform. Surveillance moved to the 'spaces between people' (Armstrong, 1983: 8) and this could be seen in practices developing in hospitals (confinement to bed, isolation and separation) and in the spatial arrangements of schools and workplaces. Scott (1990) notes how surveillance and dispersion were used to eliminate social spaces and ties in places where it was feared that unauthorised discourses might develop, notably forests, taverns and churches.

As a result, cleanliness came to symbolise discipline and order, with both disease (physical disorder) and criminality (social disorder) viewed in terms of contagion. Surveillance and disciplinary partitioning became control mechanisms for both.

Since disease in institutions had moral as well as physical causes, hygienic rituals were designed to fulfil disciplinary functions. To teach the poor to be clean, it was necessary to teach them to be godly, tractable and self-disciplined. (Ignatieff, 1978: 61)

The new hygienic practices which were introduced also aimed to remove the prisoner's identity. As with many aspects of the reform movement, the distinctions between 'humane' as opposed to 'coercive' measures were blurred. Separate and solitary confinement, originally developed by the Christian church, became a mode of operation in prisons and hospitals alike to halt the spread of both medical and moral contagion. Medical ideologies became popular in interpreting and controlling both criminality and insanity and their effects were evident in the isolationist prison regimes which developed. This was particularly prevalent in the incarceration of women (see Dobash et al., 1986; Sim, 1990; Zedner, 1991) and was emphasised in the separate treatment provided for women in the 1820s following the work of Elizabeth Fry and other reformers.

THE DEVELOPMENT OF PRISONS FOR WOMEN

If we cling to a unidimensional picture of penal institutions and their inmates, we cannot begin to understand the nature of the prison's power over the individual. By broadening the focus to include prisons for women, we immediately see that prisons function to control gender as well as crime. (Rafter, 1990: xi)

Prior to the nineteenth century penal reforms, little distinction was made between those incarcerated, be they men, women or children. Heidensohn (1981) points out that this meant that women were subjected to a regime designed for men. However, with the reform movement in the early part of the 1800s and its second wave in the latter part of the nineteenth century, moves were made, notably by John Howard and Elizabeth Fry, to change conditions for women.

Not all women in prison at this time were incarcerated for crime. Penal institutions also housed 'free' prisoners: women who voluntarily submitted themselves to prison because of the harshness of the conditions outside. Forsythe (1993) notes some of the factors which led to this situation including violence and sexual exploitation by men, poverty and the vulnerable position of many women if their partners died or left them. It would appear that prisons were frequently used as a form of asylum for some women (see Dobash et al., 1986; Zedner, 1991).

In 1817 Elizabeth Fry founded the Ladies Association which aimed to provide craft work, religious education and an orderly regime for women prisoners. Fry and other philanthropic women also attempted to change the appearances of women prisoners by inculcating the importance of cleanliness and domesticity (Rose, 1980). This led to the development of regimes based on 'domestic routine and paternalistic surveillance' (Sim, 1990: 132). Although the intentions of the reformers were undoubtedly benevolent, the new regimes were often met with resistance from the prisoners themselves as acts of individual indiscipline or collective rebellion (see Sim, 1990). This served to reinforce individual notions of 'wickedness' and 'indecency' on those who failed to comply, notions which already oscillated around criminal women and women perceived as 'deviant' (Ehrenreich and English, 1978; Hester, 1992).

While many accounts suggest that prison administrators overlooked the position of women, Zedner (1991) points out that this was not the case. The emphasis on classificatory systems meant that women prisoners were differentiated from men and later from each other largely in moralistic terms (i.e. the prostitute, the lunatic and the criminal). Zedner (1991: 3) suggests that, rather than ignoring women, policy-makers 'debated anxiously how to adapt the official regime to accord with their assumptions about women'.[10]

Although making up a larger proportion of the prison population in the late 1800s than is the case today, women were always numerically the minority. This was not true in the asylums, where there were more women during the 1850s (Sim, 1991) and differences were evident in the treatment they received. There are varying views as to whether women were treated more or less harshly than were men, with Forsythe (1993) and Zedner (1991) arguing the latter case and Dobash et al. (1986) the former. Yet they agree that significant differences were evident.

Forsythe (1993) notes that women could earn one third remission compared to only a quarter for men; they were more frequently placed in 'refuges' on leaving prison (perhaps indicative of the extension of measures of surveillance over women); they were not whipped or flogged for prison offences; they were not subject to the treadmill after the 1830s; non-communication was not as rigidly enforced as for men; women were more likely to be reprieved from the death penalty and after 1909 the routine use of cellular confinement was abolished for them. However, women were more likely to be in receipt of other forms of punishment notably stoppage of diet, solitary confinement or the dark cells. As Zedner (1991: 169) notes, because of the prohibition of certain forms of punishment in their application to women, warders were likely to employ more 'subtle stratagems'.

Dobash et al. (1986) have argued that women were more heavily punished than men because they were seen as deviating from perceived notions of womanhood, and they cite figures from Millbank Penitentiary in the 1860s to illustrate this. Forsythe (1993) counters, however, that the women at Millbank presented specific discipline problems. He states that statistics from other prisons during this period do not suggest major differences in the frequency of punishment and contends that there was no 'overall selective and disproportionate use of punishment for prison offences to condition women as opposed to men' (Forsythe, 1993: 528).

Nevertheless, the differential treatment meted out to women illustrates distinctive and subjective forms of control which although arguably less severe, were ultimately more restricting. Lady visitors and female matrons were introduced to instil notions of domesticity to counteract the corrupting influence of vice among women which was viewed as 'contagious'.

The resultant emphasis on establishing personal influence over each woman prisoner was in marked contrast to the quasi-militaristic, anonymous, and strictly uniform regime imposed on men. (Zedner, 1991: 4)

This 'personal influence', however, enabled the development of a more scrutinising and constricting regime shaped largely by beliefs concerning the nature and role of women:

As far as women were concerned, almost all prison discipline theorists argued that a close, tutelary, controlling, protecting relationship-oriented regime was particularly necessary for many women because these were creatures of emotion at the mercy of calculating, instrumental males, easily lured into vice and crime. (Forsythe, 1993: 528)

This notion of protecting women from the 'patriarchal public order' had certain profound implications, not least for the increased numbers of women locked up in asylums by husbands and fathers who considered them to be 'difficult'. This was facilitated by developing notions of 'femininity' and the increasing scrutiny of women's behaviour which resulted (see Porter, 1987). Women who stepped outside these generalised ideals of womanhood were considered to be at risk of 'psychiatric collapse' - closely linked to biological theories of the period. However as Porter (1987) illustrates, literary evidence from this period such as Ibsen's *The Dolls House* and Charlotte Perkins Gilman's *The Yellow Wallpaper* shows how in many cases the *reverse* was true. It was the physical and intellectual constraints which were placed on women that were inherently damaging.

Nevertheless, Positivist and neo-Darwinian theories played a major role in dictating expected female behaviour and were used to explain female criminality in terms of biologistic imperatives. This continued throughout the nineteenth and twentieth centuries, notably in the work of Lombroso and Ferrero (1895); Thomas (1923) and Pollak (1950) (see Smart, 1976; Heidensohn, 1996). In general, traditional explanations of female crime pointed to the failure of women individually to adapt themselves to social roles couched in terms of biology and sexuality.

Sexual immorality was believed to be profoundly linked to squalor and filth and as Mort (1987) outlines, professional representations of working-class sexuality as problematic (as opposed to middle-class 'hygienics') had a particular application for working-class women (see Smart, 1992). This, combined with the moralistic overtones of the period, resulted in the intense scrutiny of women prisoners. Following the Contagious Diseases Acts of 1864, 1866 and 1869 such vigilant attitudes led to the remand of women accused of prostitution, forcible vaginal inspections by male doctors and the confinement of women in hospital regimes that were similar to those in prison.[11] Morality and health were inextricably linked with legislation directed at those whose morals were in doubt. As Mort (1987: 76) notes:

It was *women* who were defined as the human agents of infection, threatening national health and security and challenging the social order by their active and autonomous sexuality.

Sim (1990) illustrates the way in which women as criminals came to have central importance with prison 'professionals' throughout this period. Attempts to 'normalise' offending women led to a network of intervention that was considerably 'more intensive' than that experienced by men (Sim, 1990: 129). Rehabilitation was largely targeted towards the acceptance of the role of wife and mother, already established in the pioneering efforts of Elizabeth Fry. Such biologically deterministic accounts of women were in force at an early stage in the development of regimes for women. As Poovey (1987: 138) notes, medicine was crucial in 'formulating a scientific justification for what was held to be woman's natural reproductive function and circumscribed social place'.

The frequent use of gynaecological explanations to account for women's deviance and the presumed relationship between that and their sexuality led to major medical interventions. Clitoridectomy, for example, was combined with discipline and regulation (Poovey, 1987; Ehrenreich and English, 1978) to create the 'sexually controlled female subject' (Sim, 1991: 139). The effect of this intense scrutiny is perhaps one reason why Dobash *et al.* (1986) fail to find many accounts of women's protest other than self-mutilation and cell-wrecking. Sim (1991), however, provides various examples of resistance by female prisoners both individually and collectively. Such acts served to reinforce notions of their inherent wickedness or resulted in the intervention of medical officers and the application of the label 'insane'. This continued throughout the 1900s, a time when, as Forsythe (1993) notes, the resistance of the suffragettes in prison led to the perceived confirmation of them as 'hysterical', justifying intrusive measures of control such as force feeding.

The adoption of the 'medical model' of female deviance can be seen by the appointment of medical men or women as the governors of women's prisons and by the installation of fully trained nurses, in some cases replacing prison officers. Both Dobash *et al.* (1986) and Sim (1991) chart this development. They illustrate the way that such ideologies impact on women's imprisonment today and consider the penal implications of 'therapeutic' regimes and the increasing surveillance this affords into women's lives.

Zedner (1991) also notes that the influence of doctors and psychologists led to the focus of attention on the worst recidivists namely 'habitual inebriates' and the 'feeble-minded' (see also Rose, 1985). For both groups, women were seen to present the most serious social problem, doubtless influenced by Eugenicist theories of propagation and degeneracy.[12] Sim (1990) notes that the Prison System Enquiry Committee of 1922 found that drunkenness with aggravation was the most common crime committed by women, followed by prostitution. The emphasis of regimes for women prisoners reflected the principles of domesticity and psychological treatment. However, punishment retained a prevalent position.

From the historical development of separate institutions for women, it is clear that factors other than attempts to transform prisoners into disciplined workers *did* operate, and that these developments were targeted at emphasising the role of domesticity for women, underlined by clearly defined ideological assumptions. Sim (1990: 143) notes:

> Women prisoners were the objects of a range of strategies, more intensive and well-developed than those to which male prisoners were subjected. The strategies met on the same policy terrain, saving the soul of the deviant woman for the heaven of normal motherhood.

As Zedner (1991) points out, not only did the revisionists ignore gender but they also underestimated the dynamics of the organizations at an agency level which have had a particular prevalence in regimes for women. Zedner (1991) critiques Foucault for his over-rationalised view of prisons which failed to take account of the continuing disorder in prisons (also noted by Sim, 1991). Complaints about prison conditions were prevalent. Lonsdale *et al.* (1943) noted the unhygienic conditions which women were expected to endure in the 1940s. One woman who had been imprisoned for her suffragist politics stated:

> What I was not prepared for was the general insanity of an administrative system in which lip-service is paid to the idea of segregation and the ideal of reform, when in practice the opportunities for contamination and infection are innumerable, and those of re-education for responsible citizenship practically nil... (Lonsdale *et al.*, 1943: 16)

Each account included in this pamphlet (Lonsdale *et al.*, 1943) notes the dirty, insanitary conditions, the lack of disinfectant and the cursory medical examinations despite a widespread and prevalent fear of venereal disease. Indeed, the *Prisoner's Medical Charter*, drawn up at this time as part of a campaign to improve the conditions within prisons, states its first aim as: 'More efficient sanitation, and strengthening of precautions against infection, particularly of Venereal Disease'.

The women who outline their experiences (in Lonsdale *et al.*, 1943) also note the effect of relationships between warders and prisoners as being of major significance during their period of custody. Prison officers could make their imprisonment a harsher experience or could assist them in minor ways which helped along the way. Zedner (1991: 297) notes, 'life inside is better understood as the sum of relations between inmates (both warders and prisoners) than as the perfect realisation of penal theory'. This has particular significance for the organization of women's prisons.

CONTEMPORARY REGIMES FOR WOMEN

The female prison population remains relatively small in comparison to the male prison population. In March 2000 the adult female prison population of England and Wales was around 2,880 out of a total adult prison population of 51,287 (figures obtained from HMPS, April 2000). In Scotland, with a prison population of 5,905 in April 2000, women accounted for 146 convicted or untried adult prisoners (figures obtained from SPS, April 2000).

Despite the relatively small numbers of women who are imprisoned, the figures have risen substantially over the past few years. The majority are sentenced for property offences (theft and handling; fraud and forgery etc.), yet there has been a slight increase in the numbers of women in custody for violence and more particularly for drug offences. This is reflected in the increased lengths of sentences for female offenders. The number of women sentenced to custody for drug offences rose by six per cent between March 1998 and March 1999 in England and Wales. By the end of March 1999 over one third of sentenced women prisoners were detained for drug offences (White, Parker and Butler, 1999).

In Scotland, the number of women sentenced to custody for drug offences rose by 109 per cent, from 247 offences in 1985 to 516 in 1995 (Social Work Services and Prison Inspectorates for Scotland, 1998: 8). Of course, many more offences such as theft and prostitution can be related to drug use. Drugs appear to be a significant factor in offending behaviour, with many women getting caught up in relatively 'petty' crime to fund their drug habit or that of their male partners (Taylor, 1993).

Concerns have also been expressed over the lengthy sentences meted out to overseas nationals convicted of drug trafficking offences. Many will be deported at the end of their sentence and, following a number of escapes, they are confined to closed conditions for the duration of their imprisonment. Their sentences are often lengthy, averaging eight years. They face a variety of problems: language difficulties; cultural differences; separation from families and racism (see Green, 1991; 1998).

Overall, the number of black women in prison is disproportionately high. In 1994, 11.8 per cent of the female prison population was black (compared to 9.6 per cent for male prisoners) despite estimates that 1.3 per cent of the general female population are black (Home Office, 1995b). In some prisons, the figure is significantly higher. HM Chief Inspector of Prisons Report on HM Prison Holloway in 1997 revealed that 35 per cent of the prison population were from 'ethnic minority backgrounds' (HM Chief Inspector of Prison, 1997b: 9).

Because women form such a small proportion of the prison population in a system run largely by men dealing primarily with male offenders, they are often overlooked and their needs neglected. 'It is easy to perceive their care and administration as an adjunct to the "main Prison Service" rather than as an integral part of a service sensitive to women's needs' (NACRO, 1992: 4). This has often led to their exclusion from official reports and enquiries. Women prisoners did not take part in the prison 'riots' of 1990, and this is sometimes taken to mean that the administration of the penal system is relatively unproblematic as far as women are concerned. Lord Justice Woolf (as he then was) (1991) decided while conducting his enquiry into the prison disturbances in England and Wales that: '. . . it would not be right to investigate or make findings about problems which solely relate to women prisoners, none of whom was involved in the disturbances' (Woolf, 1991: para 2.18).

Recommendations and decisions focus on the larger, male prison system resulting in the neglect of the needs of minority prisoners. As NACRO (1992: 4) point out 'many aspects of custody which in principle apply equally, have different meanings and different implications when put into effect for women and for men'. NACRO attempted to compensate for the exclusion of women in the Woolf Report by producing, *A Fresh Start for Women Prisoners: The Implications of the Woolf Report for Women* (NACRO: 1992). More recent concerns about the penal estate for women resulted from the deaths of seven young women in HM Institution Cornton Vale, shortly followed by an eighth and conditions in HMP Holloway that so appalled an HM Inspectorate team that they walked out in protest. This led to the production of two more recent reports which focus specifically on the imprisonment of women (*Women in Prison: A Thematic Review*, HM Chief Inspector of Prisons, 1997; *Women Offenders: A Safer Way*, Social Work Services and Prisons Inspectorates for Scotland, 1998).

However, as outlined previously, when considering the historical development of prisons for women, it would be incorrect to allow a belief in the 'official neglect' of female imprisonment to ignore the very *specific* interventions and dominant assumptions which determine the way regimes operate with regard to women. Female imprisonment may often be overlooked when policies are developed to deal with the more public issues relating to the overwhelmingly male penal system, but it is crucial to note that interventions into the female prison system tend to be based on particular ideological assumptions. Johnson and Toch (1982: 205) point out that in attempting to understand the differences between male and female prisoners' experiences, an awareness is needed of the:

> . . . context of structural and cultural influences such as the historical imbalances in priorities given to women's prisons, different cultural and social expectations (before and during imprisonment) and theoretical perspectives that influence the treatment of male and female offenders.

This is evident from the Home Office publication *Regimes For Women* (Home Office, 1991) which set out guidance to 'assist governors and staff in the provision of appropriate and humane regimes in establishments holding women and girls' (Home Office, 1991: 1). It makes use of previous research findings and in its implementary form outlines and suggests solutions for many of the problems experienced by women in custody.

However, the rehabilitative language and therapeutic orientation which is presented around women's prisons by official agencies obscures the reality of incarceration as it is experienced by most women. Conditions clearly *differ* from those in men's prisons. The problems of overcrowding and insanitary conditions are less and women tend to have more association time than men do. However, this is not to suggest that women's prisons are problem free. Food and medical treatment are poor, facilities are often limited and there is little or no privacy for most women. Indeed they face a different set of problems. The distance and small number of prisons makes regular contact with family and friends difficult and costly. Children may be taken into care and getting them back may be very difficult, particularly if the woman has lost her home. So while there is great emphasis placed on developing family relationships, evidenced by the architectural design of many female prisons, the physical constrictions severely limit this (HM Chief Inspector of Prisons, 1997; Carlen, 1998; Devlin, 1998; Social Work Services and Prisons Inspectorates for Scotland, 1998).

In many ways, the operation of regimes within women's prisons is indicative of a more insidious form of social control. This is partially veiled by the language prevalent in describing female prisoners' experiences. Cells are called 'rooms', security and discipline becomes 'supervision' and 'award' describes punishment. As Mandaraka Sheppard (1986: 109) points out:

> Linguistic games are often used in custodial institutions and mainly purport to give a picture which does not correspond to reality. However, the arbitrariness of the words used may also serve other purposes: first those kind words make the guards feel less guilty (if they ever do) and second they make the prisoners forget their status at least temporarily.

This links with Zedner's (1991) argument concerning the need to understand the interaction between staff and prisoners, which is of vital significance in women's prisons given their emphasis on 'therapeutic' regimes and inter-personal relationships.

However, this veneer of language which suggests a more relaxed regime tends to conceal operational practices which are more intrusive. All mail coming into and going out of the prison is opened; officers at certain establishments can listen in to the women's rooms by intercom and monitor any conversation; all phone calls are taped and visits are monitored. Officers can enter a cell at any time and it is not uncommon for a prisoner to be wakened during the night by an officer shining a torch in her face. Women have to learn to function without privacy. As a prison officer stated in relation to drug use:

> You detect the women easier than the guys - and I don't mean it's just women being women or anything like that - but they're not as fly as the men, not so cute, not so crafty. Some of them can be, but men are more conscious that walls have ears if you like. I've heard some of them talking in here about drugs where that wouldn't happen with the men when people were about. It would still be there but they wouldn't make so many mistakes

as women make. (Prison officer, interview: September 1993)

Men are not monitored so closely. Indeed the very organization of many women's prisons (small 'family' units) allows for more vigorous disciplinary emphasis. Carlen notes that:

> . . . the general features of the hierarchical discipline combine with the domestic work programme, with the denial to prisoners of sociability and adult womanhood and with the organization of the women into small family units, to ensure a mental and bodily surveillance which denudes the prisoners' daily life of all dignity and independence. (Carlen, 1983: 111)

Not surprisingly, there is a much higher rate of disciplinary offences in female prisons. This, to an extent contradicts the argument of Dobash *et al.* (1986) who state that women are more likely to turn their frustrations inward. At the same time, however, this results from them being disciplined frequently for trivial offences. The inconsistency in rule interpretation and enforcement are primary causes of stress in prisons leading to frustration. Maden *et al.* (1994) showed from their study that women were more likely than men to have at least one disciplinary offence on record, the majority of these were disobedience or disrespect (Maden *et al.*, 1994: 184). They also note that the greater freedom of movement and association in women's prisons 'allows more interaction with prison officers and increases the potential for transgressing minor prison rules'. Arguably this may result in a more oppressive regime. The greater likelihood of association is also likely to increase the potential for offences of violence to occur.

The enforcement of minor rules and prohibitions in women's prisons has been recognised by the Home Office. The document *Regimes For Women* (Home Office, 1991) notes that women are more often disciplined than men, although they are unlikely to be any more disruptive. It emphasises the need to establish that a charge is necessary before being instigated and it expresses the need to avoid unnecessary rules and regulations. While outlining the necessary procedures for disciplinary action it states:

> Resorting to disciplinary charges of disobedience or disrespect is sometimes an indication that a member of staff lacks the confidence to establish more normal relationships with prisoners - if it becomes standard practice for staff to bring essentially trivial disciplinary charges before a genuine effort of communication has been made, the disciplinary system will rapidly come to undermine prisoners' respect for all staff. (Home Office, 1991: 27, para 106)

It also notes:

> 'Informal' punishments, such as the imposition by staff of unpopular chores on prisoners considered to be 'difficult', are illegal and must not be allowed. (Home Office, 1991: 27, para 107)

Although women are less likely than men to be transferred to another prison for a disciplinary offence (Maden et al., 1994), their punishment is similar to men: loss of remission; confinement to cell; withdrawal of privileges such as tobacco or association.

The use of strip cells and silent cells is not uncommon for 'disruptive' prisoners or those deemed in need of monitoring. Strip cells are cells which have been stripped of all furnishings, including the bed. Cardboard furniture may be provided, but generally they contain only a sleeping-bag made from reinforced material (strong canvas) and a raised plinth on which a mattress is placed. Prisoners will be stripped of clothing before being placed in this accommodation and given a tunic and shorts to wear, made out of the same reinforced material as the sleeping-bag. Offenders are locked in these cells as punishment or if they are considered to be a risk to themselves or others. They are regularly used for people withdrawing from drugs.

Silent cells are similar to strip cells but have been specifically designed for punitive containment. They have reinforced walls and double doors (padded) to contain effectively any noise the prisoner may make. There will be no windows and a dim overhead light will be kept on at all times. There are peepholes high up on the walls for prison officers routinely to observe the prisoner who is held inside. The existence and regular use of such cellular accommodation clearly belies the therapeutic focus of women's prisons.

Strip searching is routinely used as a security measure for both men and women for its deterrent effect and as a means of discovering 'unauthorised' articles. Failure to submit to a strip search leads to being placed in the punishment block or an enforced strip search.

Medical 'care'
As Sim (1990) has illustrated, historically medical officers and professionals have been keen to rescue women from debauchery and deviance. Medical power has a long history as part of the network of regulation and control in state institutions, particularly regarding women. It is important to consider medical provisions when examining the experiences of drug users, given their medical requirements during and after withdrawal.

Many of the problems experienced by women in prison are trivialised and this is especially true of healthcare. Many health problems, such as diabetes, asthma, peptic ulcers and epilepsy are exacerbated by imprisonment, as are mental health problems, particularly nervousness and anxiety (Wilson and Leasure, 1991). Frequently requests to see the medical officer are denied or access decisions made by prison officers with no medical experience who are able to act as the gatekeepers between prisoners and a variety of social agencies.

Studies, such as Shaw (1992) have shown that many women prisoners believe their healthcare to be inadequate:

They wanted better access to health services, some choice in who they can see - access to outside consultants, for example, and not just in a crisis. They wanted less medication or more appropriate medication. (Shaw, 1992: 446)

Menstrual problems are often brought on or exacerbated by stress and prison conditions. Patients are frequently refused 'alternative' medicine and the Prison Healthcare Service is repeatedly criticised for malpractice. Moreover there is often no continuity between medical treatment inside and outside prison, with no formal transfer of medical documentation from the National Health Service to the Prison Service.

In 1999 the HMPS and NHS working group on healthcare in prisons recommended a formal partnership between the NHS and the Prison Service (Joint Prison Service and NHS Executive Working Group, 1999). This is yet to be fully implemented. Brazier (1982) demonstrates the need for independent control of medical care in British prisons, precisely because of the 'enforced' relationship between doctors and patients and the nature of coercion in the very operation of regimes. As she points out, 'The prisoner is an involuntary patient every aspect of whose life is regulated by the prison authorities on whose behalf the medical officer undertakes the care of his [sic] health' (Brazier, 1982: 286). This has profound consequences for the doctor–patient relationship. She states that the prison doctor:

> . . . is part and parcel of the prison hierarchy intimately involved in the maintenance of order and discipline. His consent is necessary before a prisoner can be kept under special restraint or before a prisoner can be subject to an award of cellular confinement. No individual, however skilled and compassionate a doctor, can maintain a normal doctor–patient relationship with a man whom the next day he may acquiesce in subjecting to solitary confinement. (Brazier, 1982: 285)

This is intended to apply to female prisoners as well!

Some of the major criticisms levelled at prison doctors relate to the over-use of drugs to control prisoners or the refusal to prescribe particular drugs when requested. The duty of medical officers to prevent a prisoner harming himself, herself or others often seems to weigh in favour of prescribing medication, particularly if suicide or violence seem to be a possibility and one which may be offset by the use of drugs. The issue of 'liability' takes a prominent position in decision-making.

> The dilemma faced by the doctor caring for a disturbed patient who is willing to accept drug treatment is whether to prescribe drugs which will pacify the patient but may result in unpleasant or in some cases harmful side-effects or whether to refuse drugs to the patient and expose him to the risk of restraint by physical means or solitary confinement. (Brazier, 1982: 291)

This clearly represents a real dilemma, but it does not explain the high prescription rate of drugs to female prisoners. The prison authorities justify the increase in use of psychotropic and hypnotic drugs as a reflection of the numbers of emotionally disturbed or mentally unstable prisoners. This is considered particularly applicable to women who have been ascribed such reputations and classifications in policy-making decisions relating to female prisoners (Allen, 1987). It is frequently argued that the higher incidence of medication prescribed to women in prison merely reflects the higher incidence of prescribed drugs obtained by women in the community. There has not yet been an acknowledgement of the relationship between high numbers of drug users in prison and high levels of medication.

Wilson and Leasure (1991: 35) point out that 'only a small proportion of inmates suffer from acute mental illness yet medication is often given for minor psychosomatic complaints or as a "cure" for behaviour problems'. In particular Largactil is alleged to be extensively used in British prisons yet it:

> . . . can cause jaundice, symptoms similar to Parkinson's disease or at best prolonged drowsiness and disorientation. Up to 40 per cent of patients treated with the more powerful psychotropic drugs will suffer some degree of side-effects. (Brazier, 1982: 283)

Maden et al. (1994) studied rates of psychosis among male and female prisoners and discovered the prevalence of psychosis was approximately two per cent in both groups. They point out however that 'whilst in custody, women make greater demands on prison health services, mainly because of higher rates of personality disorder, substance abuse, and neurosis' (Maden et al., 1994: 172). They note that women in prison report higher rates for all forms of adult psychiatric treatment but that this is consistent with gender differences in the general population. They point out:

> All hospital officers in women's prisons are trained nurses and may be seen as more sympathetic by inmates than hospital officers in male prisons, where only a minority have a nursing qualification. In addition, the culture of male prisons often saw emotion as a sign of weakness, so that distress may result in an act of violence, rather than a request to see the doctor. (Maden et al., 1994: 186)

They qualify this however:

> Treatment facilities in women's prisons may be better than those in many male prisons but this is not to say that they met the needs of all or most women. Many women did not regard nursing or medical staff as sympathetic, seeing them as primarily agents of the institution. Lack of confidentiality was often cited by both men and women as a reason for not revealing personal problems to officers. (Maden et al., 1994: 186)

The emphasis on the need for 'treatment' was fundamental in the developing ethos of Holloway as a secure hospital rather than as a prison. Medical and psychiatric facilities were its main focus. This clearly failed. 'Mentally disordered women were punished rather than treated or transferred to hospital whilst other women resented being treated as if they were not responsible for their own actions' (Maden et al., 1994: 173). They point out that Holloway 'now operates more effectively, having reverted to the conventional separation of disciplinary and medical services that is found in male prisons' (Maden et al., 1994: 173).

Clearly, as Usher (1989) notes, the psychologising and psychiatrisation of women serves to depoliticise and individualise their experiences.[13] This is particularly true of penal regimes for women where medical interventions often serve this purpose, concealing as they do, a wider range of practices which are aimed to punish and enforce discipline. The continued incidence of self-mutilation and attempted suicides in women's prisons is high and serves to illustrate the inefficiency of the regimes. Access to doctors is often denied, suicide threats are sometimes minimised and the conditions in prison serve to increase the problems for women who are ill or depressed (Carlen, 1983; 1998; Dobash et al., 1986; Casale, 1989; HM Chief Inspector of Prisons, 1997; Devlin, 1998).

The objectives of imprisonment for women, many of whom are there for relatively minor offences, run counter to the claim that incarceration is necessary for those deemed to be either deserving of punishment or a danger to the public. In contrast women sentenced to imprisonment are there largely due to their inability or lack of desire to conform to a particular lifestyle. As Carlen et al. (1985: 182) state:

. . . . women are primarily sent to prison because of either their unconventional domestic circumstances, the failure of the non-penal welfare or health institutions to cope with their problems, or their own refusal to comply with socially-conditioned female gender-stereotype requirements.

It is clear that professionals - social workers, psychiatrists, and the judiciary - define certain 'types' of women as suitable candidates for punishment. The insidious and ideological nature of the institutionalised distinction drawn between 'good' and 'bad' women raises serious questions across the criminal justice system. As this chapter has argued, dominant ideologies relating to appropriate constructions of femininity are institutionalised and come to affect policies and practices both inside and outside penal regimes. These ideological constructs profoundly affect the ways in which punishment and social control are regulated and the manner in which resources, such as medical care, are distributed. These measures can impact significantly on drug-using women as prisoners.

The next chapter will focus on the discourses around drug use and drug users, particularly women, to highlight the mechanisms which operate to distinguish between punitive and therapeutic policies and practices. Fundamentally, it will illustrate the operation of official discourses and their impact on those considered to be appropriate targets for state intervention.

ENDNOTES for Chapter 2

[1] Masculinist accounts are those which take male perspectives, values and experiences as the 'norm', assuming they apply to both men and women. Howe (1994) argues that social revisionists largely neglected the experiences of women and when they did include them it was as an addendum to male experiences. She points out: 'The implicit assumption is that penal regimes impacted uniformly on male and female offenders' (Howe, 1994: 72).

[2] This is not to suggest that all women will acquiesce in this. Many women resist normative constructions of femininities but there are consequences to be paid for doing so. 'The disciplinary power that inscribes femininity is everywhere and yet it is nowhere; the disciplinarian is everyone and yet no-one in particular' (Bartky, 1990: 74). Although women may refuse to submit to this, the result will be the 'refusal of male patronage' and the sanctioning of non-compliant behaviour. It must then be understood as a much wider and oppressive mechanism which maintains sexual subordination.

[3] It is this recognition that leads Cain (1990b) to advocate three strategies for a transgressive criminology: reflexivity, deconstruction and reconstruction

[4] The constant threat and reality of mental, physical and sexual violence acts to control women, placing restrictions on space, work, leisure, definitions of appearances etc. All are areas where male (hetero)sexuality is exercised as a form of control. Under patriarchy, male power is both personal and institutional and as a result, 'the law both serves and legitimates patriarchal power' (Freeman, 1984: 57).

[5] It is crucial to recognise that 'woman' is not an all encompassing category. As feminists have recognised, relations of class, race, (dis)ability continue to operate as determining contexts, in conjunction with patriarchal relations, for the experiences of individual women.

[6] From the 1500s the poor and the 'criminal' were exiled to the developing colonies. Beier (1985) notes that it was estimated that thousands of paupers, especially the young, were sent overseas and many were forced into military service from around 1560. The exiled were generally indentured for service with a colonial master in conditions that were often tantamount to slavery.

[7] Beier (1985) argues that the existence and intent of the Bridewell contradicts the contention made by Foucault (1977) that the prison, with its emphasis on regimentation and moulding only developed in the late eighteenth century.

[8] The workhouse, which dates from the seventeenth century, was intended to provide a means for controlling vagrancy. It provided the unemployed with food but forced them to work very hard, spending most of their time inside the institution. Workhouses became places of internment for those with no-one to look after them, notably the sick, the aged and the mentally ill.

[9] The growing popularity of Harteian and Lockean forms of materialism led to the mind and body being viewed as of equal material importance. Mental and moral behaviour were related to physical wellbeing. It was believed that immorality could lead to a breakdown in the body's functioning and therefore to disease. As a result the importance of both physical and mental regulation became linked.

[10] See Rafter (1990) and Feinman (1994) for similar discussions as they apply to the development of penal systems for women in the USA.

[11] Corbin (1987) documents the importance of social regulation which developed from France in the nineteenth century. The main aims of this legislation were: to regulate prostitution; to protect 'public morality'; to ensure the protection of 'male prosperity'; and to protect the nation's health from disease.

[12] Further evidence to illustrate this can be drawn from the operation of institutions other than the prison (the asylum, the Magdalene House).

[13] At the same time, mental illness is often taken to be indicative of the transformation of the individual prisoner. An example of this can be seen from a discussion on *The Moral Maze* (Radio 4, 11 August 1994). It was pointed out that if the character of the prisoner is

not fundamentally altered by imprisonment then they have not been changed by prison. In a discussion of Myra Hindley and Ian Brady, the 'Moors Murderers', one of the panel noted: 'At least Brady had the decency to go mad'.

CHAPTER 3

The Social Construction of Drug Use

The experiences of women in prison are determined, to a considerable extent, by the structural determinants that characterise the prison system. For drug using women, the ideological constructs and official discourses that relate to drug use further affect their experiences. This chapter examines the response of state institutions and agencies to individuals who use and/or supply substances which are controlled and/or prohibited by the state. The political and economic context within which certain substances are defined as 'dangerous' is also considered, with particular emphasis given to the development of controls aimed at drug users and suppliers. Policies of surveillance, regulation and rehabilitation are highlighted in order to analyse the particular emphasis given to the differential practices of treatment and rehabilitation, which operate alongside policies of regulation and punishment.

Specifically, the social constructions of drug use and drug users is examined as they apply to and affect the experiences of females. When women's experiences of imprisonment and/or drug use are studied, it is evident that a very different set of assumptions operates ideologically and in practice, compared to those for men. The area of drug use combines behaviour that is prohibited by law with an activity which is also considered to be 'unfeminine'. This compounds the perceived 'deviance' of the female drug user. From *Chapter* 2, it is evident that the combination of 'treatment' and 'punishment' in women's prisons, governed by medical and legal ideologies, provided a very specific response to female prisoners. This chapter looks at how these discourses are operationalised and institutionalised towards women drug users in policy and practice.

'DEVIANT' DRUGS

An important aspect of any social phenomenon is the propensity for perceptions relating to it to change over time. This is particularly true of drugs and is indicative of the social and cultural constructions which lead to certain substances being either acceptable or proscribed (Weil, 1972; McDermott, 1992; South, 1994). As McDonald (1994: 11) states, 'A substance's meaning or reality, its capacity to attract or repel, varies according to the cultural context in which it is placed'.

A variety of factors affect the legal status of a drug, including its properties, its country of origin and the current social/historical climate. In the UK, certain substances are controlled and/or prohibited under the Misuse of Drugs Act 1971. They are classified (Class A, B or C) - with specific regulations and punishments applied accordingly.[1] However, a drug's potential for harm clearly does not determine legal status. Many drugs that can in certain circumstances be harmful are acceptable if their use is medically regulated, while others are available with relatively few restrictions. Cigarette and alcohol use are both legal[2] but are responsible for considerably more deaths than any other substances. The legal status of a drug is instead closely linked with social and cultural influences (see Szasz, 1974; Boyd and Lowman, 1991; Strausbaugh and Blaise, 1991; Kohn, 1992). The concept of 'drugs' is not a scientific classification but is based on moral and/or political evaluations (Lidz et al., 1980; Husak, 1992; McDonald, 1994).

The control and/or prohibition of certain substances is not static but changes with and within different cultures (see Szasz, 1974; McDonald, 1994) and in different historical periods. Many proscribed drugs today were considered acceptable in the past (Zackon, 1988; Strausbaugh and Blaise, 1991). Opiates and cocaine which are presently Class A drugs with penalties of up to life imprisonment for unlawfully supplying them, could be purchased with relative ease up until the Dangerous Drugs Act 1920. Indeed, opium use was common during the nineteenth century and opiates were eaten, drunk as tea and administered for medical purposes (Edwards, 1981).

Britain, which had been a major tenderer of Indian opium, using it in an attempt to regulate trading patterns with China (Dorn, 1977; Zackon, 1988) participated in the 1912 International Opium Convention largely due to pressure from the USA. This required those states involved to control 'dangerous drugs', leading to the Dangerous Drugs Act 1920 in Britain, which placed certain substances under the control of the medical profession and pharmacists. The 1920 Act was also justified through fear of poisonings from particular drugs such as cocaine and opiates.

The development of legislation governing the use of certain substances has arisen within specific cultural contexts, usually with particular intent. Attempts to regulate the use of specific drugs can be linked with attempts to regulate particular populations. This was notably evident in attempts to control immigrants following World War I in the context of disappearing labour shortages and increased competition for jobs. The legislation which developed led to the criminalisation of certain substances, particularly opiates, cocaine and, in 1925, cannabis. Many of these substances were linked with immigrant communities: notably opium with the Chinese, and cocaine and marijuana with black immigrants. The implicit racist connotations associated with legislative controls on drug use have been outlined by several authors (Szasz, 1974; Zackon, 1988; Kohn, 1992; McDermott, 1992; McDonald, 1994; South, 1994).

Kohn (1992) argues persuasively that the panic which developed in the early 1900s around the use of drugs related more to major social changes arising in the post-war period than to the physical composition of drugs themselves. In the wake of World War I, drugs became a focus of blame for the relaxation of the old sexual roles and hierarchies in terms of class, race and gender (see also Lidz et al., 1980; McDonald, 1994). In particular, the social and economic emancipation of women was viewed as a threat to the traditional role of women and thus to the social order itself. Women were moving into the public sphere, their dress and behaviour altered and it was no longer so easy to distinguish between 'respectable' women and those of 'a certain class'. Anxieties were expressed about the cultural influences of 'men of colour' (Kohn, 1992: 2) and their fraternisation with white women. Kohn (1992) demonstrates how the sale of narcotics became enmeshed in a 'moral campaign' leading to the extension of the power of the state over private lives and personal choices.

> In this state of tension, drugs presented themselves as an explanation for some of these disturbing developments, and as a way of expressing profound anxieties about the social order as a whole. Alien, in nature, dope was invested with magical properties by being prohibited. Existing in marginal zones of society where conventional boundaries were unstable, it was understood as the agent that dissolved these boundaries, rather than as a symptom of instability. (Kohn, 1992: 176)

The situational context of social anxieties continues to influence the development of drug policies to the present day, both internationally and nationally. How the 'drugs problem' is defined and the attempts made to control it, reflect both overt and insidious methods of controlling both individuals and populations considered to pose a threat to the stability of the social order. These definitions regularly reflect responses to a 'moral panic'. As Hall *et al.* (1978: 16) argue:

> When the official reaction to a person, groups of persons or series of events is *out of all proportion* to the actual threat offered, when 'experts', in the form of police chiefs, the judiciary, politicians and editors *perceive* the threat in all but identical terms, and appear to talk 'with one voice' of rates, diagnoses, prognoses and solutions, when the media representations universally stress 'sudden and dramatic' increases (in numbers involved or events) and 'novelty' above and beyond that which a sober, realistic appraisal could sustain, then we believe it is appropriate to speak of the beginnings of a *moral panic.*

Indeed, the discourse surrounding drug use today is dominated by metaphors. Successive government campaigns have used powerful images of decay and disease ineffectively (see Faulk-Whynes, 1991). To portray the danger of drugs, the media regularly equate drug use with drastic increases in violent crime and extensive measures are used to combat what is perceived as a 'social menace'. Such representations of drug use are used to define the form which law enforcement will take and influence official definitions and thereby policy. They also determine the focus and direction of the political management of the 'war on drugs'. This was emphasised in recent times with the appointment of a 'Drugs Czar', officially known as the Anti-Drugs Co-ordinator (Keith Hellawell), in 1997.

Government commitment to fighting the 'war against drugs' has led to a massive expansion in police powers, both nationally and internationally. In response, contemporary policing methods include the use of high-tech surveillance and co-operation between regional and international police forces (see Dorn and South, 1991b). There has been increased support for joint operations between customs and police both nationally and internationally and agreement over the need for the maintenance of frontier checks (*The Guardian*, 11 January 1990; O'Connor, 1993).[3] Concerns were expressed (*The Herald*, 31 October 1992) that drug trafficking would be exacerbated by the removal of European borders, causing the drugs 'problem' to 'spill over' into Britain. This threat of terrorists and drug traffickers being afforded easy access to Europe has led to persuasive arguments for the expansion of policing and law enforcement (*The Independent*, 3 June 1993). Indeed, such efforts can be likened to an industry that continually reinforces and extends its powers and resources (Chambliss, 1994; Christie, 1994).

The use of intrusive surveillance measures which clearly infringe on the rights of an individual or group is justified by the creation of a discourse on the 'dangerousness' of particular drugs. During the 1980s, trafficking in heroin and cannabis was perceived as the main threat. This has now been replaced, to an extent, by fears about an increase in synthetic drugs (notably 'ecstasy') and the supply of cocaine. Cocaine, particularly crack,[4] is blamed for increasing levels of crime and notably violent crime. Rose and Hugill pointed out in *The Observer* (15 November 1992) that 'The police and government strategy on drugs is in disarray, as evidence grows that the use of crack cocaine has become a national epidemic, responsible for a wave of violent crime'. The reaction to crack is clearly indicative of a moral panic.

Similar ideologies operate at a national level. While law enforcement is extended and increased to 'control' drugs, individuals become targeted and criminalised as a direct result of their drug use.[5] Both nationally and internationally, individuals who consume particular substances are the focus for social controls. As Husak (1992: 2) discusses in relation to the 'war on drugs':

> The war, after all, cannot really be a war on drugs, since drugs cannot be arrested, prosecuted or punished. The war is against persons who use drugs . . . And unlike previous battles in this apparently endless war, current campaigns target casual users as well as drug abusers.

Domestic control: policing and prescribing

In Britain, perceptions of drug use (as enshrined in policies and legislation) have been governed largely in terms of legal and medical definitions and controls. This is reflected in the subsequent responses to users as 'sick' or 'deviant' (Collison, 1993 and 1994; Whynes, 1991). Bifurcated definitions have resulted in the operation of two systems of control, which tend to interact rather than to operate independently of each other. Medical control leads to the medicalisation of users; legal controls to the criminalisation of users.

A supply-and-demand model of response can be seen to operate. Attempts to reduce demand are tackled through education and 'treatment', while attempts to thwart supply are dealt with by law enforcement, punishment and deterrence. The British approach to defining and responding to drug use has been distinctive, taking into account medical, legal and social issues (Whynes, 1991) in contrast to the USA where the emphasis has been largely on criminalisation.

Systems of surveillance operate explicitly in relation to structures of class, race and gender. McDermott (1992: 197) argues that a split occurred with the development of legislation on drug use between:

> 'respectable' therapeutic addicts and hedonistic or recreational drug use. These definitions have an explicit class basis; it was acceptable behaviour for the well-to-do, but there was always a concern to regulate the pleasures of the 'dangerous classes'.

How behaviour (or people) become defined and managed as a 'social problem' has to be understood within a broader context - how 'official' definitions become institutionalised and operate as ideologies. This is clear with regard to drug use where a myriad of negative images and reputations exist. Drug enforcement policy is thereby used to legitimate the further criminalisation of already marginalised groups. As Scraton and Chadwick (1987: 213) point out:

> the intervention of the state's institutions - its very political management - reflects, transmits and reinforces the ideological construction of identities and reputations. It is this *range* of responses - economic, political and ideological - which cuts into people's daily lives and which, taken together, forms the process of marginalisation.

Once marginalisation has occurred, law-enforcement agencies will be instigated in an attempt to regulate and control those deemed to require it, in this case drug users. In this context, marginalisation is closely tied to the process of criminalisation, affecting policing and law enforcement practices and priorities. McConville *et al.* (1991) provide some explanation as to how this operates with regard to police perceptions of what they term the 'suspect' population.[6] They argue that the 'suspect' population is a police construct, of which the 'criminal' population is merely a sub-set. 'The suspect population is constructed on the basis of a complex interaction of rules and principles. But they are *police* - rather than *legal* - rules and principles' (McConville *et al.*, 1991: 15). These are heavily weighted by wider structures of class, race and gender. In this way, McConville *et al.* (1991: 15) argue that the major contentions of labelling theory are correct: 'that suspicion, accusation, conviction and criminal self-identity are not objective characteristics of "criminals", but they are the products of law enforcers as well'.

Historically, control of drug users has been advocated, whether through medical or legal means, in an attempt to prevent the perceived threat of crime and disorder and the spread of disease. Singer (1993: 43) notes:

Both criminality and disease are conceived as outlaws, invaders with secret ways, as well as forces of disorder. Both criminality and disease (and their postulated equivalence) are used to rationalise forms of power in the name of maintaining a healthier, that is, crime-free and disease-free, society. Both rationalise power as management.

For drug users, both crime (through drug use as an illicit activity) and disease (through the potential for transmission of infection) are allegedly juxtaposed. However, the potential for spreading 'harm' to the 'general public', more accurately the law-abiders, frequently contextualises measures to assist drug users. In a handbook designed for workers in the drugs field, Dickson and Hollis provide a chapter entitled 'Facing Up To Aids' (Bennett, 1989: 115). They state:

> Drug abusers have never bothered about hepatitis, overdoses, choking to death on their own vomit, thrombosis, gangrene or heroin cut with strychnine—so why should they worry about AIDS? The fact that more and more drug abusers are being identified as HIV-positive is unlikely to influence them.

Notions based on 'contagion-fears' around disease and crime enable medical and legal strategies to be used as a two-pronged approach to this phenomenon. However responses to drug users can also be evidenced in what Pitch (1995: 20) discusses as the 'metaphor of bifurcation' where social control policies are increasingly seen to be moving in two separate directions. This model can effectively be applied to policies and practices relating to drug use. One direction is determined by punitive and repressive custodial regimes for those viewed as the 'residual hard core of untreatable offenders' (Pitch, 1995: 20). In tangent with this is a form of control that is viewed as 'softer'. This is comprised of community-based therapeutic and rehabilitative programmes and educational practices and is designed to operate for 'the rest', those deemed amenable for reform/change and 'construed as a population capable of being reclaimed . . . through education, rehabilitation and re-socialisation' (Pitch, 1995: 20) (see also Cohen, 1985).

Lidz et al. (1980: 97) discuss the distinction between ideologies around treatment and punishment, stating: 'The treatment ideology responds to internal states as reflected in behaviour, and the punishment ideology mandates response only to behaviour'. Thus for an individual to be deemed worthy of 'treatment' requires that they respond to or should actively seek 'help'.[7] As discussed in *Chapter 1* this entails significant regulation of the individual and operates as a powerful form of social control. Those who fail to exhibit a desire to change are considered unworthy of rehabilitative interventions and, with the blame laid firmly on the individual, punitive sanctions will be introduced. More aptly, those who do not comply become redefined as 'dangerous' (see Castel, 1991). Pitch (1995: 21) argues that this bifurcation is fundamental in distinguishing further interventions:

It now functions as a legitimation for incapacitation, as the criterion of classification within the prison system itself and between custodial strategies as such and the policies of 'soft' control . . . It functions as a residual category: all that which is not amenable to treatment or rehabilitation is therefore dangerous.

This certainly applies to the 'chronic addict' of medical terminology and those who express no desire to give up their use of drugs. Welfare agencies are implicated within this process and function to enable this distinction and enhance this control. This clearly influences demands for criminalisation which Pitch (1995: 78) discusses with specific reference to 'new' social movements but which also applies to drug use:

> Criminalisation has the following characteristics: it simplifies the objective, medicalises and rigidifies the conflict, it requires and produces a 'friend-enemy' logic. Additionally, it both requires and produces a climate of moral indignation.

This claim for 'morality' is also discussed by Boyd and Lowman (1991) in relation to the politics of censure which operate in relation to the criminalisation of prostitution and drugs (see also Sumner, 1990a; 1990b). They point out that the criminalisation of certain drugs enables 'moral' values to be levelled at those who use particular substances. 'A practice of social censure distances the legal smoker from the illegal drug (ab)user' (Boyd and Lowman, 1991: 114). Thus analysing present policy and its effects, it becomes clear how this 'bifurcation' operates and, furthermore, the moral stance it entails. For Sumner (1990a: 28) moral censure is a technique that forms part of the process of 'normalisation', particularly as it is expressed through legislation:

> Normalisation involves, then, a combination and generalisation of 'panoptic techniques', subsuming other forms of power. In this process the censorious ideological formations and knowledges which feed the will to regulate, are reformed, strengthened and reinforced by their role in the exercise of this new modality of power; indeed new ones arise in the course of regulation itself.

Policies and practices

Initially, UK legislation was aimed at increasing punitive measures against the use of certain substances and at increasing the control of the medical and pharmaceutical professions (e.g. the Dangerous Drugs Acts of 1916 and 1920). In 1926 the Rolleston Committee defined drug use in terms of disease, introducing the concept of 'addiction' and advocating the medical prescription of drugs to the small number of known 'addicts' in an attempt to reduce or end their drug use.[8] Following their report (*Report of the Departmental Committee on Morphine and Heroin Addiction*) drugs controlled under the Dangerous Drugs Act 1920 could be medically prescribed in certain circumstances. These were where:

(a) addicts were undergoing treatment by the method of gradual withdrawal;
(b) complete withdrawal would produce serious and otherwise untreatable symptoms; and
(c) a 'normal' life could be led with the taking of a non-progressive maintenance dosage. (Whynes, 1991: 2)

The Brain Committee, set up by the Ministry of Health, reviewed this policy in 1961, but change was not considered necessary due to the small number of 'addicts' believed to exist. However, a distinction had been made between 'addicts' who were to be 'treated' and 'non-addicts' (recreational users) who were to be left to the criminal justice system. This marked the development of the 'British system', although as MacGregor and Ettorre (1987) point out, 'system' suggests a much more coherent order than was actually the case. Nevertheless the 'British system':

> consisted of a combination of punitive measures against a class of illegal users and the treatment of, including the supervised administration of drugs to, legitimate users, a policy of 'policing and prescribing'. (Whynes, 1991: 2)

The Brain Committee was reconvened in 1965 due to a number of concerns during the 1960s about the extension of drug use, particularly among young people. Stricter controls were urged for prescribing practices and these were eventually embodied in the Misuse of Drugs Act 1971. GPs were then required by law to notify the Home Office of 'addicts' who came to their attention and drug dependency clinics run by the NHS became the major source of maintenance prescriptions - introducing a multi-agency approach.

The divergence between 'legitimate' and 'non-legitimate' users had been made, those categorised 'legitimate' were defined as 'addicts' and placed under the control of the medical profession, while those categorised 'illegitimate' were not. MacGregor and Ettorre (1987: 129) point out the divergence in the effects and direction of policies:

> ... it is only in respect of dependent users of heroin (and other opiates, and to a lesser extent, cocaine) that maintenance prescribing has been a feature of the British response. Against occasional (non-dependent) users of opiates and against users of other drugs, the British system has resorted to law enforcement just as the United States has.

More fundamentally, this distinction was based on wider ideologies reflecting definitions of certain categories of drugs and drug-taking and on social and political perceptions of users (Young, 1971; Dorn, 1977). This is resonant of earlier legislation, outlined previously, and its attempts to control the social activities of certain ethnic groups and newly 'emancipated' women (Kohn, 1992). Young (1971: 54) discusses the emphasis on regulation and control and points out:

The legal prescription of amphetamines to troops and factory workers during the war, the blind eye turned to the medical student taking Benzedrine in order to swot for his exams, when compared to the severe reaction against youngsters caught with 'purple hearts' at an all-night club, would seem to suggest that the use of drugs to aid productivity is seen as innocuous whereas their use for pleasure as an end-in-itself is heavily reprimanded.

Present policies have been affected by the supposedly substantial increase in the number of drug users in Britain today (Pearson, 1987; Parker *et al.*, 1988; Giggs, 1991; Gilman and Pearson, 1991; Home Office, 1995; 1998). This was contextualised throughout the 1980s by the threat of HIV/AIDS which was frequently associated with drug users,[9] particularly intravenous users (see Berridge, 1991). The fear of drug users spreading disease among the 'non-drug using population' led to the development of a variety of government interventions. In 1988, the Advisory Council on the Misuse of Drugs (ACMD) produced its first report on the implications of AIDS and HIV for services for drug misusers. *AIDS and Drug Misuse, Part 1* (ACMD, 1988: 1) emphasised the importance of harm-minimisation policies: 'The report's first conclusion is that HIV is a greater threat to public and individual health than drug misuse'. Harm-reduction and multi-agency approaches were prioritised in a clear attempt to bring drug users into services:

> ... we emphasise that prevention of drug misuse is now more important than ever before and in the longer run the success or failure of efforts to prevent young people from embarking on a career of drug misuse will have a major effect on our ability to contain the spread of HIV. (ACMD, 1988: 19)

The focus of 'harm-reduction' interventions included needle exchanges, prescribing practices[10] and the provision of relevant information, designed towards: (a) attracting more drug misusers to services and keeping them in contact; (b) facilitating change away from HIV risk practices (ACMD, 1988: 48).

These policies were reinforced in subsequent reports by the Advisory Council in *Aids and Drug Misuse: Part 2* (ACMD, 1989; 1993). Multi-agency responses were prioritised and harm-reduction activities encouraged. By 1993 the objective of abstinence was being encouraged within a context of measures that would reduce the spread of HIV/AIDS:

> Greater measures are now needed to reduce the extent of drug use itself, and particularly of drug injecting, together with a wider recognition that *all* interventions to discourage drug misuse will contribute to HIV prevention. (ACMD, 1993: 1)

While emphasis was given to harm-reduction strategies to change behaviour, law enforcement continued to be prioritised in tangent to this.[11] The 1995 White Paper *Tackling Drugs Together* (Home Office, 1995) set out a new agenda for dealing with drug use with less emphasis on harm-reduction, and more on abstinence and overall prevention. The emphasis given to crime prevention and 'community safety' illustrated a clear 'anti-drugs' policy aimed at reducing drug-related crime. The White Paper (HMSO, 1995: 1) set out its strategy:

> To take effective action by vigorous law enforcement, accessible treatment and a new emphasis on education and prevention to increase the safety of communities from drug-related crime; reduce the acceptability and availability of drugs to young people; reduce the health risks and other damage related to drug misuse.

These policies are continued in the Government's White Paper (1998) *Tackling Drugs to Build a Better Britain* (Home Office). This reiterates the need for treatment for those with drug problems, law enforcement measures for the processors, distributors and sellers of drugs and also emphasises the need to prevent the increasing problem of drug-related deaths.

The problems of deaths linked to drug use have been prominent in Scotland (Ministerial Drugs Task Force, 1994; Scottish Affairs Committee, 1994; Scottish Office, 1999). They give greater emphasis to the need to reduce harm from drug misuse. Clearly the national contexts have contributed to this disparity. While the English reports have addressed voters' fears over drugs and crime, the Scottish Office has had to address significant rates of HIV infection in some of its major cities,[12] and an extremely high death rate among injecting drug users in Glasgow.[13] Both countries have attempted to reinforce an approach that tackles drug use on a variety of fronts. This combination of strategies attempts to enhance rehabilitative and preventative measures and to bring increasing numbers of drug users under the control of medical or legal services. These objectives are backed by punitive measures. As Collison (1993: 383) notes:

> To put it simply, the legitimate get oral methadone or, if geographically lucky, injectable drugs of choice; those on the margins of legitimacy get free syringes and harm-minimisation advice; and the illegitimate get prison.

For drug users to be considered deserving of treatment, they are required to present themselves as having a drug 'problem' and as willing to work towards change. However, the traditional emphasis placed on heroin use in defining 'treatment' bears little relevance to the newer types of drug currently favoured by young people (such as MDMA and LSD) where they play an integral part of a cultural lifestyle. Where treatment is inapplicable it is likely that punishment will be used and for the 'newer' forms of drugs this is inevitable. There has, however, been an attempt to extend non-custodial alternatives aimed at bringing 'less serious' offenders into community-based programmes.[14] This has been identified as seriously problematic due to the reluctance of many of those providing custodial alternatives to deal with drug users (Buchanan and Wyke, 1987; Hayes, 1992; Pearson, 1992).

Dorn (1977) notes that responses to drug users are dependent on a number of factors. While it might be recognised that many problems associated with drug use are *structural*, agencies remain limited in directing their response towards the *individual*. In relation to agency personnel he points out:

> They must respond to the problem in a way within their capabilities of response, and these capabilities determine the types of deviance categories and rationales that become dominant. (Dorn, 1977: 29)

Thus for users to be deemed worthy of 'help' it is required that they illustrate the potential to be helped and that such help is within the capabilities of the relevant organization or agency. In many ways, therapy and rehabilitation operate conditionally. Collison (1993) argues that for the user to receive treatment, he or she will have to play the 'sick' role, presenting himself or herself as a 'victim'. Gilman and Pearson (1991) discuss a similar point, suggesting that for the accounts of drug use by ex-users to be taken seriously there is a requirement imposed that they deny the pleasure gained from drug use.[15] As noted earlier this is likely to have repercussions for users, particularly users of the newer synthetic drugs, who do not view their drug use as problematic but see it in terms of recreation and lifestyle (see Collison, 1994). These recreational practices are not viewed as necessarily 'dangerous' to those involved but seem to be problematic for the state.[16] Gilman and Pearson (1991) question the extent of voluntarism that will exist for the user entering treatment (see also Parker *et al.*, 1988). For them, however, this should be made more structured (and thereby coercive) to be effective:

> ... it is about stacking the odds through the threat of penal sanctions so that the drug user is more likely to recognise that entering some form of treatment is a rational choice; forcing people to be free, in fact. It is an ambiguous morality at best, but nevertheless a serviceable one. (Gilman and Pearson, 1991: 117)[17]

What this leads to is a form of intervention which operates as a social control but is couched in the language of 'therapy and healing' (Gilman and Pearson, 1991: 32). This is evident in the literature governing drug use (from an agency response) and the way in which individuals and agencies perceive their roles in dealing with or 'treating' drug users (see Bennett, 1989; O'Hare *et al.*, 1992).

Controlling drugs: controlling crime

The supposed relationship between drugs and crime has already been identified as an influential factor in developing strategies of drug control. The costs of drug-related crime are estimated to be immense as it is believed that drug 'addicts' engage in crime as a means of 'feeding their habit'. The Government White Paper *Tackling Drugs to Build a Better Britain* (Home Office, 1998) argues that drugs present a major threat to 'community safety' in terms of acquisitive crime and anti-social behaviour. Figures presented in the document suggest that possibly half of all recorded crime has some drug-related element to it with general costs to the criminal justice system of at least £1 billion every year. Indications from a random sample of suspected offenders arrested by the police suggest that over 60 per cent of those arrested have traces of illegal drugs in their urine (Home Office, 1998).

It is clear that the illegal status of drug use enables a thriving illicit economy to operate. The links made between this economy and crime are based on the assessment of how much an addict requires to maintain his or her habit and, given the high cost generally involved, that they must be funding it by crime. The White Paper supports this view by quoting figures from a study of 664 addicts who apparently committed 70,000 offences over a three-month period (Home Office, 1998).

The Institute for the Study of Drug Dependency (ISDD) (in Dorn and South, 1987) point out that drug users may be involved in delinquent sub-cultures prior to illegal drug use. They also note that many studies suggest that users fund their habit within the drug network by dealing in drugs rather than turning to property crime. Auld *et al.* (1985) argue that involvement in crime may lead to heroin use rather than the reverse, noting: 'There is a sense, then, in which crime can lead to heroin use: the very opposite of the conventional view' (Auld *et al.*, 1985: 8). They show that heroin use plays a significant part in the informal or 'irregular' economy, with unemployment creating the opportunity for 'episodic' use. Involvement in the irregular economy is often due to necessity, but through participation in it individuals may 'come to buy, exchange, sell and consume heroin' (Auld *et al.*, 1985: 8).

While those convicted of a drug offence are considered as 'criminal', those convicted of supplying drugs are further vilified and sentencing is considerably more severe. Even though it is possible to refute the characterisation of 'user' and 'supplier' as separate categories (Dorn, 1977; Ruggerio and Vass, 1992) this does not prevent this distinction being made explicitly in the media and popular cultural views. Dorn (1977) notes that the development of the debate around drug use and supply in terms of the 'corrupt' and the 'corrupted' was fuelled by the Dangerous Drugs Act 1967 and Misuse of Drugs Act 1971. The evidence is that the distinction between users and dealers (as opposed to large scale traffickers) is tenuous. Nevertheless, the depiction of such distinctions, as enforced by the legislature, judiciary and law enforcement agencies, reinforces the differential approaches to supply and demand. This highlights the point made by Pitch (1995) that those not deemed 'treatable' are viewed as 'dangerous'.

Ruggiero and Vass (1992) argue that the notion of the 'pusher' is fundamentally flawed (as do Gould *et al.*, 1974; Dorn, 1977; Pearson, 1987) and they note: 'Most commonly, heroin use spreads via personal relationships and peer groups in areas where use is already endemic' (Ruggerio and Vass, 1992: 273). Individuals are often introduced to drugs through friends and acquaintances, and women are likely to try drugs in the company of female friends, boyfriends and husbands (see Taylor, 1993) rather than being the victims of heavy-handed drug 'barons'.

The development of heroin habits takes place through social routes and the majority of heroin users learn to experiment and subsequently 'live' with the drug in a circle of friends and family networks. (Ruggerio and Vass, 1992: 274)

However, powerful but flawed images of 'dealers' and 'pushers' will exclude certain individuals from anything other than a punitive response. While some individuals are identified as needing and deserving help, the emphasis remains that help is restricted to those 'worthy' of it. The depiction and creation of reputations for drug users remains ideological and political, defining and sustaining the methods that are required to deal with the 'problem' as defined by popular ideologies and official discourse.

The importance of popular discourse in the creation and maintenance of 'negative' reputations that, in turn, define official responses reflects the justification for the state to control drug users. The methods employed, be they 'welfarist' or punitive, are aimed at bringing those who fail to conform within the auspices of the state. The fears which are fuelled by drug use in terms of the perceived links with crime and disease are used to justify these measures as 'necessary' by ensuring that those who use drugs illegally are portrayed as quite distinct from the typical 'law-abiding' citizen. As discussed in *Chapter 2*, these ideological depictions have further resonance when gender is considered as an additional dimension.

WOMEN AND DRUG USE

The moral condemnation of drug users and the methods used to control drug use are influenced by cultural practices and social constructions. When issues of gender are considered, or more specifically when issues around 'women' and 'femininity' are discussed, this becomes inherently problematic. As argued in *Chapter 2*, many insidious forms of control operate to morally regulate and socially control women. Indeed as Hutter and Williams (1989) argue, the dominant constructs of appropriate femininities affect all women. Women who use illegal drugs are seen as double deviants - engaging not only in an illegal activity but in one that goes against acceptable notions of femininity.

The presentation of the 'unfeminine' nature of drug-taking is explicit in images of hedonistic pursuits and the scapegoating of independent women by the portrayal of scandal related to sexual freedom and illicit drug use (Kohn, 1992). Auld *et al.* (1985: 13) note: 'Both conditions - being stoned and being straight - are constructed as experiential states through the mediation of sexual identity and social relations'.

Drug use has traditionally been viewed as a 'masculine' preoccupation leading to the deployment of patriarchal definitions of both men and women. Although some important and thorough research has been carried out in this area, specifically relating to women as drug users, stereotypical assumptions remain dominant. Women's role in drug use is identified as peripheral or as an adjunct to the main, male participants. These assumptions reflect notions of femininity and reproduction and are the focus of much advice to women users which generally relates to pregnancy, breast-feeding, children and overdose. These issues are frequently referred to when issues of drug use and HIV are discussed.

There is, however, a major contradiction in the use of drugs by women, which cannot be applied to men. This relates to how women's 'illegal' drug use is morally condemned (as hedonistic) while medically prescribed drugs are administered to large numbers of women (as 'coping mechanisms'). Thus, illegal drug use by women is considered to be a 'social problem', while medically controlled drug use by women is not (see Ettorre and Riska, 1995).[18]

Clearly the definition of a 'social problem' is constituted by the power relations which prevail.[19] How an issue becomes defined as a 'problem' reflects and propagates these power relations, and the resultant discourse influences the construction of 'reality' (McGrath, 1993: 159). Morrissey (1986: 159) acknowledges: 'An examination of how we define and discuss a problem or fail to address it is essentially an examination of relations of power'. Drug use by women, as constructed by medical, legal and gendered discourse illustrates this.

> Choice and control of drug use by women is one of the sensitive areas where traditional norms and pressures for social change come into conflict. Female dependence is a reality - female drug dependence is an inappropriate and undesirable side-effect to be redirected to more convenient and controllable forms of dependence. (Perry, 1991: 1)

Perry (1991) considers the dichotomy between medically prescribed and illicit drugs in terms of their acceptability. She notes the role of the medical profession in providing drugs to ameliorate 'problems' attributable to social circumstances. Drug use and, ultimately, dependency are unproblematic if the drugs are used to help a woman cope with the pressures of her life and are controlled externally. When they are not officially prescribed the implied images are those of hedonism and pleasure - however incorrect this may be - and users are strongly condemned in popular discourse. While dependency is considered acceptable if it is focused upon a doctor or a husband (Perry, 1991; Ettorre, 1992), dependency on drugs, particularly illegal drugs, leads to a woman being perceived as *more* deviant than male users. This ascribed deviance is further compounded if she has children as it is assumed, incorrectly according to Taylor (1993), that her dependency negates her ability as a 'good mother'. Taylor (1993) notes that drug use has additional costs for women, particularly in relation to children. Women are often made to feel that their drug use is an indication of negligence towards their children. This is often used to manipulate them into services for drug users. As Foucault (1977) has pointed out, degrees of guilt equal degrees of punishment.

While research into drug use has rarely acknowledged women's experience not all studies have omitted or excluded women. Women have been included but the focus has tended towards their experiences as users rather than as distinctly female users (Pearson, 1987; Parker et al., 1988). Auld et al. (1985: 12) note how young working-class men use heroin as an 'excuse' to obtain sexual servicing from women, particularly their mothers and girlfriends. They argue that the male role as an 'addict' places women in the role of 'nurse or social worker'. Often this is simply an extension of men's demands on women within a patriarchal system. However, the 'sick' role can be initiated as required, enabling men to use 'addiction' as an 'emotional lever'. This does not work so readily for women as 'addicts'.

Ettorre (1992) argues that patterns of drug use as a coping mechanism differ between men and women, with women using drugs as a social support to a greater extent than men. Indeed, prevailing notions of dependency and drug use suggest that women consume drugs and/or alcohol due to 'stress' or 'alienation' (Henderson 1990 and 1992a; 1992b; Perry, 1991; Ettorre, 1992), portraying women as passive, influenced by and dependent upon men. Taylor (1993) and McDonald (1994) argue that this view is regularly incorrect in relation to non-medical drug use. Taylor (1993) in particular illustrates the active role that women take in their illicit drug using 'career' and how engagement in drug using activities often increases their independence, despite the disadvantages it can bring.

Women's marginalisation in studies has been lessened over the past few years, with a growing recognition that they have been neglected in this field, both in terms of research and of resource allocation. This is the consequence of action taken by women, largely influenced by feminist theory, and is due to an increasing recognition that women now represent a significant proportion of the drug using population. However, the number of women coming to 'official' attention may well be weighted by the reluctance of many to seek help for their drug use (inadequate resources; fear of children being taken into care) or the lower likelihood that they will come into contact with the criminal justice system. There is now a recognition of the need for more research related to women and for more resources to be made available to draw them into services, such as child-care provisions, female drugs workers and women-only groups. However, this has rarely been carried over into policy and practice.

A number of studies have attempted to move beyond the limited consideration of illegal drug use by women in terms of reproduction (Perry, 1991; Ettorre, 1992; MacDonald, 1994) and to outline the experiences of female drug users in terms of drug using 'careers' (notably Taylor, 1993). Several texts have also successfully highlighted the lack of appropriate and relevant resources for women as drug users (Henderson, 1990; 1992a; 1992b; Ettorre, 1992). Treatment programmes and strategies are largely dominated by men, both in terms of supply and demand. Consequently, many women find such programmes of little relevance to their own experiences. Several organizations have been founded, run by and designed for women. Largely based on self-help models and generally run within the voluntary sector, these projects often operate to empower women by shared experiences and the provision of support.

Similarly, there have been moves from within the statutory sector, mainly health services, to draw more women into their provisions or programmes by directing resources towards women and encouraging them into 'treatment'. As discussed previously, frequently this operates as an extension of social control, although it is recognised that many female workers and service users have demonstrated the inadequacy of resources for women. However, as Morrissey (1986: 175) notes, attempting to address such issues means engaging with the very agencies (medical and legal) which operate to control: 'Members of the subordinate group, in producing discourse in and with established structure, become accomplices in constituting the very relations of power in which they are oppressed'.

Indeed, women campaigned *against* alcohol and illicit drugs in attempts to establish the role of women as 'carers' and 'good' wives and mothers. As McDonald (1994: 22) points out, again reflecting the social constructions of the (un)acceptability of certain substances:

> In the nineteenth century, nice women campaigned against rum and took opium-laced tonics; their great-granddaughters have been able to find their femininity in campaigning against alcohol and opium alike, and in dutifully taking tranquillisers.

As previously discussed, the domination of medical and legal discourse has profoundly affected the way illegal drug use is portrayed in relation to women (see *Chapter 2* for similar arguments in terms of 'crime'). Not only are female drug users portrayed as more 'deviant' than their male counterparts but the additional employment of 'disease' models leads to them being viewed as more 'disturbed' (Showalter, 1985; Allen, 1987; Ettorre, 1992; Taylor, 1993). Women have frequently been defined as 'sick' in terms of their biology (Ehrenreich and English, 1978) and this tends to fit in with notions of addiction, with women who use drugs regularly portrayed as 'neurotic'.

Drug use by women, then, is contextualised by a discourse dominated by images of criminality and disease. While the use of drugs is in itself illegal, women who use them are frequently believed to engage in minor property crime and/or prostitution. There is thus a tendency to link drug use and prostitution (Plant *et al.*, 1990; Hoigard and Finstad, 1992) which itself leads to discussions of HIV/AIDS (Kinnel, 1989; Plant *et al.*, 1990; McKeganey *et al.*, 1992). Women drug users are thus portrayed at an intersection between sex, drugs and disease. It is not surprising, therefore, that women become the focus for harm-reduction strategies and a potential priority for services. Although women are under-represented in many services, particularly for drug users, those who are involved with state agencies are frequently identified as appropriate recipients of harm-reduction policies (such as medical examinations, distribution of condoms). This is similar to how women have been identified as an appropriate focus for moral interventions into the family (Donzelot, 1979). In the realm of sexuality, however, women are targeted as a focus for safer sexual practices, a responsibility they have always held (Patton, 1985). Singer (1993: 85) notes:

> In an era of panic sexuality, the family is being repackaged as a prophylactic social device. In the age of sexual epidemics, the family can be marketed as a strategic and prudential safe sex practice.

In the present political climate, dominated by a renewed emphasis on the 'family' which has informed a range of political thinking (Ethical Socialism, Blairism), women are readily targeted as an appropriate focus of state intervention. This operates at both a physical and moral level (Patton, 1985). Singer (1993: 84) discusses state intervention in targeting the bodies of women in this respect (in terms of HIV/AIDS): 'This consequence should not be surprising in light of the utility of sexual epidemics as occasions for reinscribing hegemonic relationships of dominance and prominence'.

Turner (1984: 34) points out that: 'The administered society involves the control of persons through the medicalisation of bodies' (see also Foucault, 1977; Sontag, 1989; Featherstone *et al.*, 1991; Singer, 1993). This has a particular resonance for female bodies which, as Bordo (1992: 92) states, are no less constituted by culture than anything else that is human.

McGrath (1993: 158) notes that HIV/AIDS appeared along with a number of 'moral panics' targeted at specific and easily identifiable 'agents', and states: 'those agents were homosexuals, drug users, ethnic groups and women'. While female drug users were, to some extent, targeted as a direct result of their use of drugs, the classification of HIV as a sexually transmitted disease (see McGrath, 1993: 160) has had profound implications for the female drug user as *female*. This is also applicable to gay men (Patton, 1985; Weeks, 1989). McGrath (1993: 160) notes: 'It consigned those who were already on the periphery to the category of the expendable'. This has similarities to the processes of marginalisation discussed earlier in relation to drug users and clearly it relates to how the state agencies, notably the criminal justice and penal systems, intervene to contain those deemed 'dangerous' (Castel, 1991; Pitch, 1994) or to de-legitimate those deemed 'useless' in terms of productive capacities (Carlen, 1983; Hudson, 1993).

In relation to drug use and the contingent fears relating to sexuality, the boundaries of the body (affected by both drug use and sex) become of major importance and the focus for controls.

> In a consumer culture, the body assumes a new social and individual significance. It becomes the site of personal strategies of health. Jogging, swimming and keep-fit programmes are designed to promote health as the basis of the good life. These instrumental strategies of health are enthusiastically supported by the state as the principal basis of preventive medicine. (Turner, 1984: 172)

This was evident in the Government's White Paper *Tackling Drugs Together* (Home Office, 1995) which emphasised 'Sports Policy' and the need for young people to become involved in sport as a preventative drugs policy. This government of the body can also be viewed in relation to diet and control:

> . . . the body is a location for the exercise of will over desire. The achievement of personal control over diet is an act of will which enhances self-esteem, but it can also be imposed from without as a denial of will. (Turner, 1984: 180)

Singer (1993: 30) takes this a step further, stating:

> Concern about health can be used to justify any number of interventions into the lives of bodies and the forms of exchange in which they move as well as to provide an occasion around which to mobilise social assets and resources. The epidemic inscription therefore functions as a socially authoritative discourse, which also both draws upon and generates mechanisms for its own legitimation.

Just as bodies can symbolise health and life, so they can also symbolise disease and death.[20] Such concerns can thus be used to justify intervention directed towards the 'body', particularly targeted towards individuals defined as members of 'high-risk' groups. This process does not operate in a vacuum, however, and in the recent past and present political and economic climate, dominated by moral authoritarianism, there is clear evidence that AIDS has been used to fuel the backlash aimed at reinforcing the nuclear family (Patton, 1985; Weeks, 1989; Singer, 1993).

This has been evident throughout the government campaign on HIV/AIDS prevention where gay men, intravenous drug users and prostitutes have been specifically targeted. However, as in the past, policy interventions which were intrusive and debilitating were frequently directed at women (Contagious Diseases Acts of 1866 and 1869: see Walkowitz, 1980; Smart, 1992). Corbin (1987) discusses the regulation of prostitution in nineteenth-century France, noting the way in which the (female) prostitute was symbolised as morally and physically linked to disease and decay: literally to the sewer or the drain. Complex relations were identified with the corpse, with prostitutes viewed as dangerous in the same way as corpses in a period characterised by notions of 'anticontagionism' and the 'war against infection'. By considering the pronouncements on the treatment of early sufferers of AIDS and policies for the disposal of their bodies, certain commonalities become evident.

The discipline and regulation of the body, then, takes on a primary importance as a function of social control. In the same way that Bordo (1992) links the anorexic's 'control of the unruly body' at the level of the individual (although set in a wider social context) the drug user's attempts to control his or her body can also be seen to emanate from an individual's desires. For the anorexic, attempts to *control* hunger identify hunger as 'a dangerous eruption, which comes from some alien part of the self, and [the individual develops] a growing intoxication with controlling that eruption' (Bordo, 1992: 92). For the drug user, particularly the dependent one, keeping withdrawal symptoms at bay takes on the same resonance. This presents problems for outside agencies in attempting to regulate the individual externally. As Birke (1992: 72) points out: 'Denial of the body is part of a wider denial of ourselves *as biological beings*'. But where certain bodies are viewed as threatening, discipline can be imposed from outside and the penal system operates in many ways to achieve this.

Amariglio (1988: 607) notes: 'Penology is concerned not with punishing the body but with disciplining it, perhaps in the hopes of recuperating it by making it docile'. This becomes problematic when drug users are the focus of attempts to improve discipline. In this case, bodily desires may not prove so easy to regulate, nor is it easy to obtain knowledge about the 'drugged' body. Nevertheless, these discourses come to form a major influence in the development of official definitions and ideologies (Scraton and Chadwick, 1987). This has already been discussed in relation to women and crime (*Chapter 2*) and drug users in general. For women as drug users, contact with the criminal justice process is influenced by such ideologies that then become translated into official discourse and practice.

Allen (1987), Carlen (1988) and Worrall (1990) have illustrated the way in which women whose personal, social and economic background becomes defined as 'problematic' are perceived within the criminal justice system as going against 'normal' womanhood. They become targets for interventions of social control and generate harsher responses than women who are not deemed to have similar 'problems'. Drug use (and any related crime) places them in 'double jeopardy' in their dealings with the criminal justice system. The notions of hedonism and recklessness, both moral and physical, associated with drug use lead to them becoming defined as either in need of 'treatment' or punishment.

From marginalisation to custody
This chapter has critiqued the prevalent discourses that operate around the use of drugs. In particular, it has examined the social constructs that are developed from ideological depictions of drug use and drug users and examined their effects on social policy and legal practices. The images and ideologies which pertain to the use of proscribed substances contribute to the processes of criminalisation that operate in relation to drug users. This results in the marginalisation of drug users, and takes a particular form in relation to women users.

As previously discussed, those deemed unworthy of 'treatment' or for whom 'treatment' has failed in the past will generally be imprisoned. Given the difficulties, and often reluctance, of operators of non-custodial measures to work with drug users, many drug using women find themselves quickly directed up the tariff scale towards custody. How these ideologies and definitions influence their experiences of custody will be examined in the chapters which follow by considering the experiences of women drug users in prison.

62 Women, Drugs and Custody

ENDNOTES for Chapter 3

1. This is dependent on the class of drugs, value, amount and whether or not the drug was intended for personal use or supply. The Criminal Justice and Public Order Act 1994 increased the maximum fine for possession of cannabis and other 'soft' drugs from £500 to £2,500 despite criticism from magistrates, police and drug counsellors. At the same time, the Scottish Home Affairs Minister was suggesting a fixed penalty system of fines of between £25 and £100.

2. Tobacco and alcohol have both been prohibited in different countries during different historical periods (see Szasz, 1974).

3. The Government White Paper *Tackling Drugs Together* (1995), Home Office, outlines the responsibilities of the police, and Customs and Excise in enforcing anti-drugs legislation. This is re-emphasised in the 1998 White Paper *Tackling Drugs to Build a Better Britain*.

4. Crack is produced by mixing cocaine with a solvent and heating the mixture. It may be taken by 'freebasing' or smoking. The psychological and physical dangers of crack are believed to be much greater than those attributed to cocaine.

5. The lengthy sentences used to deal with foreign couriers, often with no remission, raises fundamental issues. While this form of punishment is intended to illustrate the severity of the offence, social revulsion towards it and to act as a deterrent to other people, it is widely accepted that the effect of deterrence is limited. The people who are presently languishing in British prisons for drug smuggling are rarely the organizers of trafficking cartels and their incarceration will have little discernible effect on the drug trade. See, generally, Green, P., *Drugs, Trafficking and Criminal Policy: The Scapegoat Strategy*, Winchester: Waterside Press, 1998.

6. See Hillyard (1993) for his study of people's experiences of the Prevention of Terrorism Acts in Britain. While the context is very different, similar constructs apply.

7. See ACMD (1991) for guidelines on the assessment of individuals for suitability for treatment within the criminal justice system.

8. See Edwards (1981), ISDD (1983), McGregor and Ettorre (1987), Whynes and Bean (1991) for a discussion of the development of these policies.

9. Along with other groups notably gay men and sex workers (see Patton, 1985; Carter and Whatney, 1989).

10. Needle exchanges provide injecting equipment to drug users in exchange for used needles which can be safely disposed of. They bring users into contact with various services, enabling service workers to make primary healthcare available as well as providing advice on drug use and safer sex. Prescribing practices enable medical practitioners to provide users with controlled amounts of medication as an alternative to their continued use of illegal drugs. Prescribing (either reduction or maintenance) is considered particularly important in tackling injecting drug use and in reducing illegal use and subsequently crime. However, there have been significant problems associated with methadone, which has become the standard treatment for heroin addiction in Britain. Methadone is more addictive and more difficult to withdraw from than heroin; it is more toxic and responsible for more deaths than heroin use. Its unpopularity with drug users has led to it being sold or exchanged for heroin with the result that it is now more available than heroin in many cities. See Newcombe (1995) and Parry (1995) for a discussion of the problematic use of methadone. Marks (1994) calculates that mortality rates from heroin yield a ratio of 1 in 2,582. In contrast, mortality rates from methadone appear to be 1 in 134, making methadone 19 times more toxic than heroin.

11. The Government White Paper (Home Office, 1995: Annex B, 51) set out estimated spending on tackling drug misuse in the UK at £526 million. This was broken down as follows:

£209 million on police/customs enforcement
£137 million on deterrence/controls
£104 million on prevention/education
£61 million on treatment/rehabilitation
£1.5 million on international action.

This is replicated in the 1998 White Paper (Home Office, 1998) which sets out the ascribed allocation for an increased amount of Government spending totalling around £1.4 billion:

Law-enforcement related spending : 62 per cent
International supply reduction: 13 per cent
Treatment: 13 per cent
Prevention and education: 12 per cent

The priorities are clear.

[12] The 1993 ACMD report estimated that around 25 per cent of drug injectors in Edinburgh were thought to be HIV positive (half the level in 1986) as were 25–30 per cent of drug injectors in Dundee. Prevalence was estimated at less than two per cent in most of the country (ACMD, 1993: 1).

[13] In 1994, 247 deaths in Scotland were drug-related. Of these, 139 were of people known or suspected to be drug dependent and over half of these were in Greater Glasgow (*Druglink*, September/October, 1995: 5). In 1997, 263 deaths in Scotland were formally identified as drug related (Scottish Office, 1999). This figure appears to be increasing.

[14] This is evident in the new drug treatment and testing orders introduced by the Crime and Disorder Act 1998.

[15] This represents an extension of the moral value attached to the rehabilitative ideals of 'coming to terms with one's crime'.

[16] For example, the attempts to prohibit or regulate 'raves' under the Criminal Justice Act 1994.

[17] This is similar to what Young (1971: 31) defines as 'humanitarianism', but which he argues often conceals a conflict of interests or moral indignation.

[18] Antidepressants and tranquillisers are prescribed overwhelmingly for women. Prozac in particular, is marketed as a 'feel good' drug and advertising is targeted towards women.

[19] See Young (1994) for a discussion of the cultural assumptions of the police and the way in which this often leads them to negotiate women out of the drug-related crime scene if their role is peripheral.

[20] Clearly the emphasis given to fitness and health is beneficial for women who have traditionally been restricted in their capacities to develop their bodies through fitness regimes. However, for women the emphasis is still directed towards maintaining an appearance that is still feminine. Overly muscular female bodies are not considered attractive in popular ideologies. The aim of fitness regimes for women is more likely to be targeted at achieving the stereotypical female body.

CHAPTER 4

Policies and Guidelines

Over the past 25 years a plethora of legislation and policy guidelines has been produced in an attempt to tackle the 'social problems' associated with the use of controlled drugs. Policy directives and legislation have targeted community initiatives. However, many official reports (ACMD, 1988; 1989; 1991; 1993; 1996; Ministerial Drugs Task Force, 1994; Scottish Affairs Committee, 1994; Home Office, 1995; 1998) have also referred to the role of the Prison Service, particularly in relation to public health and more increasingly with regard to crime prevention. This chapter examines the policy developments that have been developed by HMPS and SPS to support and enhance government initiatives aimed at tackling drug use.

THE CONTEXT FOR PRISON SERVICE POLICIES

In 1971, the Advisory Council on the Misuse of Drugs (ACMD) was set up under the Misuse of Drugs Act to review regularly the situation relating to the use of proscribed drugs. By the 1980s concern around drug use had increased due to the high numbers of young, working-class heroin users and, for a brief period, emphasis was given to policies which favoured 'cure' and rehabilitation. The need to implement effective policies was recognised within the Prison Service and in 1987 HMPS produced a circular which provided detailed advice on the need to provide care and treatment for drug users in custody (HMPS, 1987). At the same time, however, details were circulated outlining new, increased security measures which were to be implemented as an initiative to reduce the extent of drugs in prison (see *Chapter 6*).

By 1988, the 'drug issue' was being defined broadly in terms of public health, with fears of the increased transmission of the Human Immunodeficiency Virus (HIV) (*Chapter 3*). The ACMD report on Drugs and HIV/AIDS (Part 1), published in 1988, highlighted the importance of treating HIV as 'a greater threat to public and individual health than drug misuse' (ACMD, 1988: 1). As a result, harm-minimisation strategies were defined as a priority for development, with abstinence as the ultimate goal. This was to be achieved largely through community-based services aimed at bringing drug users into contact with appropriate information and resources. Education was prioritised along with an emphasis on harm reduction. Syringe exchange schemes were proposed in addition to needle supplies being available for purchase from chemists' shops. Prescribing (particularly of opiate substitutes such as methadone) was advocated as part of a 'package' of treatment tailored to meet the needs of the individual.

Throughout the report, the main emphasis was the reduction of the spread of HIV/AIDS. Injecting drug use through shared (contaminated) equipment was identified as transmitting the virus in 16 per cent of UK cases of HIV infection and over 50 per cent of all known cases in Scotland (ACMD, 1988: 6). The main emphasis, therefore, was to educate individual behaviour away from 'high-risk' activities through the provision of and access to relevant resources. A multi-agency approach was advocated as the most effective means of realising this difficult objective.

Prescribing practices and needle exchanges, as well as the provision of free condoms, were considered to be a valuable asset in providing an opportunity to maximise contact with drug users and to change behaviour. While prescribing practices were seen as giving an important dimension in harm reduction, the report emphasised that this was not 'a panacea' (ACMD, 1988: 47). Although vital in assisting withdrawal, prescribing (either reduction or maintenance) also provided the opportunity to bring drug users into contact with services which could ostensibly help the user to change his or her behaviour, thereby reducing the risk of the transmission of HIV/AIDS. It also served in no small measure to increase an element of social control over identified users through 'treatment' agencies and to supposedly support a move away from criminal activities.

The ACMD addressed the significance of prisons, given the high number of drug users receiving custodial sentences. The report recognised that many of those incarcerated were likely to have injected. The report (ACMD, 1988: 61, 8.2) noted:

> Thus prison represents a unique opportunity to reach large numbers of drug misusers for the first time, educate them towards safer practices and draw them into contact with a network of help that could reduce the risks to themselves and others.

Two areas of 'risk' specific to prisons were identified: the small number of syringes available which, it was believed, would be likely to lead to wide sharing; and homosexual acts among male prisoners. The report considered, but did not recommend, the provision or exchange of needles in prisons (ACMD, 1988: 65, 8.11). It did recommend, however, that access be made available to condoms (ACMD, 1988: 65: 8.13), although this has not resulted in condoms being made available *within* prisons.[1]

The low rate of success in identifying drug users on reception to prison was recognised in the report, and it was advocated that availability of resources might encourage individuals to identify themselves as drug users and seek 'help'. One of the conclusions (ACMD, 1988, 67: 8.20) stated: '. . . efforts to identify drug misusers in prison and to encourage them to identify themselves should be further increased'. (The related difficulties of attempting to do this are discussed in *Chapter 5*.) Thus, emphasis was placed on:

- better training for prison medical officers;
- thorough medical examinations; and
- the provision of incentives and the minimisation of deterrents to encourage identification and/or self-disclosure.

Easier access for outside agencies, particularly probation, was advocated as was the need for general education to reduce the risk of HIV/AIDS. The intention was to combine education programmes with individual counselling. These recommendations were contextualised within a general framework that argued against custodial sentences and for the provision of appropriate alternatives.

Subsequent ACMD reports continued in this vein, reiterating concern at the high number of drug users in prison and recommending remands to treatment rather than custody when pre-sentence reports were required. In addition to re-emphasising the need for education, the second report (ACMD, 1989) also urged prison medical officers (PMOs) to consider a range of treatment options. These included the prescribing of substitute drugs, such as methadone, as part of a harm-reduction strategy (ACMD, 1989: 65, 8.17). This was backed by guidelines produced in 1991 by the Medical Working Group of the Department of Health and the Scottish and Welsh Offices for the clinical management of drug users. Prescribing was encouraged, for rapid or gradual withdrawal and for maintenance, but only as part of a broader strategy of care. Detailed recommendations were outlined for the management of opiate withdrawals by the provision of substitutes and other beneficial treatments. Abrupt discontinuation was recommended for withdrawal from stimulants and hallucinogens. Doctors were required to inform the Home Office Addicts Index when coming into contact with any individual addicted to a notifiable drug.

For such measures to be effective it was clear that users had to be identified. An ACMD report published in 1991, *Drug Misusers and the Criminal Justice System (Part 1)*, identified the difficulties, yet necessity, of identifying 'drug misusing offenders' (ACMD, 1991: 8, 3.2). It outlined the importance of encouraging self-disclosure directly connected to the provision of incentives for identification and the reduction of disincentives. The report recognised a number of obstacles to self-disclosure. These included: fear of receiving a harsher sentence; fear of being remanded in custody; lack of confidentiality; the prospect of increased surveillance in prison; the over-riding fear that children may be taken into care. Lack of treatment facilities further increased the level of disincentives to disclose.[2]

The increased attention given to the treatment of drug users, and the more therapeutic concerns that were evident at the time, contributed to the form the developed policy guidelines took within the Prison Service. In 1991 the Prison Service Medical Directorate published *Caring for Drug Users* (HMPS, 1991). This respected the commitment of the service to tackling both the supply *and* demand aspects of drug use within the prison environment. However, much of the report provided guidance aimed at helping drug users in prison to reduce/end their use of drugs.

Multi-agency approaches to education, counselling and treatment were prioritised in a context based on the development of trust, confidentiality and co-operation (see *Chapter 7*). The broad aim of the guidelines was to provide an inter-disciplinary approach to the problems experienced by drug users in prison. The guidelines set out a strategy that was intended to provide an opportunity, within prison, for the drug user to stop or to reduce his or her use of drugs. This was considered particularly important given the relationship between injecting drug use and the transmission of HIV/AIDS. The guidelines recommended that resources should be made available throughout the prisoner's sentence, with an emphasis on a 'holistic' approach taking into account both the physical and psychological aspects of drug use.

Policy guidance for Scotland developed with a slightly different emphasis. A series of drug-related deaths among young people in Glasgow (see *Chapter 3*) and a growing concern about drug use and HIV in Scotland led to the commissioning of a Parliamentary Report by the Scottish Affairs Committee. The Scottish Office also set up a Ministerial Drugs Task Force to investigate an appropriate response to the drugs 'problem' in Scotland. Both continued to advocate detoxification services and substitute prescribing as a matter of urgency and recommended that needle exchange outlets be extended in their range. Consideration was also given to the role of the SPS and concern was noted over the lack of accurate information on the numbers of drug users in prison in Scotland. This followed the transmission of HIV and Hepatitis B among male prisoners in HMP Glenochil which was largely attributable to shared injecting equipment. While 13 men were shown to be HIV positive, the actual number who may have been infected could lie between 22 and 43 (Scottish Affairs Committee, 1994: para 152). The failure to continue methadone treatment on entry to custody was identified as particularly problematic. While some prisons did prescribe opiate substitutes on a reduction basis, others were reluctant to, a matter in which the prisoner had no choice. The report of the Scottish Affairs Committee noted (xli: 145):

> There appears to be no standard practice for dealing with drug misusers on admission to prison. Treatment, if required, is determined by the prison doctor, and varies between prisons.

It was recognised that this could lead to illicit drug use within prisons. Indeed, prisoners most at risk of sharing injecting equipment appeared to be those who were being maintained on methadone prior to sentence (see Shewan *et al.*, 1994). As a result, the reports of the Scottish Affairs Committee and the Ministerial Drugs Task Force advocated the continuity of treatment for users on a reducing basis, developed in accordance with the individual's own GP. In line with the ACMD Report (1989), these recommendations emphasised the need to view prison as providing an opportunity for detoxification and the possibility of a drug-free lifestyle. The report of the Scottish Affairs Committee (1994: xlv, 161) recommended that the Scottish Office: 'examines the possibility of providing six to 12-month residential rehabilitation within the framework of the prison service'.

In March 1994 the SPS produced its policy guidelines *Guidance on the Management of Prisoners who Misuse Drugs*. There were many similarities to the guidelines of HMPS in England and Wales. The SPS stated that detoxification should be provided (maintenance being offered only in exceptional circumstances), noting that methadone was available in some institutions. Continuation of methadone for a prisoner held on a short sentence of remand, and who was on a maintenance programme outside, was left to the discretion of the prison medical officer. Detoxification or appropriate medical care 'must be given to ensure that the transition from drug misuse is as humane as possible' (SPS, 1994: 12, para 6.5). The following areas were outlined as key elements in 'managing' prisoners who misuse drugs: research; security; drug treatment; education for prisoners and staff; healthcare and throughcare (SPS, 1994: 1). The SPS also recognised the need to detail accurately the extent of illegal drug use in prison, gaining information through recorded offences and drug finds.

Despite the events at HMP Glenochil in 1993, no plans were to be made to introduce needle exchange schemes. The guidelines stated, however, that sterilisation tablets should be made freely available to prisoners in recognition that some would continue to inject drugs in prison. Guidance should be issued to prisoners on the use of these tablets to help sterilise injecting equipment (SPS, 1994: 10). This denoted a significant distinction in policies between Scotland and England and Wales. In line with the English prison strategy, security was prioritised in an attempt to prevent drugs getting into prison. However, the SPS (1994: 11) also noted:

> Drug misuse cannot be tolerated within prison and a priority is the exclusion of all illicit drugs. Any attempt, however, to achieve absolute success in preventing the smuggling of drugs into prison would require the introduction of unacceptably stringent control measures, particularly in relation to visit arrangements. The key to successful exclusion lies in a balance between security measures and programmes designed to reduce the demand for drugs in prison.

This was recognised in the report of the Scottish Affairs Committee (Scottish Affairs Committee, 1994: xlii, 148) which stated:

> SPS have taken specific security measures to stop drugs being brought into prison. But they admitted that a balance had to be struck between the level of security needed to stop drugs being brought into prison and the maintenance of good order and avoidance of disturbances. It would appear, therefore, unrealistic to assume that the problem of drug misuse within prisons can be eradicated by stopping the supply of illicit drugs, although this should remain the target.

In 1995, a change in policy (England and Wales) became evident with publication of the Government White Paper *Tackling Drugs Together* (HMSO, 1995) which set out a drugs strategy for England and Wales. Its statement of purpose established its main aims. The strategy was targeted at reducing drug-related crime, reducing the availability of drugs to young people and lessening the health risks and other damage caused by drug misuse (see *Chapter* 3). It discussed drug users in prison, emphasising the measures required to reduce the supplies of drugs, while also advocating a multi-disciplinary approach to the care and support of drug users. In line with Government agendas this placed more emphasis on tackling the 'fear of crime'. Abstinence was prioritised at the expense of harm reduction, which was given negligible mention in the report.

As an offshoot of the Government's strategy, HMPS introduced a new policy and strategy document *Drug Misuse in Prison* (1995). In essence, it brought together many of the priorities outlined in previous strategies into the one document. It also introduced new measures to tackle drug use and it reflected a change in tone. The document began:

> Reducing the level of drug misuse is one of the seven strategic priorities in the Prison Service's Corporate Plan. The Prison Service will not tolerate the presence and use of illicit drugs in its establishments. (HMPS, 1995: 2)

This new strategy was focused on three areas: reducing the supply of drugs; reducing demand for drugs; and reducing the 'potential for damage to the health of prisoners, staff and the wider community, arising from the misuse of drugs' (HMPS, 1995: 2). While measures to provide help for drug users were to be continued, measures to prevent use of drugs were to be monitored by the introduction of random drug tests. The need to develop procedures to prevent drugs entering prison was reaffirmed and there was to be: 'an assessment of local needs and priorities which takes into account the equal opportunities implications of tackling drugs in prisons' (HMPS, 1995: 3).

These procedures were to be incorporated into a strategy taking account of the need to provide treatment, counselling and support. More emphasis was placed on obtaining information concerning the extent of drug use within the prison population. The new initiative of mandatory drug testing was emphasised:[3]

> The Prison Service is to introduce a mandatory drug-testing programme for inmates during 1995. Inmates will be required to provide a urine sample for testing purposes and, for the first time, it will become a disciplinary offence within prison for an inmate to use a controlled drug without appropriate medical authorisation. (HMPS, 1995: 7)

Further, a number of measures were outlined to reduce the supply of drugs into prisons: improved perimeter security; searching; supervision of visits; intelligence gathering; the use of informants; increased control of prescribed medication. While these measures were not new, the statement and emphasis given to this bifurcated strategy indicated a change in priorities.[4] The report indicated a marked shift away from the therapeutic and educational orientation of *Caring For Drug Users* (HMPS, 1991) and introduced a hard-hitting strategy geared to the restriction of drugs in prison and to an expansion of punishments for those caught in possession or under the influence of illicit substances.

The policy strategies of the SPS (1994) and HMPS (1995) were based on multi-dimensional approaches to drug use in prison. Both stated their intentions to provide throughcare services for drug users, educational programmes and treatment plans as a way of reducing the demand for drugs in prison. Both emphasised the prioritisation of halting the use of drugs in prison and, ultimately, the supply of illegal drugs. This was not a new approach for either Prison Service, but the unification of these two dimensions suggested an innovative attempt to direct a two-pronged attack against drugs within the penal system, combining measures to reduce both supply and demand.

The policy of HMPS has been emphatic in its plans to halt drug use in prisons (aiming towards the total exclusion of all non-prescribed drugs). It sets out a variety of means through which it aims to achieve eradication including: increased surveillance and observation of prisoners, particularly known drug users, and the introduction of mandatory drug testing (see *Chapter 6*). Even the emphasis on the provision of throughcare facilities such as treatment, counselling and education (see *Chapter 7*) are apparently provided as measures which will 'enable the Prison Service to reduce the level of drug misuse in prisons' (HMPS, 1995: 14–15). This indicates a shift from the more therapeutic and preventative emphasis of the 1992 policy and reflected wider policies that were being implemented in the community.

The Government's national strategy on drugs, *Tackling Drugs to Build a Better Britain* (Home Office, 1998), reiterated the role of the Prison Service in responding to illegal drug use. The measures outlined were incorporated into the Prison Service strategy document *Tackling Drugs in Prison* (HMPS, 1998). This publication emphasised the efforts to control the presence of illegal drugs in prisons and outlined provisions to target individuals suspected of drug use rather than focusing on random drug testing. Drug-free behaviour was to be rewarded through the use of incentives and earned privileges.

In the light of Government policy, developments are under way in the Prison Services of England, Wales and Scotland to provide a co-ordinated response to the problems of drug use in prisons. A new unit has been set up within the Directorate of Regimes of HMPS to respond to the national strategy. As a result of this development, a fresh drug treatment service framework has been initiated (CARATS: Counselling, Assessment, Referral, Advice and Throughcare Service). This will facilitate the development of programmes to assist and support drug users to become and remain drug free (but see the further comments at the end of *Chapter 8*).

This is similar to developments in Scotland where a Drug Strategy Co-ordination Group has been formed to co-ordinate the key elements of the SPS drugs strategy (prevalence, treatment, education and links with external agencies). This reflects Scottish policy responses to Government action and is outlined in *Tackling Drugs in Scotland: Action in Partnership* the Scottish Office, 1999). Under a Drug Strategy Co-ordinator, the Co-ordination Group will update the 1994 prison policy. Emphasis is being placed on increasing drug free places; expanding the use of CCTV, searches and introducing intelligence analysts. Also included will be mandatory drug testing along with the piloting of new drug detection equipment.

The research findings that follow highlight the difficulties inherent in providing therapeutic/rehabilitative programmes in penal environments due to the incompatibility of distinct but conflicting goals (see *Chapter 1*). The increased emphasis on security and surveillance both philosophically and in practice contrasts with rehabilitative measures. The difficulties in providing treatment or therapeutic measures in a prison environment, where the overall emphasis is on secure custody and the maintenance of order, will be examined throughout the following case studies.

In essence, there are two significant and connected difficulties over the role of treatment provisions in a prison environment:

i) the concept of 'less-eligibility'; and
ii) treatment versus punishment.

In an environment where resources are limited, for both economic and ideological purposes, the operation of policies aimed at the maintenance of discipline and order will have a profound effect on the development of therapeutic/rehabilitative opportunities.

i) Less eligibility
The notion of 'less-eligibility' is based on the assumption that prisoners should not be entitled to a better standard of care within prison than that available to citizens outside. Garland and Young (1983) note that the political, economic and ideological power of the prison operates to marginalise the prisoner. Restrictions on available resources form part of this process. As Duff and Garland (1994) point out, this can operate as a punitive measure in societies where large groups of people are very poor. Sim (1990 and 1994) provides a concise historical account of the application of the notion of 'less-eligibility' as it applies to healthcare in prisons. He notes that this principle persists and 'undermines any move towards a more humane or benevolent delivery of health provision' (Sim, 1994: 11). He goes on to discuss how this impacts on *all* aspects of a prisoner's life including medical care, nutrition, exercise and freedom from fear.

The availability of resources in prisons relating to healthcare *should*, but rarely ever does meet the standards of care available in the community (limited though such 'community' resources often are). The Healthcare Service for Prisoners (until 1 May 1992 called the Prison

Medical Service) has been criticised consistently for its inadequacies (see Chapter 2). As Sim (1990: 119) states:

> While the rhetoric of rehabilitation had allowed the managers of the penal estate to argue that prison healthcare was similar to that provided by the NHS, the reality for those behind the walls was a healthcare system caught in the disciplinary vice of appalling conditions and the legacy of less eligibility.

The discrepancies between resources and medical provisions in the community and those in prisons are easily discernible in the treatment of drug users. Government guidelines, as previously discussed, emphasise the need to give serious consideration to the resources made available in prisons, particularly given the increasing threat of HIV/AIDS. Despite the guidelines, however, the resources available in prisons continue to fall short of those available outside. Needle exchanges do not exist in prisons and opiate substitutes are not readily available, nor are condoms (despite the recognition that each initiative would play a fundamental role in harm reduction).

Since the mid-1980s many drug agencies have been relatively well supported through HIV/AIDS related funding. After a decade, much of this funding was reduced and this has had a profound effect on services for drug users.[5] The opportunity for community-based groups to provide services in penal institutions has been limited and left the dilemma that services already under way in prisons could not be sustained to provide effective contacts with community groups for prisoners on release. This is expected to be resolved through the CARATS programme. Sparks and Bottoms (1995) touch on this debate in their discussion of Lord Justice Woolf's 'new framework' within penology (1991). They note that Woolf considered the disturbances of 1990 in terms of the Prison Service's failure to meet prisoners' 'legitimate expectations' (Sparks and Bottoms, 1995: 46). His recommendations, therefore, contributed to the argument of reform groups that certain minimum standards were required in penal institutions. For Lord Justice Woolf, these minimum requirements were essential to the promotion of stability, and fair/just conditions were presented as fundamental to the attainment of security and control. This interdependency between justice, security and control forms the key underlying factor in HMPS's recent drug strategies. What is raised here is the distinction between 'rights' and 'privileges'.

The pursuit of policy objectives, which are defined by less eligibility, can lead to the introduction of measures that are closely related to punishment. When resources are limited their distribution will be scrupulously monitored and decisions will be made as to whom is 'deserving' or 'undeserving' of them. These assessments will be based on official definitions and the ideological standpoints of those in positions of authority. Those who are not considered 'treatable' or for whom available provisions have 'failed' will be assessed as 'untreatable' (Pitch, 1995) and correspondingly 'dangerous' (Castel, 1991). Punishment can then be justified as deserved.

Treatment versus punishment

In considering the role and function of the penal system it is clear that the concept of punishment impinges on every aspect of imprisonment although this is frequently neglected by criminologists (see Carlen, 1994). Hudson (1993: 182) also notes:

> Thinking about penal reform without thinking about punishment, then, leads to muddle and ambiguity, and leaves any apparent progress prone to unintended but predictable consequences of either strengthening segregative institutions or extending segregative traits in supposedly non-carceral sanctions.

De Haan (1990: 80) points out:

> Up until now the concepts of treatment and rehabilitation have provided a justification for punishment by masking the very character of it - the deliberate infliction of pain. However, the credibility of these options is rapidly deteriorating as deterrence and retribution come to the fore.

Indeed, this dichotomy requires consideration from a philosophical *and* political perspective. The relationship between treatment and punishment is certainly far from simplistic and in a penal environment the boundaries often become blurred. Walker (1980) raises the dilemma that treatment, with its objective of altering behaviour may be more coercive and damaging than punishment *per se*, which may be shorter and treat the offender more rationally (see also Feinberg, 1970). Certainly the ethos of rehabilitation implies that imposing internal change on the recipient changes behaviour. External controls are targeted at internal transformation. This is applicable both within prisons and in diversionary programmes provided in place of custody.

For some theorists, however, the only function required by the prison is to deprive the prisoners of their liberty, not to punish beyond this. Therefore rehabilitation is essential to offset the damaging effects of imprisonment:

> Institutionalisation is an alienating and depersonalising environment, without opportunities to combat degeneration or foster positive human development; [it] is a source of various harmful effects that play no part in the design of legal sanctions. (Rotman in Duff and Garland, 1994: 297)

In this respect, Rotman argues that while rehabilitation may be necessary it does not justify larger sentences as a means of rehabilitating. The compulsory imposition of 'state-obligated' rehabilitation is also advocated by Carlen (in Duff and Garland, 1994: 307) who believes that requirements, such as the provision by prisoners of urine samples, may be reasonable in return for rehabilitation programmes. However, within the penal setting, the enforced relationships between service-providers (prison staff) and service-users (prisoners) contradicts the objectives of contractual arrangements and informed choices.

Given the opposing aims of each objective (treatment/rehabilitation versus punishment) it is not surprising that the pursuit of one is often at the expense of the other.[6] As Sim (1990: 128) points out:

> Discipline, individualisation and normalisation are cornerstones of these institutions within which the emphasis on security, order and control invariably vanquish any notions of rehabilitation and reform.

Historically, rehabilitation was presented as an 'end-in-itself', but recent policies governing drugs (as discussed above) indicate that rehabilitation has come to be presented as a *means* by which to tackle the demand for drugs in prisons. Thus, it sets out as a controlling and security-dependent measure. Hudson (1993: 144) suggests that the erosion of the rehabilitative ideal within prisons has been replaced by the threat of punishment regimes. While not explicitly stated, there is no doubt that prisoners who refuse to participate in drug groups/therapy will be placed on more austere regimes. In the present economic and political context, overall conditions are likely to deteriorate rather than improve, to create this distinction. It is clear that the introduction of such measures serve particular purposes. As Sim (1994) notes, the emphasis on rehabilitation removes attention from structural flaws by blaming the individual. Blame can be further individualised if/when rehabilitation fails (Wright, 1982).

The next three chapters consider how effective the penal system has been in its attempt to implement programmes for drug users within prisons. Many of these initiatives are relatively new or are still in the process of being implemented. Nevertheless, new policies contain very similar assertions to current policies which have been circulating for a number of years. The case studies dealt with in those chapters examine the official discourse that defines the policies and practices of services for drug users, contrasting this with the experiences of prison staff who implement the policies, and of prisoners who experience their effects.

More specifically the case studies examine the ideological and economic significance of official constructs around women drug users and how this is used to determine policies, whilst the text considers the operation of these discourses at an institutional level (prison policies) and the individual level (practices of prison staff). The impact of therapeutic/rehabilitative measures are considered within a context where less eligibility is emphasised in terms of resource provision. The punitive aspects of resource provision - or lack of provision - are also emphasised.

ENDNOTES for *Chapter 4*

[1] Condoms are made available to prisoners when they leave the prison on release or home leave. Although the Prison Service Director of Healthcare stated that condoms should be made available where appropriate *within* prisons (1995), the BMA Foundation for AIDS

discovered that this was not a recognised practice in many prisons (BMA Foundation for AIDS, 1997).
2   See Briton (1995) for a discussion of the disincentives for drug users to disclose their drug use to probation officers.
3   The introduction of mandatory drug testing in prisons was not without its critics (ISDD, *Druglink*, May/June, 1995: 4). Prison officers expressed concern that it could increase conflict between staff and prisoners. Harry Fletcher (General Secretary of the National Association of Probation Officers) reiterated this. He further criticised the linkage of compulsory testing to withdrawal of privileges (*The Guardian*, 26 April 1994).
    Senior members of the Prison Service also objected to compulsory drug testing without the implementation of treatment and rehabilitation, pointing out that this could threaten order in prisons. The need to complement drug testing with adequate treatment services was shared by the Association of Chief Police Officers, (ACPO), the Police Superintendents' Association and the Police Federation (letter to *Druglink*, May/June 1995).
    Prisoners who tested positive or who refused to be tested could face up to 28 days being added to their sentence as well as loss of privileges and earnings (see HM Prison Service, 1995). *The Guardian* (1 April 1995) reported that instructions to prison governors enabled staff to hold prisoners in a secure room and administer 'controlled amounts of water' if the prisoner was unable to provide a urine sample. Initially, rates of refusal to be tested were reported to be as high as 80-90 per cent in some prisons. The costs of drug testing are considerable. In 1997, 159,000 days were added to prisoners' sentences as a direct result of mandatory drug testing (MDT) costing about £7 million in additional running costs (Edgar and O'Donnell, 1998: 4).
4   On 31 August 1995, Michael Forsythe, then Scottish Secretary of State, announced that compulsory drug testing would be introduced in Scottish prisons. The cost of this was to be met from within the Prison Service's current budget (*The Daily Telegraph*, 1 September 1995).
5   In 1992 the Government announced that the reorganization of community care would not provide a separate grant for drug and alcohol services, leaving them to compete for funding with other local authority services. Drug and alcohol service providers were concerned that this would force staff cuts and closures, particularly in the residential sector, with local authorities directing limited funds towards more 'popular' services.
6   This was evident in the Prison Service's decision to make it mandatory for all women prisoners on escort for medical or welfare appointments to be handcuffed to a prison officer. The decision to remove the handcuffs (i.e. during labour) was to be left to the doctor or midwife. This policy was introduced due to an increase in the numbers of women absconding. Harry Fletcher (General Secretary of the National Association of Probation Officers) was highly critical of this policy which was not, in his view, justified: 'This is a frightening example of the absurdity of ministers' obsession with security and punishment. As a consequence of it, women in labour will be chained and those at child care hearings will wear cuffs' (*The Guardian*, 15 July 1995).

CHAPTER 5

Disclosure and Withdrawal

This chapter considers prison policies in relation to the disclosure of drug use by prisoners and the management of drug withdrawal within the prison system. As with many elements of institutional practices and procedures there is often a discrepancy between policy objectives and what has been or can be achieved in practice. This is the case when a 'problematic' issue - such as drug use - is taken into consideration. Given the clandestine use of drugs, it is usual for drug users to attempt concealment of such information from the authorities, both in the community and in the criminal justice system.

Policies are defined and determined by a variety of assumptions and are informed by influential discourses. As previously discussed (*Chapters 1, 2* and *3*), there is a range of specific discourses which dominate drug use and criminality. Penal regimes are based on prevailing assumptions that come to define policy and practices. Within these regimes, however, staff and prisoners may or may not share those assumptions and ideologies which come to dominate. The following chapters will consider the significance of such tensions, examining policy objectives and their operation through the realities of the experiences of staff and prisoners. Central to this discussion is an analysis of the dynamics which inform the relationship between political expediency, operational policies and priorities and the actual practices negotiated, formally and informally, by staff.

As noted in *Chapter 4*, during the 1980s the recognition of an emergent drug 'problem' in Britain was reflected in changes in penal policies and attempts to cater for the growing number of drug users in prison. In 1987 HMPS (England and Wales) issued a policy statement on the throughcare of 'drug misusers' outlining the importance of a co-ordinated approach capitalising on the period of custody to encourage users to abandon their habit. These guidelines recognised that not all drug users would disclose their drug use on entry to custody (HMPS, 1987: para 13). As a result, a medical examination was proposed,[1] which aimed to identify drug users for whom withdrawal arrangements could be instituted. The actual treatment would be at the clinical discretion of the prison doctor (HMPS, 1987: para 14).

Criticising the guidelines on provisions as vague, Gunn *et al.* (1990: 115) called for a standard opiate withdrawal regime for every prison and an assessment procedure for all 'hard' drug users. To an extent, this was incorporated into new guidelines produced in 1991 by the (then) Prison Medical Directorate. The new guidelines *Caring for Drug Users* (HMPS, 1991) outlined a full and comprehensive strategy for dealing with drug users in the prison system, emphasising a co-ordinated and multi-disciplinary approach. The creation of an environment in which drug users would disclose their drug use on reception to prison establishments was prioritised:

> Every effort should be made to identify, during the reception process and after, inmates with a history of drug misuse, and to encourage them into treatment. (HMPS, 1991: Section 1, 3)

Further, the guidelines emphasised 'careful adherence to the principles of confidentiality, and the establishment of trust between staff and inmates' (HMPS, 1991: Section 1, 3). Making detoxification programmes available was seen to encourage disclosure, particularly by users of opiates and benzodiazepines, for whom withdrawal could be painful and/or dangerous. This was recognised by the Prison Medical Directorate, which outlined the benefits of providing detoxification programmes:

> It gives the addict a feeling of security about their immediate future in the establishment and the knowledge that some treatment is going to be immediately available. Secondly, it encourages a climate which leads to a higher level of self-disclosure about drug habits at the time of reception and reduces the level of illicit activity in the establishment. (HMPS, 1991: Section 2, 1)

The guidelines stated that a detoxification programme should be offered 'unless specifically contra-indicated' (HMPS, 1991: Section 2, 2) and they provided guidance for a routine detoxification programme to be administered, where possible, in the prison hospital under the supervision of hospital staff. It was emphasised, however, that this was *guidance* and that the clinical judgement of individual doctors was to remain intact.

The Medical Directorate, using contemporary research, hoped that making resources available for drug users within prisons would encourage greater disclosure:

> Currently, most prisoners who have drug problems seek to avoid them being identified by the prison. This is because, rightly or wrongly, they believe that the risk[s] of admitting the problem (in terms of extra supervision by officers, less favourable consideration of parole or home leave applications) outweigh the possible benefits (in terms of treatment or advice). Welfare organizations working with prisoners with drug problems report that only ten per cent of their clients have actually reported their problems with drugs to the prison authorities. It is important in the management of this issue that the percentage be increased. This will only be done by providing more treatment options that will fit their range of needs. No two prisoners are the same, and there is no one method or treatment that can be assumed to work for everyone. (HMPS, 1991: Section 5, 1)

Following the release of the guidelines, there was an increase in the number of drug users identified on entry to custody, although this could have been due to the continued increase in numbers of drug users in general. A 1991 study into the psychiatric profile of the sentenced prison population estimated that 19.6 per cent had substance abuse/dependence problems (Gunn *et al.*, 1991). Since then, and following policy changes, the number of notifications to the Home Office Addicts Index by prison medical officers (PMOs) has steadily increased. Forty-six per cent more addicts (1,180) were notified by PMOs in 1993 than in 1992 (Home Office, 1994: 17). The study went on to note:

> Recent prison service initiatives such as the new manuals on care for drug misusers and on HIV/AIDS may have been factors in encouraging misusers to come forward and in reminding officers of the need to notify.

Despite the attempts that have been made to identify and detoxify drug users within prison, this has not been without problems. While the guidance provided undoubtedly is useful, the function of penal regimes in incarcerating a population held largely against its will, makes it impossible to establish an atmosphere of co-operation and confidentiality (see *Chapters 1* and *2*). This makes the provision of incentives to encourage individuals to disclose drug use an operational imperative. Detoxification programmes may be an essential means of achieving this, but how they are implemented is dependent on the discretion and perspectives of individual medical officers. Consequently, practices vary significantly between prisons. Indeed, in certain institutions the guidelines have been ignored or only partially implemented.

Previous studies have identified problems in disclosure of drug use and the clinical management of withdrawals. Turnbull *et al.* (1994) identified the difficulties that prisoners experienced as drug users, noting the discrepancies between different penal institutions. Many prisoners have no alternative but to disclose, for example if their offence was drug-related or physical signs of drug use are evident. But in the study by Turnbull *et al.* (1994) many tried to conceal their drug use because of fear of official repercussions, notably extra surveillance. Drug users did not consider their treatment or medication to be adequate and many experienced severe withdrawal symptoms.

Turnbull *et al.* (1994) discuss the availability of medication during withdrawal from drugs. Out of 40 respondents who requested medication, 22 (55 per cent) received some (Turnbull *et al.*, 1994: 28). The medication provided was either opiate substitutes (Physeptone tablets, methadone linctus, dihydrocodeine), minor tranquillisers or drugs to relieve the physical symptoms of withdrawal. The length of time and the amounts prescribed varied considerably. The drug users often viewed this divergence in standards as more than circumstantial:

> Drug users perceived that doctors' judgements of them, and their circumstances, were often moral rather than clinical, the symptoms of drug withdrawal being viewed as the result of a self-inflicted problem, and being non life-threatening. They also reported that doctors often said that they were constrained by prison resources or treatment policy. (Turnbull *et al.*, 1994: 31)

A number of respondents in that study experienced difficulties in obtaining medication for alleviating symptoms relating to their use of drugs, particularly if they had been on methadone prior to imprisonment (see also Shewan et al., 1994). One prisoner (male) was placed in strip conditions and refused any medication for withdrawals (Turnbull et al., 1994: 26–7).

Where medication for opiate withdrawal was provided as part of a detoxification regime or to provide symptomatic relief, this tended to be for a maximum of 14 days, with some prisons adopting a routine course of medication for all prisoners reporting drug dependence, regardless of the amount used outside. Respondents reported that their individual withdrawals lasted on average between two and four months. Consequently, some used illegal drugs to offset the effects of withdrawals or longer-term insomnia. Similarly, Ross et al., (1994: 192) argue:

> the prescribing of very short courses of methadone does not seem to form part of a coherent clinical strategy to address the individual drug misusing prisoner's clinical needs.

In their recommendations, Turnbull et al., (1994: 55) state:

> Drug users on the whole, believed that the medication and treatment available was inadequate, and said that they experienced severe withdrawal symptoms as a result. Continued drug use among prisoners has to be understood in the context of the lack of adequate services for helping and treating this group.

They advocate measures to provide incentives for disclosing drug use on reception to prison and throughout the sentence with appropriate help, treatment and education, rather than the persistent emphasis on disciplinary measures.

Shewan et al., (1994) carried out a study into drug use before, during and after imprisonment in four Scottish prisons (male establishments). They noted that the respondents expressed dissatisfaction with the prison medical and nursing service. In 94 per cent of the cases where respondents were prescribed substitute drugs in the community this was stopped on entry to prison, although, in a few cases, short-term alternative medicine was provided (Shewan et al., 1994: 15). Of the sample, 25 per cent who reported withdrawing in prison had received medication for their withdrawals, most commonly benzodiazepines although there was no consistent pattern. Several prisoners identified particular aspects of the regime that had made their withdrawals worse (Shewan et al., 1994: 136). These included: the lack of medication on offer; less opportunity to gradually reduce their own level of use; unsympathetic response of staff; the feeling that being placed on observation was degrading.

This study suggested that 71 per cent of those injecting before imprisonment were either identified by prison doctors or nurses, or identified themselves as drug users. However, half the sample (and 96 per cent of injectors) had gone through withdrawals at some time in their prison career. It was discovered that those being prescribed methadone in the community, who had then had this stopped, were at greater risk of sharing injecting equipment in prison. This led the authors of the report to argue for a routine detoxification programme based on oral prescribing directed towards gradual withdrawal, particularly for opiate users.[2] From interviews with staff there appeared to be broad agreement for a harm-reduction approach, including a detoxification programme. Shewan et al., (1994: 2) noted that any emphasis on harm reduction should be placed within the context of prisons as 'secure places of custody'. Ultimately, they recognised that identifying drug users is of major importance if there is to be any attempt to change behaviour towards safer practices or abstinence.

The significant problems of standards of medical provision in prisons (*Chapter 2*) impacts on processes of disclosure and identification of drug users. In a study carried out by Mason *et al.*, (1997) with adult male remand prisoners at HMP Durham, the prevalence of drug users was high. The researchers considered that 71 per cent of the drug/alcohol using respondents required some form of help, with 36 per cent judged to be in need of a detoxification programme. However, reception health screening significantly underestimated the extent of drug and alcohol use amongst prisoners. Illicit drug use was identified at reception in only 24 per cent of cases, with problem drinking identified in only 19 per cent of cases. As a result, only 9 per cent of prisoners were prescribed treatment to ease withdrawal (Mason *et al.*, 1997).

WOMEN, DRUGS AND CUSTODY: FINDINGS

Practices between individual prisons vary due to a number of factors. These include: the rate of turnover of prisoners; the category of prisoners held; and staffing levels. Certain requirements however, are expected of medical staff. Once a prisoner has been identified as a drug user, appropriate withdrawal arrangements should be made, if considered necessary. These are dependent on the clinical judgement of the doctor. Prison guidelines suggest that withdrawal symptoms should be treated in the hospital wing although this varies across institutions.

Different drugs require different responses for withdrawals and medical intervention may not be required. However, the Medical Directorate (England and Wales) issued guidelines for the detoxification of individuals addicted to opiates and recommended the use of a reducing schedule of methadone administered over a period of seven days. The normal starting dose is approximately 40–50 mgs of methadone on the first day, although it is recognised that some individuals require larger or smaller doses. How these guidelines are administered is left to the discretion of the medical officer and the policy of methadone provision remains under review. As guidelines, however, their operational significance depends on clinical discretion and this leads to significant variations between institutions. Different prisons operate different regimes and the requirements of prisoners vary. It was essential in developing the research for this book, therefore, that the practices of detoxification in the participating prisons should be investigated and assessed.

HMP One

Prisoners should theoretically have gone through any withdrawal symptoms by the time they are sent to an open prison. However, many women were on some form of medication and so follow-up treatment was generally provided. HMP One had a healthcare centre staffed by nurses with a part-time GP from the local community. Short-term prescriptions, each reviewed weekly, were provided for withdrawal symptoms and included triazolam, temazepam, Valium and Lomotil.

> The doctor gives them short-term treatment. Sleep is usually a problem, cramps are a problem with the withdrawal symptoms that they get. (Nurse sister, HMP One)

> Everyone is interviewed and asked if they wish help while they're here. If they choose it then appointments are made for them. At the moment, nearly two-thirds of our population are drug users and I've hardly seen anyone. (Nursing sister, HMP One)

> From all accounts we're a very generous prison, or our doctors are very generous because a lot of prisons don't give them anything, they have to do without. And they can bawl and shout, but I don't think it's just to appease the person. Well I think it is a lot of the time because they can be horrendous. If they're helped to sleep or just calmed down we have less problems. I don't know whether it's because of our doctor or what, but it's choosing the easier option. (Nurse, HMP One)

HMP Two

An NHS medical practitioner supplied medical provision. No hospital accommodation was available within the prison, but a healthcare centre operated, staffed by nursing officers. Symptomatic relief for opiate withdrawals was provided with Lomotil, tranquillisers (such as Valium and Mogadon) and painkillers. A recent development meant that prisoners who were 'stable' on a methadone programme in the community could be retained on the drug in the prison. However, only around three per cent of methadone users were deemed to be 'stable'. Sometimes Largactil and anti-depressants were prescribed. Wide use of temazepam was a problem among many prisoners and women who had been using this were given a withdrawal regime of diazepam. Women who disclosed drug use were placed initially in a secure, observation block and monitored as was deemed necessary.

Although medication was provided, generally in the form of tranquillisers with a diazepam withdrawal regime for women on temazepam, the standardisation of provision was recognised as problematic by staff:

They couldn't go into depth with rehabilitation or with the withdrawal regimes other than the standard one they use here. They can't individualise it to the girls' requirements. That's the trouble, there's no individualised care, it's standard. (Nursing officer, HMP Two)

Women with a history of drug-taking fits or established temazepam users were placed on observation, carried out by discipline staff:

> All we can do is give them a bed on the floor and an officer will check them every 15 minutes. (Nursing officer, HMP Two)

> Time-wise, drug addicts are our biggest problem. When they come in at first they're so demanding - needing to see the doctor, needing more medicine, saying they're not sleeping, abscesses, the fits are the worst thing. We have a sheet of observations every day and that's nearly all drug addicts. (Nursing officer, HMP Two).

Nursing staff universally agreed that much of the medication prescribed in the institution was directed towards drug users:

> I would say about 150 out of 170 women are on medication. We go through about 1,000 Valium a week which doesn't leave a lot of them who aren't getting Valium or Mogadon at night. In a male jail the night medication round for 600 prisoners would take me an hour. Here it takes about two hours. (Nursing officer, HMP Two)

HMP Three

This prison held women who had been sentenced, so in theory prisoners should have withdrawn at another institution before arrival. As a result no reduction programme operated here and women were not prescribed opiate substitutes. A number of prisoners did, however, arrive directly from court after being on bail and some came from other prisons. Thus some women entered HMP Three with a 'habit'. Withdrawal symptoms were, therefore, treated medically - although it was not usual for women to be placed in the healthcare centre during this time unless it was felt necessary. HMP Three had a full time healthcare centre staffed by nurses and covered by a locum doctor. Prisoners reported being prescribed Largactil, Heminevrin, dihydrocodeine, chloral, Mogadon and Melleril as well as Valium and other anti-depressants:

> This is a sentenced prison with only a few Justice Remands, so theoretically women will have withdrawn before they get here, but with so much stuff around that's not happening and women are withdrawing here because they're able to get stuff in. We don't use a methadone reduction programme here, we tend to try and treat them symptomatically (Nursing Sister, HMP Three).

> Detox is individual for each woman. I'd like to see a doctor here who would be keen to use it if he thought it was necessary, but unless you get a doctor who's trained in substance misuse they have a totally different perception of what it does to people. The last doctor had absolutely no sympathy at all for

drug users and we had a locum who would give them anything to shut them up (Nursing sister, HMP Three).

HMP Four

HMP Four holds a high number of remand prisoners and a significant number of drug users. Opiate substitutes were not provided and, despite this being a reception prison, many women stated that they were refused any medication. Staff verified this. Prisoners on withdrawal were sometimes placed on the hospital wing staffed by nursing officers. The majority, however, were placed in normal accommodation, although some were located two to a cell for the first night if there was an identified cause for concern. A high proportion of prisoners recounted being prescribed Largactil and chloral.

> Basically they don't get any help, they don't get any medication. (Prison officer, HMP Four)

> If they were very bad [withdrawing] they would go to the hospital but the majority come onto the wing. They just seem to be left in their cell, they don't seem to take them in the hospital now. (Prison officer, HMP Four)

Some officers believed the most important help available for women on reception to prison, where little or no medical help was offered, was from other prisoners:

> They all help each other in here, particularly the girls on drugs - they'll stay with one who is withdrawing; they even clean up the vomit from each other's cells, or they'll help their mate along the corridor while she's throwing up. They really support each other. (Prison officer, HMP Four)

HMP Five

In 1987, a seven-to-ten-day methadone detoxification programme was established for opiate users in HMP Five, with a non-negotiable reduction to zero. Prescriptions for hypnotics and analgesics were also made available as necessary. When the research was carried out in this prison, Physeptone was being administered to drug users in decreasing doses over a five-day period during which women were located on the hospital wing. HMP Five has a two-unit hospital wing staffed by medical and discipline staff. The amount distributed was based on set guidelines and was the same for all women regardless of the extent to which they were using on the outside. Various medications were prescribed for symptoms of withdrawal including Valium, temazepam, chloral, diazepam, Heminevrin and various anti-depressants.

In HMP Five where medication was provided for women coming off opiates, prison and medical staff recognised that something was available for the women and viewed problems as discipline-based rather than medical issues. Ninety-six per cent of officers in HMP Five who participated in this study believed that drug users were more of a discipline or security problem than non-users. Nevertheless, they recognised that withdrawal often presented problems:

If a woman is coming off drugs then she will have bad mood swings and can be aggressive towards staff. (Prison officer, HMP Five)

They tend to have very bad mood swings and depression. (Nurse, HMP Five)

Disclosure of drug use

Across the prisons, officers were asked to estimate the number of women on the unit/wing where they worked who had been regular drug users prior to imprisonment. Sixty-three per cent of officers estimated that half or over half of the women had been regular drug users. The officers believed that many of the offences for which women were imprisoned were drug-related although not necessarily drug offences:

> A good 70 per cent have had drugs involved in their offences like shoplifting to feed their habit or someone else's, or offences committed under the influence of drugs. (Prison officer, HMP Three)

> I would say most of them have used drugs. They even say the crimes they commit were because of drugs, to get money for it or whatever. (Prison officer, HMP Two)

This was borne out by the prisoners themselves. Of drug using respondents, 91 per cent believed that their charges were drug-related. Sixty-seven per cent stated that they had committed the offence(s) to get money for drugs, 18 per cent had been charged with a drug offence, while 15 per cent stated that they were under the influence of drugs at the time of the offence.

> If I didn't take drugs there's no danger, no *way* I would be in here. I wouldn't be stealing, I wouldn't be soliciting, I wouldn't be doing anything to get money to keep the habit, because I wouldn't need it. (Prisoner, HMP Two)

> It's all been drug-related, but don't get me wrong, I admit that now it's become a way of life for me, become a habit. Even if I came off the drugs now I don't think I'd be able to stop stealing . . . stealing has become as much of a habit as a way of life, I can't stop it. (Prisoner, HMP Two)

> I don't think I would have offended at all if I wasn't taking drugs. Because our savings were finished from using I needed to get money from somewhere. I wouldn't turn to prostitution so the best thing was fraud . . . Most of the time I have to take something to do it . . . If you've got something in you it gives you the confidence to go out and steal. (Prisoner, HMP Two)

> I was robbing for crack and done a section 18 wounding. I shouldn't have done it but I was out of my face on temazepam, crack, drink and butane gas. (Prisoner, HMP Three)

In a very few cases, drugs were a by-product rather than a goal of crime:

> Basically I don't go out stealing for drugs, when I do robberies it's not

because I want money for drugs. I've always got credit so to speak. But I've always got a bit of money for drugs - so my problem isn't drug-related. It's a way of spending the money I make, I'm not a drinker you see. (Prisoner, HMP Four)

Many officers noted that the number of drug users in prison recently had increased significantly:

> A lot, the majority are users. It's changed a lot over the last six years. It's got a lot worse, from being about 50-50 to about everyone now. (Prison officer, HMP Four)

This was recognised in all five establishments. In Scotland previously there had been a significant number of prisoners with an alcohol dependency and this had been surpassed recently by the growing number of drug users.

> Previously it used to be all alcoholics but most of them are drug users now. (Prison officer, HMP Two)

> About 80 per cent of the clientele in here were in for alcohol-related crimes, then we discovered more inmates were coming in for drug-related rather than alcohol-related crimes. (Prison officer, HMP Two)

> I've been in the Prison Service for fourteen-and-a-half years. When I first came in there was one drug addict came into prison and it was like wildfire going round the prison. You expected someone with horns. We'd never come across a drug addict, we didn't know what to expect, we didn't know how to deal with them or anything. Since then obviously the numbers have got higher and higher. Alcohol has got less and less. (Prison officer, HMP Two)

The speed with which numbers of drug users has increased in prisons has led many staff to feel unable to deal adequately with the problems presented by women withdrawing from drugs. They felt that appropriate medical conditions had not been provided and it was difficult to regulate the movement of drugs into prison. This was due mainly to the failure of training methods available to prison staff to provide enough information on the subject or help develop an understanding of the issues that relate to drug use. As a result, many discipline and medical officers relied on the images and stereotypes of drug using women presented in the media and popular discourse (see *Chapter 3*).

Prison officers' views on why prisoners do not disclose drug use

> Even the women who have had cannabis on them didn't recognise that was a problem although they were there as pushers. They were using as well and taking advantage of their position. But they didn't see it was a drug problem. (Prison officer, HMP One)

> A lot of these girls will stand and say they don't take drugs but when you

see their eyes like pin-pricks you know they do. I think a lot of them have a problem admitting it. (Prison officer, HMP Three)

Some officers were confident in their ability to identify drug users:

> Some girls come in very desperate, in need of help but their mental and physical state gives them away. You would pick it up and I think after years of experience you do tend to notice this kind of behaviour in a person. (Prison officer, HMP One)

Other officers identified the difficulties of accurate identification:

> I have been conned myself. I use my own judgement. If they look bad then you know. But if they look alright and say they haven't used for a while, don't have any great trackmarks, then I would give them the benefit of the doubt. Then a few days later you might find they're having fits, shakes, vomiting and they would have to go back on observation. Quite a lot of the girls actually look fairly normal when they're quite heavily under the influence of drugs, because it's their lifestyle. (Medical officer, HMP Two)

Drug use on entry to prison was not disclosed by 31 per cent of drug users. Of the 69 per cent who identified themselves as users, the majority told medical staff while going through reception procedures. Several women were aware that their records (from previous periods of custody) stated that they were drug users. Eight women stated that they were showing signs of withdrawing on arrival at the prison, or had required medical assistance due to withdrawals occurring while they were held in police cells. One woman had gone into convulsions on arrival at prison.

Women who had not disclosed their drug use gave various reasons for this. Ten per cent stated that they did not want to be put on observation or the hospital wing:

> Because if you say you've been using they send you to the observation block and its all crackpots so you feel worse than anything, so you're better off just saying you don't use anything. You don't get anything off them anyway. (Prisoner, HMP Two)

> If you say they put you on observation and when you go to work in the cutting room you don't get a decent job. (Prisoner, HMP Two)

> If you come in and say you've been using drugs they put you on 15-minute observation, down the stairs, you get a blanket on the ground, you have your light on *all* night, *every* night, constantly, until the doctor takes you off 15-minutes obs. That's worse than everything else. It's bad enough not being able to sleep, but rattling around with your light on all night . . . (Prisoner, HMP Two)

> Its hard when you're on obs. because you're trying hard to get a sleep and there's someone looking in every 15 minutes shining a torch in your face. (Prisoner, HMP Four)

Some women (six per cent) did not want staff to know of their drug use, fearing that more stringent security measures would be enforced. This was linked to their views or expectations of available medication, a form of cost–benefit analysis:

> Your visits will be watched constantly. It's pointless admitting it anyway because you don't get any help from the health centre. (Prisoner, HMP Two)

> It can lead to strip searches and closed visits. I brought in my own supply. (Prisoner, HMP Five)

A further 12 per cent did not think that the medication they would receive was sufficient or appropriate and, therefore, did not consider that it was in their interests to make their drug use known to prison staff:

> I'd never tell them unless I was in such a bad state it was showing on me . . . As far as the medication is concerned I don't think it would be worth saying for three Valium and one Mogadon. I wouldn't waste my time going down to the health centre for that. You're better off getting nothing. (Prisoner, HMP Two)

> A lot of people are put off by the idea that they come in and admit to the doctor they were using drugs but they don't get any help with their withdrawals . . . So they come in thinking if they're not getting help, not getting medication, then what's the point of telling them that. (Prisoner, HMP Four)

The influencing factors which determined whether a woman would disclose her drug use or not turned on the 'probable' consequences as she believed them to be, either due to previous experience or word-of-mouth from other prisoners. The main considerations were:

- the location on which the prisoner expected to be placed (i.e. the secure wing or hospital unit);
- the physical conditions which were likely to result (i.e. observation);
- increased security measures which may be implemented (this includes observation as well as more generalised scrutiny by staff);
- the likely medication which would be made available.

This last item appeared to be an over-riding concern for many women and was used to balance out the others. For example, if the medication available was deemed a necessity by the woman then this would take priority over her other concerns. However, if she thought the medication would be of limited value and she felt able to do without it, or that she would be able to obtain more adequate medication from other (illicit) sources, then the added fear of stigmatisation, unpleasant conditions and greater scrutiny were considerable disincentives to disclosure. Some officers were confident that most women *did* disclose drug use:

> I think the majority do, because we do the reception board in the morning

and that's one of the things they're asked. I think the majority admit it. (Prison officer, HMP Four)

They have to fill in a form for their security category, telling what they've been using and things. Quite often they don't admit it then, but once they're in the units they'll talk to the other girls or to you. (Prison officer, HMP Two)

We have to see all the women who come into the prison as receptions and the format for screening involves asking if they're a drug user. What I've found is that none of them say 'No', apart from one or two odd ones. (Nursing Sister, HMP Three)

According to the officers, however, certain types of drug use were less likely to be disclosed than others:[3]

Usually they're quite happy to admit taking drugs . . . There may be the odd new one coming in who might not admit to taking drugs but I think you find that particularly among the youngsters. They're not injecting so it's not quite as obvious as other drug users. They're more into the party drugs and obviously they're not going to admit it unless they're going through severe withdrawals. (Prison officer, HMP Two)

The young ones don't see themselves as drug users. They just think, 'Oh, it's party time', take a few pills then need something to bring them down - they don't see that as being a drug addict. (Prison officer, HMP Two)

This was reiterated elsewhere by other prison staff:

They seem quite happy to talk about their drug use. By the time they reach us, if they've had a serious drug use like heroin, they're quite used to it. They've been into the system, they've tried to come off it, they're committing their crimes to feed their habit and they're used to it being part of their personality. As for recreational drugs - they don't really talk about it except as a taken-for-granted thing that they do. They don't see it as a problem. (Education worker, HMP One)

Staff believed that if medication were available, prisoners would be more likely to disclose that they were drug users:

Yes, they will admit it. If anything they will tell us that they take more in the hope that they'll get more from us. (Nursing officer, HMP Two)

Initially it used to be that people didn't disclose because they thought there would be restrictions on them. They thought everyone would keep a closer eye on them, that they would be restricted from doing a certain number of jobs within the prison. Now I think the attitude towards drug use has changed as society has changed. So I'd say that a high proportion of them want some form of medication. (Nursing Sister, HMP One)

Prisoners' reasons for disclosure

As noted previously, 69 per cent of drug using prisoners in this study disclosed their drug use to access medication or some form of medical assistance. Several women stated that they had disclosed because they felt they had to, either because they were withdrawing on arrival at the prison or because the authorities were aware that they were drug users.

> I told the doctor I was a drug user because it was down on my records as well as being in for drugs. (Prisoner, HMP Five)

> I just answered 'Yes', because you can't lie - they're going to find out sooner or later. (Prisoner, HMP One)

> Well they've got it marked down if you've been in before. They just ask you what you've been using from the last time you were in. They can tell by looking at you. (Prisoner, HMP Two)

The drug using respondents in this study had used a variety of drugs over different periods of time. However, 97 per cent of them had been regular (illicit) users for over one year with 64 per cent having used for over four years. A number of women (28 per cent) had been using drugs for ten years or more. The longest period identified concerned a woman who had been taking amphetamines for over 20 years (initially prescribed by a GP). The majority of respondents combined different drugs. Most took a wide variety, combining non-medical drugs such as cocaine and cannabis with drugs that may have a medical purpose (tranquillisers, opiates) but were not prescribed to them. Seventy-two per cent had injected (see *Chapter 6*).

Many women (49 per cent) were receiving medication in the community directly related to their drug use (i.e. as a maintenance prescription or as part of a withdrawal regime). Of this group, only two women, were *not* using illegal drugs at the same time. Those in receipt of authorised medication (related to drug use) were prescribed a range of drugs, but predominantly opiates (85 per cent) and tranquillisers (87 per cent). Sixty-seven per cent of this group was prescribed methadone, but only 30 per cent received methadone alone.

Many women had considerable habits combining various groups of drugs in significant quantities. They were also likely to sell or exchange some of the drugs that they received legally for their preferred drug of choice (for example selling or exchanging methadone for heroin). This meant that their drug intake was chaotic, leading to extreme discomfort on entry to prison:

> I was getting dihydrocodeine and temazepam from my GP but I was taking what was for a week in the one night and then going and buying more the same night. (Prisoner, HMP Two)

> By the time you start using uppers a lot you need something to come down off them so I was getting downers. At first I was buying them, then I got them on a script, but it wasn't just from one doctor. I had three doctors going, three chemists going, my sister-in-law worked in a chemists so I was getting double my script in there. I was maybe getting four or five times more than my doctor was giving me. (Prisoner, HMP Two)

Provision of medication

Of regular drug users, 70 per cent received medication on entry to prison, either as detoxification or as symptomatic relief from withdrawal symptoms. As previously noted, policies varied between institutions and 30 per cent of drug using women stated that they did *not* receive medication for withdrawals on arrival.

A wide range of medication was issued. In only one establishment was an opiate substitute (Physeptone) available, generally for five days. In this prison, 74 per cent of women who received medication for withdrawals received Physeptone, although only 39 per cent received that alone. The majority were given a variety of other drugs in addition: chloral; tranquillisers; anti-depressants and Heminevrin. In the other prisons a mixture of medication was provided. In certain prisons Largactil and chloral were regularly distributed, while another relied heavily on Valium and Mogadon. Of the women who, on entry to prison received some form of medication directly related to drug use, 66 per cent continued to take non-prescribed drugs (see *Chapter 6*).

Although there were significant differences between prescribing practices in different establishments, women with a history of drug use were significantly more likely than non drug-users to attempt to obtain medication during their sentence. None of the non-drug users who participated in this study were receiving medication for anything other than a medical condition (such as asthma), or during pregnancy, although women were prescribed medication such as tranquillisers and/or anti-depressants where it was considered to be appropriate. Such medication did not appear to be heavily prescribed to non drug-users. Indeed high levels of prescribed drugs appeared to be a direct result of the high numbers of drug users in prison, many of whom required and/or requested a range of medication particularly tranquillisers.

> I would say over two-thirds of our population of 200 are drug users. About 48 people here were receiving anti-depressants *but* that was a fortnight ago, it's increased since then - so that's about 25 per cent receiving medication ... not all of those are drug users. (Nurse, HMP One)

> Approximately 70–75 per cent of the population is on medicine at the one time. Approximately 60 per cent of that will be drug-related, tranquillisers or whatever they need to support them coming off drugs. (Nursing officer, HMP Two)

> It feels like two-thirds of them are junkies. There has to be at least half ... half of them are on a Valium regime anyway. (Nursing officer, HMP Two)

This seemed to be particularly problematic at HMP Two where Valium and Mogadon were prescribed as symptomatic relief for drug users on entry and over a period of three to four weeks. In most prisons, many drug users wanted medication (particularly tranquillisers) after the allotted time for withdrawal had passed, but they were unable to obtain it. Although drugs such as antibiotics and paracetamol were available for *medical* conditions, they were often refused (particularly at HMPs One,

Two, Three and Four) if the request was believed by medical staff to be related to drug use. In particular, sleeping tablets and tranquillisers were closely controlled, despite previous concerns that certain types of medication are freely available. This was not the case in HMP Five which, historically, has had a medical emphasis and where 65 per cent of prisoners continued to receive medication following detoxification. This generally took the form of tranquillisers and/or anti-depressants.

While it would be reasonable to argue that the notion of 'less-eligibility' (*Chapters 1* and *4*) is fundamental to what many women believed to be inadequate treatment, it is also necessary to consider the recent role of campaigners against the perceived over-prescription of drugs notably tranquillisers and anti-depressants in women's prisons and hypnotics in male prisons. It was argued that such high doses of certain drugs were being used as control mechanisms to subdue and restrain prisoners. This led to a growing concern that has had some effect on the prescribing practices of many medical officers. Certainly this was the view of many members of staff, particularly medical staff, who were concerned at the high levels of medication available:

> To my mind there's total over-prescribing, particularly your sleepers and Valium; a lot of the lassies don't need anything. At one point I was sitting in with the doctor during a clinic and he actually gave a lassie something just to get her out the door. He said, 'Why did I do it?' I *know* why he does it, to get peace and quiet the same as any GP on the street, giving them anything they want . . . The girls here, they see it as a crutch to hold them up, although it's only a minute quantity compared to what they've been using on the streets. It's still far too much. (Nursing officer, HMP Two)
>
> I think a lot of the lassies could do without it. I just think the doctors could be a bit harder to say 'No' to some of them, particularly with Valium or it will just keep going on forever. (Nursing officer, HMP Two)

Nevertheless, for many women who had been regular drug users prior to imprisonment, their main concern was that they desired *more* medication and often felt they were prescribed insufficient amounts. Indeed, many perceived the lack of medication available in certain prisons to be a form of punishment that impacted directly on their status as a drug user.

Prisoners' perceptions of medication

Prisoners were not, on the whole, satisfied with the medication available to them. Of those who received it, only 28 per cent *were* satisfied. Those who were not, attributed this to the following factors:

- not enough medication (47 per cent);
- medication was not prescribed for a long enough period of time (24 per cent);
- it did not help or was ineffective (30 per cent).

As previously noted, many women were taking considerable quantities of drugs prior to imprisonment, generally a combination of prescribed medication and illicit drugs. The medication that they received in prison was often negligible in comparison to this and many women felt it had little effect.

> I was on prescribed medicine outside as well [as heroin] - dihydrocodeine and temazepam - so they give you Mogadon and Valium to stop you fitting. Valium to stop you fitting and Mogadon for sleeping. But if you compare what you're getting outside to what they give you in here - one Valium and one Mogadon - it's not touching you. (Prisoner, HMP Two)

> You come in here and see the doctor and it's up to him whether he gives you anything. If the doctor doesn't give you anything then that's you, you need to cold turkey. But he usually gives you something if you fit. (Prisoner, HMP Four)

> Now it doesn't matter what kind of habit you have, you get Valium, maybe a Mogadon at night and that is it . . . It doesn't help, you don't get a sleep, you feel ratty and everything. There is a lot of girls coming in here and fitting, really badly. These Valium aren't doing them any good. They're taking maybe 40–50 Valium every day outside so one Valium isn't doing them any good. (Prisoner, HMP Two)

Some prisoners believed that it was important that medication was limited:

> When you're on Valium you only get it for a few weeks unless you really need it. He tries to get you off it as soon as possible which I agree with. I don't think you should be going out of here with a Valium habit. (Prisoner, HMP Two)

However, many women felt that the five-day period of detoxification was inadequate:

> It's too fast - not even out of your system. (Prisoner, HMP Five)

> Medication should last longer, I'm still withdrawing. (Prisoner, HMP Five)

Several prisoners were not told what medication they were being prescribed, others felt that the type was inappropriate:

> I was getting Largactil to calm me down and help me sleep, but I cut it down because I was getting side effects from it. It just starts working on its own, it doesn't take away the withdrawals it just makes you sit there all the time and there's not a lot you can do about it . . . I had more problems getting it stopped than I would have had getting it. I don't know how they get away with it because Largactil does produce very bad side-effects. (Prisoner, HMP Four)

> They should give out normal sleeping tablets, chloral does your head in and you get addicted to it. (Prisoner, HMP Five)

> The medication is crap. They're giving me Largactil now, to try to calm me down, but it's for schizophrenics. The doctors aren't any help in here. I've blagged everything out of these doctors: Heminevrin - I'm not even an alcoholic, DF118s for toothache ... I'd save it all up and take it at once. (Prisoner, HMP Three)

For many women, one of the main problems was their inability to sleep at night (discussed further later). Several women would tell medical staff (incorrectly) that they were alcoholics to obtain medication that they felt would be more appropriate:[4]

> Its got to the stage that lassies coming in sentenced this year are kidding on that they're into alcohol so they get Heminevrin cos that gives you a sleep. (Prisoner, HMP Two)

> If you come in and say you've been using drugs they just give you Valium and that doesn't do anything. So my pal told me to say I was an alcoholic because then you get Heminevrin so that's what I got even though I can't handle drink at all, and it gets me sleeping so that's me a lot better. (Prisoner, HMP Two)

As one woman stated:

> You do get the situation where women attempt to pull a fast one to try to get medication but the whole system of providing drugs is so arbitrary, not just in prisons but outside as well. It depends on the doctors. A lot of them have no idea about drug dependency or addiction as such. (Prisoner, HMP Five)

Withdrawing

> There's no one specific thing among females that we could say started them off on drugs. But it's either drug offences or shoplifting and prostitution that brings them back in. So when they get lifted for shoplifting they're usually full of drugs. In fact, about 90 per cent of them are full of drugs when they come in. (Prison officer, HMP Two)

For drug users, entry to prison regularly meant their intake was abruptly discontinued or drastically reduced (although some were able to maintain their drug use in prison: see *Chapter 6*). As previously discussed, medication was generally provided by PMOs, either as a short detoxification regime or to provide symptomatic relief. This was often minimal compared to the quantities used by the women outside. As a result most respondents, both those who had disclosed their drug use to the authorities and those who had not, experienced withdrawal symptoms. The extent and nature of these depended on the drugs and quantity used, length of time the drugs had been used for and individual tolerance.

Clinical management of withdrawal varies and depends on the nature of the drug. Withdrawal from opioids may be managed by symptomatic relief using less addictive medication or by using a substitute opioid (i.e. methadone). Withdrawal from benzodiazepines and other sedative/hypnotic drugs should take the form of a regularised daily dose which is gradually reduced. Diazepam is particularly suitable in this respect (Department of Health, 1991: 44). Withdrawal from this type of drug is problematic due to the potential risk of convulsions. In prisons where a high proportion of women used this type of drug (particularly temazepam) 'fitting' was a regular occurrence.

The guidelines recognise the importance of psychological support for withdrawal regimes to minimise discomfort and note that additional drugs may be required if this is not effective (i.e. for anxiety reduction or to relieve depression). Within the prison environment there is often little opportunity to make such support available and, clearly, confinement and isolation will exacerbate many of the symptoms noted above. This contributes to the relatively high levels of anti-hypnotic drugs such as Largactil which are prescribed in prisons, perhaps in an attempt to reduce drug-related psychosis. It is often difficult to distinguish between withdrawal and anxiety in individuals coming off benzodiazepines and symptoms can be particularly severe if withdrawal is too rapid, causing 'convulsions, hallucinations and psychotic episodes' (Hamlin and Hammersley, 1989: 110). Such medication can have severe side-effects and is no substitute for the psychological support many women require during drug withdrawal.

Stimulants and hallucinogens do not, according to official guidelines (Department of Health, 1991: 46) produce major physical withdrawal and abrupt discontinuation is recommended. However, anti-depressants or benzodiazepines may be provided to offset depression and anxiety. Doctors use medical discretion. This is based on their clinical judgement as well as guidance such as the above. However, as medical staff were aware, the individual's drug use was often more complex than allowed for in guidelines, with very few using one category of drug in isolation:

> In the main it's heroin, amphetamines, cocaine. Usually heroin and cocaine together. A few benzos [benzodiazepine] but they usually use that in conjunction with the heroin or with the coke. Most of them are quite bad users . . . There are many who have controlled use, being maintained on methadone, who have been bizarre users but managed to get it under control by getting methadone, probably long-term. The ones we get here haven't got to that stage, they've got a totally chaotic habit and will take anything and use any means to get what they can. (Nursing sister, HMP Three)

This was a position adopted by staff throughout the study.

Most prison officers from all institutions (91 per cent) and a significant number of non-discipline staff, said they believed that drug users presented more of a 'problem' within the regimes in terms of discipline and security. While it was felt that this was manifested in attempts to use drugs within the prison (see *Chapter 6*) it was also considered that disruptive behaviour was due to the withdrawal experienced when coming off drugs. This was stated in all prisons, regardless of whether substitutes were prescribed as part of a withdrawal regime or not:

> Those using drugs behave irrationally, those who are coming off or cannot get hold of drugs are aggressive and abusive. (Prison officer, HMP Five)

> Well sometimes they can be a bit moody and they're always desperate to get medication, whereas ones that don't tend to use don't bother the same. (Prison officer, HMP Two)

> If they're still withdrawing and haven't managed to get anything in to calm themselves down they tend to be harder to handle than if they're calmer. (Prison officer, HMP Three)

This presented particular problems for staff in open prisons:

> The biggest problem here is women who have been sent on from HMP Four and are still withdrawing - they might only have been there for one day. About 50 per cent of them will try to run away to get drugs. (Prison officer, HMP One)

Many of the prisoners also identified the problems:

> This is the hardest part [cold turkey], especially when you go to an open prison like this and you're going cold turkey and there's just a little fence and it's just edging you to run for drugs. It's easy for some to hold back but it's not for others. (Prisoner, HMP One)

> You'll find a lot of the absconders are the ones that are withdrawing. The prison are doing a lot for that person if they help them over that withdrawal stage. (Prisoner, HMP One)

From the interviews with prisoners it was evident that many women suffered severe withdrawals, largely due to the combinations and quantities of drugs used outside. While in some cases medication alleviated the most severe aspects, the physical and psychological aspects of imprisonment clearly contributed considerably to the distress experienced by many women, particularly users of opiates and benzodiazepines:

> *M:* What do you experience when you come in if you're going through withdrawals?
>
> *Answer:* I can't really explain it . . . your head's up your arse to put it politely. You're banged up behind your door . . . and the nurses in here are in a worse state than China . . . Some of them just think it's self-inflicted. Well it is, but some of them are really snide. When you're sitting there with a chanty full of sick, they won't even let you out to empty it. (Prisoner, HMP Two)

In prisons with a hospital wing, women considered 'at risk' of convulsing were located there to be regularly observed. In prisons where this facility was not available, they were placed on observation, frequently under strip conditions. The physical conditions and locations contributed significantly to their discomfort:

> In remand they keep you down the stairs but here if you're fitting there's a room along there where there is just a mattress on the ground. That's all you get until the doctor thinks you're all right to go into a room. It's even worse because you don't get blankets, it's just like a big sleeping bag and it's more uncomfortable because you're strung out. No drugs and it's hard to sleep; it makes you worse, lying on the floor on something hard. They say it's for your own safety but I don't think so because it makes you feel worse. (Prisoner, HMP Two)

> If you come in and you're full of drugs you are automatically put down the back cells. They say it's for your own safety but how long you're kept down there is literally up to them and up to the governor. You can be kept in there for up to seven days. There's other ways of securing people's safety than taking their dignity and everything else away from them and throwing them in the back cells with a riot dress on. It's whatever is the easiest way out for them, whatever is the quietest. They can't hear you in these cells, if they shut over the door it's a silent cell. Some people could be screaming out for help and they just think they're at it. (Prisoner, HMP Two)

Restrictions, such as observation, enabled staff to keep a watch on prisoners in case of medical difficulties. However, in the prison environment this was again contextualised by issues of security that had serious consequences for the prisoner:

> When you're coming off you've got sickness and diahorrea at the same time but you're not allowed out of your room, not even to empty your pot which is made of paper. It's disgusting. It's not only unhygienic, it's degrading. (Prisoner, HMP Two)

Many women reacted to these conditions by banging on doors, shouting for medication and ringing emergency bells to attract the attention of staff. From the experience of many respondents in this study, such attempts were ignored as far as possible by staff who relegated it to 'attention-seeking' behaviour or put the prisoner on report for being 'disruptive'. Not surprisingly, it had a very different meaning for the prisoners involved:

> If you ring the bell and someone answers and says that someone will come and you don't bother ringing again, no one will come. You've got to keep banging the door all night for someone to come out. Sometimes they say the nurse isn't here, she's over on the other side, they try to fob you off. But I've been banging on the door all night and they've said she isn't here and then she eventually comes. (Prisoner, HMP Four)

> Last night I rang the bell from quarter to eleven and no one came till 12 o'clock. I wanted paracetamol although I didn't have a pain. I think I just wanted to talk to someone. It was a civvie who came eventually and they –

[the prison officers] had just sent him up to tell me I couldn't get anything. (Prisoner, HMP Four)

The hospital strips are used for people who are withdrawing, if you're banging and that. It's strange but your mind goes, you're not really in that room. You see yourself and say, 'get yourself together' but you just want to bang the door down you're in that much pain. But you know no one will come; you won't get to see the nurse or whatever. (Prisoner, HMP Four)

For many women, one of the most difficult aspects of withdrawal was the inability to sleep. Being locked up, usually alone, and experiencing withdrawals with nothing to do but lie awake compounded feelings of isolation and depression:

I think they should give you something stronger to help you sleep. Cos you lie there hour after hour, every night, wide-awake. The hours just drag. It gets you down. (Prisoner, HMP Four)

I was bad for about three weeks till the sweats had gone. But it takes about six months before you can get your head down. It gets better each night but it's about three or four o'clock every morning before I'm getting to sleep. I'm still craving for it. (HMP Four)

What I really found hard this time was that I couldn't sleep at all at night. I'm lying there asking what time it is all night, just going demented in that wee room. You just can't fall asleep, it's horrible. (Prisoner, HMP Two)

This was why many women did not wish to be placed on observation or the hospital wing (unless medication was made available but was conditional on the location). They felt that it was more advantageous to be placed with women who were no longer withdrawing but were sympathetic to their plight, rather than to be placed with a number of other prisoners who were also withdrawing.

Several women stated that the combination of lack of sleep, feeling ill, uncomfortable physical conditions and little or no organized activity, left them overwhelmed by their problems:

I think most junkies can cope with it during the day when they're out but it's when you're alone in your room that your head starts racing. You've got problems out there and you're not feeling like yourself. Sleep's the best thing you can get; that's what most junkies are wanting - to get a sleep, but they're not getting that help. (Prisoner, HMP Two)

When you're coming off you just feel so bad and then you start thinking about everything that you've done and you just feel like topping yourself. Me, I'm too much of a coward to do something but I can see how someone would. That's when these things happen. (Prisoner, HMP Four)

Some people have been heavily depressed and cut their wrists and things because they can't stand withdrawals. I'm not saying everyone will be like that - but it happens. I don't think they've got enough time to sit down and listen to you, and even when you go to see the doctor when you're first admitted, there's an officer in the room - that's not right. You're limited to what you say and a lot of people are nervous and if you're coming off drugs you're easily upset, your temper goes quick. If they think you're starting to get ratty they get up and put you out. (Prisoner, HMP Two)

It was not only the physical conditions of imprisonment that added to the women's difficulties. Women perceived many aspects of the regime as unnecessarily harsh; for example, the requirement to work. Although this was not obligatory for women on observation or on the hospital units (and some women welcomed the chance to participate in a structured activity) it was felt by some that they were required to work before they felt able:

> You can tell by their attitudes that they don't like drug users . . . I don't know if they know much about what we're going through when we're withdrawing. A few of them understand what you're going through and some of them are all right to you. But you get the odd one who will just come in and say, 'Right, get your unit order' and you can be dying. Some of them would make you work, but I wouldn't work, they can just put me on report, I couldn't work. (Prisoner, HMP Two)

> You feel like grabbing them and saying to them that if they had the flu bad they wouldn't come in to work, never mind want to wash corridors and buff them. You can't be bothered moving, you just want to sit there, all I want to do is listen to music, daydream. One of them said to me: 'I've no sympathy for them' (drug users) 'they're all the same, all no hopers'. I thought what was she wanting a job in here for if she thinks that, they're supposed to be helping us so we're alright when we go back out but she just wasn't interested, she just thinks we're all the same. (Prisoner, HMP Two)

Although most women acknowledged that some staff were sympathetic and helpful, this was not always the case. Many staff had little knowledge about, or understanding of, drug use and many held strong beliefs and attitudes towards drug users, largely derived from popular discourse and media stereotypes. This often came across in the way drug users were treated. Individual members of staff, as medical or discipline officers, were in powerful positions in relation to prisoners and it was not uncommon for their attitudes to affect their work. Within the penal regime, the gulf between staff and prisoners, necessitated by the need to secure custody and control, meant that prisoners regularly felt that the attitudes and behaviour of staff led to what they felt was punishment inside the prison. It certainly exacerbated those tensions, which are ever present, between those who are imprisoned and those who are required to keep them so:

> There's so much tension in the block between officers and inmates. They say our attitude stinks but you should see theirs. And okay, there has to be rules and people have to abide by rules, but the petty rules are unreal. On their minds all the time is drugs - it's as if they're the Drugs Squad not the Prison Service. Some of them shouldn't be in this job with their attitude . . . They

could ask you to do *anything* and if you don't do it they say they'll put you behind your door . . . But it's some staff more than others. (Prisoner, HMP Two)

I think they [medical staff] have no sympathy whatsoever. I wouldn't call them nurses because they're officers first and nurses second and that is the way they're trained to do their job. (Prisoner, HMP Two)

Medical staff were viewed as part of the apparatus of discipline and many prisoners felt that medical officers held moralistic attitudes which influenced the treatment received by drug users:

Well the impression I get is that you're just another junkie, not just from the doctor but the nurses as well. Self-inflicted, that's the way I think he thinks about it. They done it themselves, let them go with it. (Prisoner, HMP Two)

With junkies, they look at you as if you're a bit of trash. That's the way I feel. I think they just put it down that we're doing it ourselves. Do they not realise it's an addiction? We can't just stop like that. Where an alcoholic coming in gets medication to stop the DTs and that, we don't. Just Valium and that doesn't do much. (Prisoner, HMP Two)

Staff just aren't interested in you. The scum of the earth—that's the way they look at you, that's the way they treat you as well. It just makes you hate the staff although there are a lot of all right ones. (Prisoner, HMP Five)

Prisoners frequently reiterated that some staff *were* sympathetic, helpful and tried to make it easier for women. One person who had started to hallucinate due to withdrawals while on remand stated:

The nurse came in and saw me and I needed that because I knew my mind was going away from me but I couldn't control it. She came in and talked to me and told me that I needed to get up and try to get myself together. I needed that push. Her voice seemed to hit a chord and I got up and tried. When I was washing the corridor it seemed like the yellow brick road. I wasn't moving, but they just let me because I was trying. (Prisoner, HMP Two)

However the combination of factors which operate in penal institutions and which underlay the ethos of incarceration, notably the emphasis on discipline and security, served to increase individual perceptions of punishment:

Most people tend to look at it that you got yourself into it, you should get yourself out of it. That's why you're in here so your punishment is that you turkey and you're in jail. (Prisoner, HMP Four)

To them we're just junkies. They don't care. We're nothing to them and they make it worse for us. Our punishment is to be in here. We shouldn't be punished more when we're in. (Prisoner, HMP Five)

The lack of parity between medical treatment provided in prison and outside was marked and angered many women. Only in exceptional circumstances does the Prison Service encourage maintenance treatment. Consequently, many women who were receiving prescribed medication from their GP or community drug team had it stopped when they entered prison. Although medication, either for symptomatic relief of withdrawals or a brief detoxification regime, was made available where considered necessary, this disparity between prison and community provision was viewed as punitive by many women. Further, a contingent mechanism of control operated for women who were on a 'script' (regular prescription) outside prison. Those who acknowledged that they had not kept to their prescribed medication, by using illegal drugs to top it up, or who had continued to inject felt they were treated unfavourably:

> If you go to the health centre and say you've been using all sorts of things he'll [the doctor will] give you a couple of Valium to get you through the night. If you say you've been sticking to your script he'll say he will keep you on your script but cut you down. So most lassies say they've just been using their script when they haven't really. (Prisoner, HMP Two)

> If you come in here and you're on methadone, say you've got your methadone on you and it's in your name, they won't give it to you. They just knock it on the head. I don't see why they don't continue it in here. I can't see the point of it myself. (Prisoner, HMP Four)

> I went along and got some medication myself. I told them I needed it to help me sleep. I knew from previous experiences that if you come in having been on a maintenance course they won't give you anything, so I wasn't going to give them the pleasure of knowing that. (Prisoner, HMP Four)

This is a clear example of the institutionalisation of discourses around the 'treatable' and 'untreatable'. When resources are made available but the individual does not fully comply, they will be punished (*Chapter 3*). Maintenance prescriptions are provided generally as a means of reducing harm from drug use, particularly injecting behaviour, and in an attempt to reduce the associated crime that it is believed drug users engage in to fund their habit (*Chapter 3*). Individuals in receipt of prescribed medication of this nature, and who subsequently commit crime, are viewed as having broken their part of the agreement. Clearly, this influences the treatment that they receive within the criminal justice system, both formally and informally.

CHAPTER 5 - CONCLUDING REMARKS

While attempts have been made to encourage prisoners to disclose their drug use, particularly through the provision of medication, many obstacles remain. Inherent aspects of the penal regime inhibit the effectiveness of any form of provision and, as shown above, increase the difficulties faced by drug users. Resources are not comparable to those available in the community and there are wide disparities in prescribing practices between prisons and the outside community and also as between individual prisons. Maintenance prescribing is not offered as a solution to this, but it is clear that the disparity between prescribing policies in prison and in the outside community requires further examination. This distinction accords with the less adequate provisions of care provided in prison, particularly with regard to medical care (see Brazier, 1982; Sim, 1990 and 1994).

Combined with the emphasis of the prison system on control and security, the boundaries between care and punishment become blurred. For example, the need to monitor the condition of an individual withdrawing from drugs in the prison environment leads to observation under secure (often strip) conditions. While some aspects of this may be necessary to ensure personal safety *under prison conditions*, the overall effect is highly punitive to the individual concerned. It is a denial of any clinical responsibility for the physical and psychological well being of the person 'in care'.

Thus the prison environment cannot, in its present form, provide an amenable setting for drug withdrawal. The environment is not conducive to the attainment of confidentiality or support. Women who do not disclose their drug use have to undergo withdrawals without medical supervision while those who do often feel the medication available is of limited value. The manifested results may vary, but are evident in the widespread use of illegal drugs within the prison itself. The problems associated with this are analysed in the next chapter.

ENDNOTES for *Chapter 5*

[1] Medical examinations have always been carried out as part of the reception process. However, staff were instructed to make particular checks for signs of drug use.
[2] This was also a conclusion of the Scottish Affairs Committee (1994) and the Ministerial Drugs Task Force (1994).
[3] This was also recognised as a problem for services outside the prison (ACMD, 1993).
[4] Heminevrin possesses sedative/hypnotic and anti-convulsant properties and is generally used for restlessness and agitation in the elderly, or the treatment of severe insomnia. It is used in prisons for the control of acute withdrawal from alcohol.

CHAPTER 6

Illegal Drugs in Prison

During the 1980s the issue of illicit drug use in prisons was contextualised largely by fears of the potential transmission of HIV/AIDS through the sharing of the apparently limited sets of injecting equipment found in penal establishments. In 1989, the Advisory Commission on the Misuse of Drugs' second report on *Aids and Drug Misuse* focused on the possibilities of HIV transmission within the prison system, noting that the problems associated with shared injecting equipment were of major concern. Between seven per cent and 17 per cent of injectors were believed to have shared needles while in custody (ACMD, 1989: 64, 8.17). Education was advocated to tackle this, as was the provision of a 'range of treatment options' to reduce 'harmful behaviour' (ACMD, 1989: 64-5, 8.17). This chapter considers the recognition and definition of the problems associated with drug use in custody. By considering recent research, it also evaluates the estimated extent of the recognition of illicit drug use in prisons - before considering the way in which HMPS (England and Wales) and SPS (Scotland) have tackled resultant problems.

THE EXTENT OF ILLICIT DRUG USE IN PRISONS

The issue of drug use in prisons has been variously defined over the past 25 years. In 1978, evidence given to the Expenditure Committee on Women and the Penal System raised questions about the problems posed by drugs and alcohol in prisons. It was recognised by staff in several women's prisons that illicit substances did get inside prison yet at this time the problem was not considered to be significant. A representative from HM Prison Cookham Wood noted that, in her opinion, a more immediate problem was the distribution of tranquillisers and sleeping pills by staff (Expenditure Committee, 1978-9; evidence from 11 December 1978).

While this has remained a concern for many researchers and campaigners, by the 1980s the focus had changed dramatically and concerns were increasingly being voiced over illicit drug use. In 1984 a Prison Officers Association (POA) survey leaked to the press suggested that 81 per cent of prisoners had a 'serious drug problem' (*The Guardian*, 3 October 1984) and that drugs had replaced tobacco as the prison's main 'currency'. The report criticised official Home Office statistics relating to drug finds in prisons, arguing that the majority were not reported to the Prison Department by governors, thereby leading to a significant underestimation of the extent of the problem.

This concern was reiterated at the 1987 annual POA conference where it was reported that POA leaders believed that more than half of all prisoners were using, holding or dealing in drugs. Phil Hornsby, the assistant secretary of the POA, called for urgent action by the Home Office to prevent 'total anarchy' (*The Telegraph*, 21 May 1987). Specifically, calls were made for measures to stop visitors bringing food into prisons as it was believed that this was a major means through which drugs were accessed (*The Telegraph*, 21 May 1987; Tippell, 1989). In 1987 HMPS issued a circular detailing instructions for the care of drug using prisoners (HMPS, 1987). A separate circular was issued detailing increased security measures. The latter outlined the need for more routine searching of visitors, and increased strip and cell searches (*The Guardian*, 18 August 1987; Padel, 1987).

Tippell (1989) notes that although fears around AIDS and overdoses were of concern in prisons, for many officers the most immediate problem related to the disruption of the informal economy of the prison, with disputes and bullying around drugs causing control problems. He states that:

> Prison governors have warned, in response to a Home Office circular ordering increased vigilance, that without more staff and a greater number of searches, they will be unable to control the amount of drugs smuggled into prisons. (Tippell, 1989: 118)

Pearce (1992) considers the particular problems caused by drug use in prison within a Scottish context. He indicates the growth of such use during the 1980s, particularly of prescription drugs (such as opioids, tranquillisers and benzodiazepines) which were often injected by prisoners. There were essentially two types of demand for drugs in Scottish prisons:

> First, there is the urgent polydrug quest of the regular misuser. The second type of demand is the more planned and considered recreational use, perhaps during weekend lock-up, of cannabis, LSD or 'snorted' Temgesic. (Pearce, 1992: 164)

However, the economy around drug use was itself problematic with pressure for payments often affecting families who were required to provide money for individual prisoners who had run up debts. Within prison it led to various control problems:

> It has been evident that illicit drugs have frequently featured either as part of the subcultural power base or as a specific problem within the siege area itself. (Pearce, 1992: 163)

Trace (1990) argues that drug use had been a problem in the prisons for some time before HIV/AIDS placed it higher on the agenda. He proposes that cannabis use in particular had been widely tolerated; however the growing extent of drugs as currency within prisons now rendered it inherently problematic. Many individuals who may not have used drugs outside were doing so in prison to relieve the boredom of prison life. Additionally, as Trace (1990) notes, many who did not inject were doing so to obtain maximum benefit from the limited drugs available. The scarcity of injecting equipment meant a wide and institutionalised sharing of implements that had merely been adapted for injecting. Attempting to prevent drug use in prison resulted in enforcement measures that increasingly restricted the limited rights of prisoners while increasing the risks of shared injecting. Trace (1990: 14) argues:

> There is a genuine policy dilemma here. The more successful the Prison Service is in stemming the flow of smuggled syringes, the more those that do get through will be shared and the greater the potential for transmission of blood-borne infections, including HIV.

Research findings in this area raised a number of concerns, despite the acknowledgement that the true extent of drug use in prison was unknown (Gunn *et al.*, 1990: 117). As Dolan *et al.* (1990: 184) note:

> The study of illegal or stigmatised behaviour while people are in prison is beset by problems of data quality. Prisoners are unlikely to provide information that could, if the confidence was broken, lead to extra cell searches, restricted visits, segregation or possibly have their chances of parole affected.

Despite this, a study by Dolan *et al.* (1990) into 183 injecting users found that 23 per cent of those who had been in custody reported injecting during their last period of imprisonment and 75 per cent of those said they had shared needles and syringes. People who were HIV positive were *more* likely to report sharing than those who were not. Other studies continued to produce alarming findings, although the figures varied. Kennedy *et al.* (1991) found that eleven per cent of their study (intravenous drug users attending needle exchanges in Scotland) admitted to sharing needles in prison. Estimates of the number of people sharing one needle ranged between five and 100 per prison.

Turnbull *et al.* (1991) found that 55 per cent of their study reported using a drug when last in prison. The majority used cannabis although a wide range of drugs was also taken. Injecting was reported only by individuals who had injected outside prison, however sharing equipment was prevalent. While 27 per cent of injecting users had done so in prison, 73 per cent of them had shared equipment. They note:

Whilst drug injectors were less likely to inject drugs in prison than in the community, those who did inject in prison were more likely to share needles and syringes than when in the community. (Turnbull et al., 1991: 31)

Maden et al. (1992) carried out a retrospective, self-report survey of a representative sample of male prisoners in England and Wales. They discovered pre-arrest injecting by eleven per cent of prisoners and argued for the need to develop services for drug users in prisons and for further research to obtain data on the extent and nature of drug use by prisoners. Increasingly the extent and nature of the problem was beginning to be officially recognised. In 1992, the Chief Inspector of Prisons remarked: '. . . society can no more expect total control over the presence of drugs in prison than elsewhere' (quoted in Turnbull et al., 1994: 3). This sentiment does not appear to be reflected in the current policies of the Prison Service.

Power et al. (1992a and 1992b) interviewed a sample of prisoners in Scotland and discovered that while 27.5 per cent of their study were injecting drugs prior to imprisonment, 7.7 per cent had injected on at least one occasion in prison. Prior to imprisonment, 17.3 per cent of their sample had shared needles with 5.7 per cent sharing at some time during their period of custody. This means that of injecting users in this study, 28 per cent had used drugs in prison with 74 per cent of them reporting to have shared injecting equipment. The implications of shared injecting in Scottish prisons presents an alarming scenario given the considerably higher number of injecting drug users infected with HIV in comparison to England and Wales. Pearce (1992: 167) records:

> In mid-1988 the Scottish Prison Service as a whole had about 15 times as many cases of HIV infection per thousand prisoners as did the Prison Service of England and Wales.

The concerns of researchers were brought to the forefront in 1993 when a number of male long-term prisoners in HMP Glenochil contracted Hepatitis B. This was attributed to the sharing of contaminated injecting equipment and, in the context of a major health crisis, counselling and HIV testing was offered to all prisoners. Of the 60 per cent of prisoners who came forward for testing, 13 were found to be HIV positive. However speculative findings suggest that overall, between 22 and 43 prisoners could have been HIV positive (Scottish Affairs Committee, 1994: para. 152).

A study commissioned by the SPS into four Scottish prisons, carried out by Shewan et al. (1994), discovered that 88 per cent of participants who used drugs in the community had used at least one drug while in prison and 29 per cent had injected drugs in prison. The study also found that some individuals who tried cannabis for the first time in prison became regular cannabis users after release, while some individuals tried drugs they had not used prior to their imprisonment.

Shewan et al. (1994) argued that the availability of drugs in prison was relatively restricted, but noted:

> Drug use is a part of prison life, and the notion of a drug-free jail is either fanciful or would involve unacceptably stringent security measures, which would have a negative impact on the atmosphere of the prison for those who live and work there. (Shewan et al., 1994, Summary Report: 8)

It was also evident from their study, however, that injectors were more likely to share in prison than in the community. Particularly affected were those on a methadone prescription in the community who had generally reduced or stopped injecting. These individuals appeared more likely to resume/increase injecting in prison and to share equipment. Similarly Ross et al. (1994) found that drugs, notably heroin, were readily available in prisons and were often used by those who had been on methadone programmes in the community and who were denied it while in custody. Turnbull et al. (1994) interviewed drug users who had completed a prison sentence and found that all respondents (44) had used drugs during their last sentence. Injecting equipment was often shared (by nine of the 16 respondents who reported injecting). Many of them recognised that the methods available for cleaning equipment were inadequate.

The impact of prison on drug use

Swann and James (1998) carried out a study to assess the impact of prison on drug use. They discovered that - for the majority - drug use decreased during the period in custody. However, nearly half of the respondents who claimed not to be using drugs before imprisonment stated that they had started doing so once imprisoned. The prison environment was not perceived as supportive to those who wished to abstain and 52.9 per cent of the study claimed that the pressure to use drugs was greater in prison than outside it (Swann and James, 1998: 262).

The study by Turnbull et al. (1994) included male and female respondents as did Power et al. (1992), although the number of women was small in comparison to the proportion of men. To date, little research has focused specifically on female prisoners despite the recognition that a significant number are regular drug users. One study which attempted to do this (Fraser, 1994) found that four per cent of a sample of prisoners in HM Prison Holloway had injected drugs there, with 2.3 per cent reporting to have shared equipment. Over 18 per cent of respondents had used non-prescribed drugs in Holloway. This was an internal self-report study carried out by the prison psychology department. It was recognised that the findings were likely to under-estimate the full extent of drug use in the prison. HM Inspectorate of Prisons, conducting a short inspection of HMP Styal, estimated that 80 per cent of prisoners were using 'hard' drugs, mainly heroin, and that almost all were taking some kind of drug. As a result, Dr Malcolm Faulk, the inspectorate's specialist in healthcare matters, was commissioned to conduct research at Styal that led to recommendations for urgent action, including consideration of a needle exchange system and methadone prescribing within the prison.

Research carried out at HMI Cornton Vale in Scotland by Nancy Loucks (1997) indicated that drug use appeared to decrease dramatically in prison although she noted that a number of women began using certain types of drugs in custody that they had not used previously.

While British prison policies allow for a methadone reduction programme, if thought appropriate by the PMO, both Scotland and England have resolutely refused to institute needle exchange schemes although cleaning materials (such as Milton and bleach crystals) are made available in Scotland. The rationale behind this, according to the Prison Service (Connor, 1995) is that prison *reduces* the likelihood of injecting behaviour, despite research indicating that sharing of equipment tends to increase dramatically (Shewan *et al.*, 1994; Turnbull *et al.*, 1994; Taylor *et al.*, 1995). New research contradicts the present assertions of the Prison Service. Gore *et al.* (1995) observed that one quarter of Scottish prisoners who injected had acquired the habit while in prison. This also suggests that rather than merely targeting known drug users for education and services, policy initiatives need to be directed more widely.

Preventative measures
Attempts to reduce the prevalence and use of drugs in prison rely on tackling both demand (through treatment, education and therapeutic programmes, see *Chapters 5* and 7) and supply. Measures taken include the use of sniffer dogs, cell searching, surveillance, and closed or closely observed visits. Body and strip searching of prisoners (conducted either randomly or on suspicion) and mandatory drug testing (MDT) are also used. These procedures are intended to discourage both the use and supply of drugs; known users are targeted more specifically.

MDT was introduced in all penal establishments in England and Wales by March 1996, a trend that was soon replicated in Scottish prisons. The success of this mechanism in reducing drug use in prisons is questionable. In a study carried out by Edgar and O'Donnell (1998) in five prisons in England and Wales, 48 per cent of prisoners who reported using drugs in custody at some time stated that MDT had not led to any change in their drug use. They suggested that MDT had, however, led to a rise in tensions with three-quarters of respondents agreeing that staff–prisoner relationships had suffered. In some cases, it was believed that MDT had led to a shift to 'hard' drugs, with 57 per cent of interviewees being of the opinion that MDT was likely to encourage prisoners to change from cannabis to heroin, which is less easily detected by tests.

Loucks (1997) discovered that over half the women in her study at HMI Cornton Vale believed that MDT did nothing to change their drug use in the prison. For many of the respondents who indicated that it had effected a change, they suggested that their use of cannabis had been reduced, while they were more likely to use harder drugs such as heroin.

WOMEN, DRUGS AND CUSTODY: FINDINGS

As previous research has illustrated, drugs have a continued presence in prisons, as is evident from MDT testing. All staff respondents in this study, in both discipline and non-discipline positions, stated that they believed illicit drugs were available in the prison in which they were working. Prisoners also were frank about the subject. Many were prepared to discuss their use of drugs in prison and how drugs were obtained, despite the sensitive nature of the issue and the likely consequences for them if identified.

> Sometimes there's more drugs in here than there is on the outside. It's just getting hold of them, 'cos everyone is mad for some. (Prisoner, HMP Four)

> I'd say there was more in here than there was outside. (Prisoner, HMP Three)

Sixty-nine per cent of drug using respondents in this study stated that they had used drugs while in prison. The drugs differed slightly between establishments, probably dependent on those most regularly used in the locality. Interviewees had used the following drugs in prison:

- opiates 52 per cent;
- cannabis 46 per cent;
- tranquillisers (not prescribed) 26 per cent;
- cocaine/crack 11 per cent;
- hallucinogens 7 per cent;
- amphetamines 7 per cent; and
- unspecified 9 per cent.[1]

Availability of drugs

Drugs were passed into the prison in various ways. They were thrown over perimeter fences. They were brought in by prisoners at reception or on return from home leave or day-release. Visits were identified by most staff as being the most likely environment for getting drugs in:

> ... they pass it at visits with a kiss. You can see them trying to take a big gulp to swallow whatever it is. But you've no proof, absolutely no proof whatsoever. (Prison officer, HMP Two)

Occasionally, attempts to bring drugs into the prison were thwarted by staff. In spite of the security measures, however, both staff and prisoners recognised it was likely that the attempts would continue:

> Some of the girls will try to be coy about it, saying the staff are all paranoid and that, but the amount of stuff they've got in here is phenomenal. Just two or three weeks ago there was £3,000 worth intercepted coming in in the fingers of a Marigold glove. Last week a home made birthday card was opened up because it was sealed and it was full of white powder. There's a vast amount coming in but we can't do anything. (Prison officer, HMP Two)

> Probably they do get it in, but here we're quite on the ball especially at visits when it tends to come in. We're not bad compared to other jails . . . We check everything that comes in but you can miss things. If they're determined they'll get it in. (Prison officer, HMP Two)

> Over the last three years drugs are much more prevalent than they used to be . . . But even without temporary leave drugs would continue to be in the prison. When you get addicts together they'll find ways and means of getting their drugs and that's the bottom line, so I'm not sure if there should be all this clamping down on it 'cos where there's a will there's a way. (Prisoner, HMP Five)

Once inside prison, drugs were distributed among prisoners in various ways. In general, they were shared among groups of friends, sold or traded:

> Some of them trade them, some sell them. If I'd a visit this week and I got a parcel I'd share it out with the unit. Maybe two or three of us would put our parcels together. It's so easy to get drugs, just so easy. (Prisoner, HMP Two)

> You can get drugs, but everyone mainly gets them for themselves. If your mates get it they'll give you some but unless you're in the right group you can't get any. (Prisoner, HMP Four)

> We trade our phone cards, we do anything. It's not that bad if you all knock around in a crowd like we do. I get it on a home visit. We all get it in on a visit, if you know what I mean. I'll get it first and we'll all have mine, they'll get it next . . . it just goes round. But you make sure you've got a couple of joints for bed for yourself. (Prisoner, HMP One)

In certain areas of the prison, drugs were more readily available than in others. Remand prisoners had greater access to drugs than sentenced prisoners did:

> There is a lot more drugs in remand, you're not really coming off so it's worse when you come over to sentenced. There's lots of visits every day in remand, except for the weekend, so there's lots of girls getting lots of visits, a lot of drugs getting passed over. (Prisoner, HMP Two)

The boredom of prison routines, particularly the unstructured regimes for remand prisoners, combined with the stress of life inside and problems prisoners had left outside, meant that many prisoners were willing to take any possible measures to escape from their surroundings or to pass the time. As a result, ten per cent of respondents used drugs for the first time in prison:

> I started using drugs when I came to prison. I was in an open jail and there was some going round so I just tried it. (Prisoner, HMP Four)

> Believe it or not I got started in here . . . When I got out I went about with people I'd met in here and after that I just got into it. (Prisoner, HMP Two)

> I started using in here when I was 28 . . . . . I started off with smack and eggs . . . When I got out I started hitting up, it was my war cry. I thought it was going to be the solution to all my problems but it wasn't. I ended up nearly killing myself. (Prisoner, HMP Two)

Other prisoners had used different types of drugs in prison, particularly if their drug of choice was not available:

> I'm a crack user. When you come here you find it's mostly heroin in here - not a lot of crack. I've taken it because I've been in here. I wouldn't take it outside, it's not my drug. (Prisoner, HMP Three)

> In my second month in remand I started getting drugs in, getting drugs from other lassies and I started using tems. I don't use tems outside. I've not touched anything since I've been sentenced as it's a lot harder to get drugs in [on the sentenced wings]. (Prisoner, HMP Two)

A number of women who were drug users indicated that this had contributed to the decision to imprison them. They felt that they had been given a custodial sentence as a means of getting them off drugs. Yet, ironically, the presence and availability of drugs in prison meant that the notion of providing a drug-free environment was a myth that had damaging repercussions:

> I was on a five-year sentence. I came in, done the withdrawals and said 'never again'. I didn't have anything for about two years, then I started having a little go of it again. Just before I got out I got right into it again. I was getting visits and all that so by the time I left the prison I was back into it, just got out and went back on it. (Prisoner, HMP Four)

> It's not the place to put you off. Prison is the stupidest place to put you because you get more in prison. You get more people using drugs in prison. I wanted to stop but I've used ganja and whizz while I've been in here. (Prisoner, HMP One)

> As a matter of fact I think you go back out worse. You could be hooked on more drugs because they're available in here. But the judge thinks he's going to stop you taking drugs by sending you to prison. (Prisoner, HMP One)

As Collison (1993 and 1994) has pointed out, the idea that prison can provide a therapeutic and rehabilitative environment for drug users is one that is fundamentally flawed. It also serves to conceal the real nature and experience of imprisonment for drug users. Anecdotal evidence suggested that due to the increased pressures placed on prisons to stamp out drug use, prisoners who were least likely to use drugs (such as elderly, long-term prisoners) were tested more regularly than those viewed as more likely to do so. Drug use was also more frequent on Friday evenings, as testing was less likely to be carried out over the weekend.

Women who had been regular drug users often used illegal drugs, when they were available, to offset withdrawal symptoms. Of drug users in this study who did *not* receive medication in prison (for detoxification or symptomatic relief of withdrawals) 40 per cent stated they had taken non-prescribed drugs in custody. Among women who *did* receive medication of this nature, 68 per cent continued to use drugs:

> There's a lot of drugs in jails. When you're turkeying all you think about is getting some gear in to stop you hurting, you don't think that you're getting through it. (Prisoner, HMP Four)

> The doctor saw me the last time, I told them I was bad and I was that time. I told them I had been injecting and whatever else. They gave me some mad tablets that didn't do anything so this time I just said I didn't take drugs, I'll get through it on my own. So I never bothered going for anything this time, I got sleeping tablets off some of the girls. (Prisoner, HMP Two)

In addition to drugs being brought into the prisons, a number of medical officers and discipline officers working on hospital wings noted that it was not uncommon for prisoners to accumulate prescribed medication (a key reason why many medical officers state their reluctance to prescribe methadone):

> It is found that women will abuse themselves with their own medication, i.e. they will collect a certain amount and then take it all at once. (Prison officer, HMP Five)

It was also stated that prisoners 'topped-up' their prescribed medication with other supplies:

> They're greedy people. We have to be careful when we're giving our medicines out here because they'll keep them. That's why we give liquid medications as much as possible even though they're more expensive. With the pills they just flog them - a bit of buying and selling - they're not fussy. (Nurse, HMP One)

This mixing of medication provided a cocktail of drugs that presented serious medical problems and the persistent risk of overdose:

When I was only a couple of months here I was sent over to one block and there was a girl who was clinically dead, she had no heartbeat or respiration and was as black as that chair. Luckily she revived in quite a short time, that was just overdosing. And the thing was, her pals had left her lying, there she was lying in the corridor. They had obviously panicked and didn't want to be roped in with her. (Prison officer, HMP Two)

Use of injecting equipment

Where drugs were available, so was injecting equipment. This was clearly more difficult to smuggle into prisons and only limited supplies were available, leading to the concomitant risks of sharing. In HMP Five prisoners were asked about their injecting behaviour both inside and outside prison. Fifty per cent of drug using respondents had injected in the community, with 45 per cent of this group stating that they had shared equipment at some time. Of those who had injected outside 30 per cent continued to do so, at some time, in prison. None of the study who had *not* injected outside used injecting equipment in prison. The majority of those who had injected in prison had washed their equipment with water alone, only one woman had used a cleaning agent. Most women who participated in this research were aware of the risks of sharing injecting equipment:

> People inject, but it's up to you if you want to take the risk of using a needle in here because half the population of the prison have probably used the one set. (Prisoner, HMP Two)

> It's very alarming really because there aren't that many needles around but there are a lot of women who want to use them. I think it's a problem that people are failing to acknowledge because it's a real breeding [ground] for various infections and things. But people are just not taking it on board because if they do have to acknowledge that there is a drug problem in prisons. (Prisoner, HMP Five)

> I don't know about numbers, but yes they [needles] do get in. Personally I wouldn't use it, I wouldn't use any works unless I'd got it myself and knew it was fresh but there is still a lot of people in here prepared to use them. It's each to their own I suppose. (Prisoner, HMP Four)

Despite the risks of injecting, it is likely that some individuals, wherever they are, will continue to engage in this behaviour. The significant difference is that outside prison they are able to obtain clean injecting equipment without any difficulty. Those who used injecting equipment in custody rationalised it in various ways:

> I used a needle and afterwards I reported it because I was frightened of catching something. I told the nurses where it came from, it was their cleaner who stole the needles. But they didn't believe me and I got put on report for making malicious allegations. (Prisoner, HMP Three)

> Someone had given me some heroin but it wasn't enough for a toot so I had to have a dig. (Prisoner, HMP Three)

Individual staff, particularly the few with some knowledge of drug use, were aware of this dilemma and many, on an individual basis, attempted to provide some information on harm reduction to prisoners. Some prison staff felt that this was hampered by the attitude of the prison management:

> Here in particular we know fine that they've got works. With the risk from HIV and other things I used to give them a wee drop of Milton, which is a bleach solution which kills HIV and hepatitis. I knew fine they were going away to wash their works out although they would give some excuse like they needed it to wash their cup. Now the powers that be stopped me giving it out. As far as I was concerned I was doing something that helped the prisoners but they said I couldn't. (Prison officer, HMP Two)

> In one block we have started giving out bleach crystals, supposedly for cleaning out the mop buckets, but I still say to them they're okay if they wash their works out with that because your blood metabolises bleach. Although I say it in a jocular manner I'm actually trying to put a wee bit of healthcare into it. I believe they should actually be shown how to inject safely and how to clean their works . . . It's never going to go away so I think we should give out that information . . . But it's resources, it's all down to money. (Prison officer, HMP Two)

Discipline and control issues

As noted earlier, many of the concerns expressed by the prison authorities relate - not merely to the health risks associated with drug use - but also to the potential disruption they cause to the internal order of the prison. For many staff, the presence of, or attempts to obtain, drugs in custody created other problems for discipline, security and control. As a result, a number of staff considered drug users to be a greater management problem than non-drug users (although as already indicated, this distinction became inherently blurred within the prison). A significant number of prison officers (63 per cent) stated that drug users were more aggressive, violent and/or disruptive than the other women:

> They tend to be far more aggressive and anti-authority. (Prison officer, HMP Five)

> The biggest problem in here isn't the murderers, it's the addicts - they're far more devious. (Prison officer, HMP Two)

Ninety-one per cent of officers stated that women who regularly used drugs posed more of a discipline or security problem:

The regular drug users are a discipline problem, thieving from each other, fighting, lying, scheming and just problems in general. (Prison officer, HMP Five)

Women who are using drugs are a disruptive influence on the unit. There are fights regularly, and usually they stem from women trying to buy drugs and deals gone wrong. (Prison officer, HMP Five)

As a result they were often the recipients of disciplinary measures. Talking about the 'back' and 'silent' cells in one establishment, a prison officer noted:

> Most of the ones in here are drug users, you find very few *ordinary* prisoners in here. (Prison officer, HMP Two, emphasis added)

Both discipline and non-discipline staff regularly remarked that the biggest problems were bullying and intimidation among prisoners based around drug use. In some cases, it was stated that women who were supplying drugs would attempt to force non-users to take drugs in an effort to extend their potential market:

> They do things to each other just to try to get them on to drugs because its big money for the girls getting it in. Women have the ideal body for getting drugs in and there's no way you can stop them. (Nursing officer, HMP Two)

> The other week an inmate disclosed to me that another inmate was getting £1,000 worth of heroin and £1,000 worth of crack over the fence every day. Several women were saying to me that they felt threatened by that because she was pushing it around the prison. Word was coming back of her dealings with people who weren't users but were made to be, basically. (Nursing sister, HMP Three)

> They hold each other down and then they inject each other so they get hooked and have to buy it off the ones who do that . . . There's a lot more of it going on than I thought there would be. (Nursing officer, HMP Two)

Staff also considered that bullying was significant in accessing drugs:

> The problem was a lot worse when we had dormitories - bullying was rife. You would have some women giving other women forced internals if they thought they had a stash on them, or they would rob them of their jewellery to sell for drugs. (Prison officer, HMP Four)

> If someone tells you there's something going on in a house you can reckon on it being a lot worse than they've told you. They're frightened of grassing. You do hear of bullying going on and people being held down and heroin stuffed up their noses, all sorts of things. If you do anything about it then the poor person who told you . . . you can forget them ever getting out of prison. The whole prison would be down on them because 90 per cent of them are using. A lot of girls get beaten up; a lot are frightened to go on home leave

because they're frightened to come back . . . they know if they haven't come back with what they were supposed to for the others they'll get done over. It's not just one-to-one, it's several to one. It's only got to be a matter of time, I'm sure, until someone gets killed . . . We desperately need to control it. (Nursing sister, HMP Three)

The responses of prisoners, to an extent verified these statements, particularly in certain establishments where they were serving longer sentences for more serious offences. For women who had several friends around them with whom they shared and traded drugs, this presented less of a problem as they were unlikely to be isolated or to run up debts. For others, however, fighting and bullying was significant:

There's always fights and bullying. I just don't get involved. If it's there for me I take it, if it's not, I don't. It's not worth having a habit in jail, you tend to get let down. (Prisoner, HMP Four)

Much of the 'trouble' occurred when someone had drugs or had received them in the prison and others wanted them:

There's a lot of bullying. They threaten you if you don't sort them out, things like that. It's over drugs, or to get something they can sell for drugs. There are some manic users here who go looking for drugs every day. (Prisoner, HMP Three)

The only time people get pressured is when they've got drugs because there's loads of fights - loads. I wouldn't touch them in here. Loads of bullying. They go mad in here when they find people have drugs, they just go round and batter them. There's not much staff can do 'cos no one will tell them what it's for. They'd just get put down the back. (Prisoner, HMP Three)

I've known it [bullying] in all prisons. If someone comes off a visit and they've got gear or whatever and they don't declare it, if you know what I mean, they'll just go in and take it, take it off them. What you would do is come off a visit and say, 'I've got some crack so you, you and you can have some'. But some people come back and don't say anything and then you see their eyes are like pins, or people will know they've got something and they'll just get it off them. There's always fighting in here. You'll always get two or three people that will go round trying to get it off people—the bullies. They know who to go to. (Prisoner, HMP Four).

If you come in here and you're a smackhead and you've got gear you will *die* before you'll give it up. You would die! You'd get yourself beaten to a pulp before you would give it up. (Prisoner, HMP Four)

During the course of the research, several women who were not drug users stated that they had been pressurised into collecting drugs or bringing them into the prison for other prisoners who believed that the non-users were less likely to be identified. Various means of coercion were used to 'encourage' them to comply with this. One woman had given up her position as a 'trustee' working outside the prison due to continual intimidation to collect parcels for other prisoners. At the time of interview she stated that threats were still being made against her, even though she had approached the governor and staff for help.

Many of the problems existing around drug use related to the informal economy that dominates trading in drugs. However, policies that specifically target individuals who are known drug users often lead to a displacement of the associated problems. At the same time, many of the measures taken to prevent drugs getting into the prison can impinge on all prisoners:

> It causes a lot of friction with girls who don't take drugs. They're sometimes treated quite badly with the precautions taken, everyone suffers in the long run. (Prison officer, HMP Three)

Regular body and strip searches (internal searches were not carried out except for medical reasons) as well as property searches were used in attempts to find any illicit substances and to act as a deterrent. The lack of privacy, which always exists in prisons, was compounded by drug reduction measures that impacted on all prisoners. Additional searches were carried out randomly using sniffer dogs. Visits were closely monitored, although staff regularly complained that there were not sufficient staffing levels for this to be effective, and women had to suffer the gross indignity of providing urine samples for MDT.

> At visits if they think someone is getting something in they'll strip search them after the visit or just stop the visit completely. Now and again they'll do a check on the landings. (Prisoner, HMP Two)

Most staff recognised that the measures taken were not completely successful in discovering drugs and were limited in their ability to prevent drugs coming into the prison:

> You can only try and watch but they'll get it in somehow, you'll never find it. We strip search women coming back from court and we're allowed to search if we've seen drugs being passed from inmate to inmate. Their rooms will be searched but we never find it on them. (Prison officer, HMP Four)

> There's guidelines. Ideally every officer would want to stop drugs coming in but we're realistic enough to know that as long as people are prepared to go to the devious lengths these people will go to, there will always be drugs in prison. (Prison officer, HMP Two)

> I've been on visits when I knew something was coming in and sat for 60 minutes without moving my eyes and not seen a thing but witnessed the results of it that night . . . You can search people but only to a certain degree. (Prison officer, HMP Three)

Both staff and prisoners recognised the limitations of these preventative measures, and the latter felt that many such initiatives were overzealous:

> It's terrible what they do to you on visits. They always put me on the hot seat and they give me it really tight . . . I've been carted a couple of times on visits. They take every bit of your clothing off and fling you in the back cells with a strong blanket, that's from the Saturday to the Monday and then you see the governor. It's degrading, really degrading. They just don't care. That's happened to me a few times in here. But I've stopped taking visits now. I wouldn't put my family through that. (Prisoner, HMP Two)

> Even when I was in here and wasn't taking drugs you were heavily watched at visits, you had no privacy. You can't even kiss your mum without them pulling you apart. It's not just visits, they think you get drugs in everything you get sent in . . . It's going to happen, it's happening right under their noses. For every person that gets taken off a visit, 15 will get through. (Prisoner, HMP Two)

The restrictive and intrusive measures could also lead to problems for staff, causing hostility and tension between prisoners and officers that could result in disruption and sometimes violence:

> It's too easy to get your drugs in. You get them through cards, trainers, everything. People think when you come here you're going to be off drugs but you're not. Every day in life there's drugs in here and they know that but they'll never, ever get them . . . They'll never stop it. They've done everything, the visiting rooms have cameras, everything is on us, they have screens up now. But even on a closed visit they tell you not to kiss, but that's the first thing you're going to do. If there's only one of them they're frightened because there's you and your visitors and you think, 'well, if I'm going to get carted, I'll get carted for something, bang!' That's what it's all about. (Prisoner, HMP Two)

As staff and prisoners recognised, the stringent measures clearly impacted on staff/prisoner relationships. They affected the operation of regimes and all prisoners but with limited success in preventing drugs being brought into and used within the prison.

CHAPTER 6 - CONCLUDING REMARKS

It is clear that both staff and prisoners are affected as a result of the illicit use of drugs in prison. The presence of drugs clearly causes various problems, both for the smooth running of the regime and for the experiences of prisoners. Official attempts to tackle the problem illustrate the influence of ideological constructs and definitions in determining policy. Specific individuals are targeted for closer monitoring and surveillance on the basis that they are 'known' drug users and likely to be disruptive. At the same time, measures such as MDT can often have a more direct impact upon prisoners who are not identified as drug users. As the research for this book indicated, this assertion is problematic. Many prisoners who are not known to the authorities as drug users will have contact with drugs in prison. The distinction and definition of 'known' users operates to marginalise a section of the prison population who then become the focus for increasingly punitive and stringent security measures. These definitions are likely to be heavily influenced by popular ideologies and reputations (see *Chapters 2* and *3*). The major problems around drug use are displaced as a result and prisoners themselves develop informal and often violent systems of regulation. Inevitably these measures come to distinguish prison regimes and have a profound effect on all prisoners.

It is evident that increasingly stringent security and punitive measures are unlikely to stop prisoners accessing drugs but they *are* likely to exacerbate problems in terms of co-operation and control within the prison. A number of prisoners shared the sentiments of one woman who stated:

> Basically at the end of the day, no matter how much you try and stop it, some of it is still going to get through and once it's in it's in, there's not a lot they can do about it. (Prisoner, HMP Four)

The provision of medication and treatment programmes may continue to encourage drug using prisoners to identify themselves to the authorities, but if the perceived consequences of this (in terms of increased control and scrutiny) outweigh the perceived benefits, this is likely to hinder the attempts made to tackle the demand aspects of drug use in prison. The introduction of MDT appears to have exacerbated this situation with prisoners required to participate or face punishment. Alongside measures aimed at tackling the supply of drugs, the Prison Services advocate measures to reduce the demand for them including education, counselling and rehabilitative programmes. The next chapter considers the development of therapeutic programmes for drug users and analyses the effects that this strategy has had on prisoners themselves.

ENDNOTE for *Chapter 6*

[1] The comparatively low rate of cannabis use is surprising, but may reflect the variation in drug use in different prisons. A study carried out by the National Addiction Centre (1998) found that women were more likely to test positive for opiates than male prisoners (6 per cent compared to 4.9 per cent for men) and less likely to test positive for cannabis (8.4 per cent compared to 22 per cent for men). Rates for benzodiazepines were 6 per cent for women compared to 1.2 per cent for men.

CHAPTER 7

Resources in Prison

The shifting policies in relation to drug use in the community have, to an extent, impacted on the development of policies within the prison system. In the mid-1980s resources for drug users were made available as an overall rehabilitative strategy. By the late 1980s there was greater emphasis on education and harm-reduction, targeted at informing prison officers and prisoners of the risks of HIV and AIDS, particularly in relation to drug use. This continued into the 1990s with the input of education, counselling and the development of treatment programmes aimed at reducing or ending individual drug use.

THE DEVELOPMENT OF POLICY

Policy documents (HMPS 1987; 1991) encouraged multi-disciplinary approaches towards services for drug users and from 1991 prison governors were required to set out in their annual reports the services which were available for drug users within individual institutions. A few years later policies were updated to emphasise and reiterate the need for effective resources to reduce the demand for drugs in prison (SPS, 1994; Scottish Office, 1999: HMPS, 1995; 1998). As this chapter illustrates, however, those resources that have developed and the financing of these areas have led to an ad hoc response to a serious and considerable task.

The dilemmas presented by problematic drug use and the potential for dealing with it have been the subject of debate for some time. In 1968 a Home Office policy document on women and girls (Home Office, 1968: para. 10) noted:

> Imprisonment as at present conceived is unlikely to serve any useful purpose in cases of drug addiction, prostitution and drunkenness. It is necessary therefore to consider what alternative punishments or treatments are available and how we can most effectively deal with the problems posed by drugs, prostitution and drunkenness.

The recognition of the need for 'treatment' for prisoners in relation to drug and/or alcohol use has persisted (HM Inspector of Prisons, 1997; Social Work Services and Prisons Inspectorate for Scotland, 1998) although there are differences in opinion as to the form and location for appropriate 'treatment' provisions. The Howard League has argued that:

> There should not be special treatment centres for drug addicts or alcoholics inside prisons, as this would only encourage their being sent to prison. Instead these specialist services should be provided by the NHS within the community, in hospitals and in residential clinics. (Howard League, 1990: 2 para. 4)

However, the courts have continued to impose custodial sentences on individuals with drug and/or alcohol problems and, as previously illustrated, the prisons have to deal with high numbers of regular drug users. The recognition of the resultant problems has led to prison staff and prisoners negotiating some form of 'treatment' services within the penal system. As outlined in *Chapter 3*, the means and methods by which drug users become criminalised and are processed through the criminal justice system have amplified and institutionalised this situation. Tippell (1989: 117) states:

> Agencies involved in the treatment and rehabilitation of people with drug problems have long been critical of the disproportionate emphasis placed on criminal justice aspects of drug-control policy and the resulting criminalisation of users.

Tippel cites a report produced in 1980 by the Advisory Council on the Misuse of Drugs (ACMD), *Report of Drug Dependants Within the Prison System in England and Wales*, which noted the need to integrate services in the prison with resources in the community. Tippel (1989: 121) argues:

> It is all very well talking in an abstract fashion about former drug use, but it does little to help you cope outside, find a place to live, or approach a job interview.

While the 1980 ACMD report was useful in establishing the Parole Release Scheme in 1983, the links between the prison system and community resources for drug users have remained problematic. Much of this is attributable to the lack of specified expenditure within the prison system to pay for such services. Local health authorities, which are responsible for funding community drug services, do not generally prioritise prisons in the distribution of what are already over-stretched resources. Problems of prisoner access to 'aftercare' services remain significant.

Measures have been taken to provide alternatives to custody for drug and alcohol users, although their success has been limited. The Criminal Justice Act 1991 enabled magistrates and judges to add treatment for alcohol and/or drug problems to standard probation orders in an attempt to avoid sending minor offenders with such problems to prison. Lee and Mainwaring (1995: 14–15) assessed these options, noting that such sentencing initiatives were rarely used. When they were, the commitment to the court necessitated by such orders often meant that probation officers, rather than drug workers, took the lead (although some orders specified residential treatment). Further, less serious offenders were placed on these orders which then failed to operate as alternatives to custody (see also Collison, 1991). This looks likely to be the case for drug treatment and testing orders, introduced in 1999.

The growing recognition of the increased numbers of drug users in prison led to the development of research which analysed 'high-risk' behaviour in terms of HIV and AIDS both in prison and in the community (see *Chapters* 4 and 6). Government and prison officials, substantiated by research, highlighted the lack of treatment resources for drug users within the criminal justice system.

Maden *et al.* (1990), who studied women prisoners in an attempt to ascertain levels of illicit drug use prior to arrest, note:

> Many of the women expressed a desire for treatment. Motivation is difficult to assess in prison; the only real test is to make treatment available.

This gives some indication of the dearth of resources that actually existed. In their 1991 study, Maden *et al.* (1991), noted that 51 per cent of male drug dependent respondents reported that they would accept treatment if offered it in prison, while 35 per cent stated they intended to seek treatment when released. Other research concurs. Gunn *et al.* (1991) in the context of their report on 'mentally disordered prisoners' argued that all 'hard' drug users should have access to some form of 'treatment', either individually or in groups, and they also urged greater links between prison and community incentives.

This was necessitated by the identification of concerns in relation to health. Kennedy *et al.* (1991) who studied drug users attending needle exchange schemes in Scotland raised concern about their 'low-risk' injecting behaviour being interrupted by periods of imprisonment where some individuals were more likely to engage in 'high-risk' behaviour. Ninety-one per cent of the respondents in this study claimed that they had not received any treatment for drug problems in prison in Scotland.

These research findings raised growing fears about the possibility of the transmission of HIV/AIDS within prisons through shared contaminated injecting equipment and subsequent concerns about transmission into the wider community. As a result, the Prison Services in Scotland, England and Wales were identified as having a major role in reducing or ending an individual's use of drugs. This was reinforced by evidence that prisons had considerable contact with drug users, notably injecting drug users, who may not have had any contact with outside drug agencies (see ACMD, 1989; Turnbull, 1992). Indeed Maden *et al.* (1991) note that several of the respondents, particularly injecting amphetamine users, had been turned away from services which were more specifically geared to dealing with heroin users. These factors were integrated into proposals to develop existing resources or to set up initiatives within the penal system.

In Scotland, England and Wales individual prisons recognised the need to provide some sort of service for drug users. Invariably this took the form either of outside drug workers providing services within the prison on an individual or group basis, or of 'interested' workers within the institution (probation officers, psychologists, education workers, prison officers and nursing staff) attempting to develop some type of provision. Such initiatives often proved difficult due to the resistance of other staff, limited resources both in terms of staffing and finance, and a minimal commitment to appropriate training. Nevertheless a number of innovative measures were in place by 1990.[1] These were intended for development throughout the prison setting when *Caring for Drug Users*

(1991) recommended that all institutions in England and Wales should set up multi-disciplinary teams within each individual prison. Governors were made responsible for providing treatment, counselling and support within each institution and for setting up links with agencies to provide continuity for prisoners on their release. However, the development of resources was often slow or, in the case of some prisons, non-existent. Although some establishments developed an impressive range of services (see Rushton, 1993) the failure to provide *effective* resources in many areas, particularly with regard to women, led Maden et al. (1994: 188) to note:

> The main unmet need for treatment within prison is from women with substance abuse and personality problems, who require a range of services, available on a voluntary basis.

The recognition that there was a need for appropriate resources to be made available was coupled with the knowledge that the presence of illegal drugs within prisons was hindering attempts to develop effective treatment services. Education offered a useful forum for presenting information to prisoners, particularly in relation to harm-reduction, but it was increasingly clear that this was, in itself, insufficient to change behaviour or to tackle many of the other issues relating to drug use.

Many institutions facing serious drug problems had little or no resources. HM Chief Inspectorate Report (1994) on HMP Styal noted that staff complained that there was no detoxification programme and little rehabilitation on offer. Attempts to develop a drug free unit had been postponed due to an increase in the number of prisoners. A self-help group had been set up by prisoners and staff but, as the inspectorate team noted, it had met with 'considerable opposition' in attempting to help drug users (HM Chief Inspector of Prisons, 1994: 11 para. 3.07). The team noted (para. 3.17):

> Staff who were struggling to make day-to-day systems work properly found it hard to give priority to combating the use of drugs. Steps should be taken to help inmates who are addicted to drugs to break free of their dependency, and to help others to avoid using drugs. The direction of the regime should be towards helping inmates to help themselves.

This highlights the inhibitions in establishing appropriate and effective resources. While there may be an obvious need for provisions to be made available, thus ensuring the continued operation of the prison regime, opposition and unwillingness from staff can easily limit, and indeed sabotage, any efforts made.

In an attempt to discover effective means of tackling the issue of drugs in prison, Britain began to look abroad, particularly to the USA and Europe to consider alternative ways of working. Other states, such as Sweden (see Bishop et al., 1987), had implemented programmes in the late 1970s aiming to reduce dependence on drugs. The recognition that drugs were being smuggled into prisons, despite security measures, and the negative influence of this on prisoners who were not motivated to participate in treatment programmes had led to the development of drug free units. These, often operated as 'privilege units' and were generally separate from normal living accommodation, although prisoners did not tend to be segregated at all times. Prisoners' participation was voluntary and dependent on an agreement on their part (often by way of a contract) to remain drug free. They were required to take part in programmes organized around work or study, group discussions and planning for life outside. Urine testing, which was a condition of participation, was used on a random basis to ensure that prisoners remained drug free.

Similar systems were implemented in certain prisons in Britain, where prisoners agreed to abstain from alcohol and drugs and to provide urine samples for testing. A delegate at the Prison Governors Association's Annual Conference in 1994 noted:

> The fact that we are setting up drug free wings is an acknowledgement that drugs are freely available in the rest of the prison. Inmates don't have to go looking for dealers, in fact they need a refuge to get away from them. (*The Sunday Times*, 13 March 1994)

However, a positive test result did not, at this time, constitute a breach of prison rules and it was often unclear how prisoners should be dealt with if samples showed unauthorised drug use. *The Guardian* (21 September 1993) reported on a 'drug free' unit at The Wolds, a privately managed remand prison[2] on Humberside, using random urine testing which, on one occasion, allegedly showed positive for the entire unit.

There appeared to be some support among prisoners for setting up drug free units and for monitoring by the use of random testing. This reflected the pressures many prisoners felt as a result of drugs in prison (see *Chapter 6*). Self-help groups set up in individual prisons often used urine testing, at the request of prisoners, to provide an incentive for them to stay drug free. A survey carried out by the psychology department at HMP Holloway found that 87 per cent of respondents were in favour of a drug free unit compared to 12 per cent against. In addition, 81.8 per cent of respondents favoured some degree of urine testing in the unit while 18.2 per cent were against it (Fraser, 1994).

Such initiatives depend on the voluntary participation of individuals and require the agreement of prisoners to undergo drug testing. This situation was overturned by the Criminal Justice and Public Order Act 1994 which introduced mandatory drug testing (MDT) of prisoners as part of a strategy to tackle drug use in prisons (see *Chapter 6*). This has created a very different situation, as prisoners who test positive can be disciplined under prison rules. The 1994 Act also introduced a new disciplinary offence: refusal to provide a sample for testing. As a result of this new initiative, the Prison Service had to find approximately £4.6 million to carry out appropriate testing. As Collison (1993: 397) had noted prior to this: 'Doing something about drugs is expensive - but prison is, and always has been the most expensive remedy'.

This is particularly relevant; given the input of extra funding to provide more effective surveillance and deterrence measures as opposed to more therapeutic resources. As the Prison Service operates within a limited budget, the prioritisation of financing measures to tackle the *supply* of drugs as opposed to the *demand* aspects of drug use (see Chapter 4) will inevitably render measures one-sided and will ultimately demonstrate their incompatibility. Although the 1995 strategy *Drug Misuse in Prison* outlined a number of useful directions in terms of resource provision this clearly required a greater injection of finance than had previously been the case. Drug testing absorbed considerable finances that had to be drawn from existing budgets.[3]

Prison policy, however, is directed towards advocating programmes of different intensity geared to changing the behaviour of individuals. This can take the form of: short educational programmes; in-depth counselling; treatment in dedicated drug units and therapeutic communities (HMPS, 1995: 18). The policy states however (1995:18):

> It is impractical for all establishments to provide all types of drug programme; consideration should be given to arranging a transfer to an establishment which can meet the individual's requirements.

This provided the first indication that different prisons may be used for different purposes, possibly resulting in a multi-tier system. Selection and assessment techniques are likely to be arbitrary and are based on views around amenability to treatment (Castel, 1991; Pitch, 1995). Nevertheless, as Collison (1994: 60) has noted, the emphasis given to the development of therapeutic programmes and initiatives conceals the true significance of imprisonment:

> ... the routine representation of the prison as a hospital and detoxification centre by the judiciary may function as a situational denial that drug use is being penalised in much the same way that women's imprisonment is an imprisonment denied.

WOMEN, DRUGS AND CUSTODY: FINDINGS

The availability of resources for drug users in prison is continually changing. At the time of the research for this book there was a wide divergence in available resources between individual establishments. There was evidence that certain prisons had well-established support systems in place (to the extent the prison regime would allow); others relied on the enthusiasm and goodwill of one or a few workers, while others had no appropriate resources.

With greater priority being given to tackling drugs, it is not clear what effects the attempts to reduce the supply aspects will have on existing or developing resources for users. The introduction of MDT, closer surveillance of visits and the increased numbers of body and cell searches which are being carried out (targeted at known drug users) will have a profound influence on the effectiveness of therapeutic initiatives (see HM Chief Inspector of Prisons, 1997).

Attempts to create 'drug free' units can lead to more specific and more focused resources but they remain reliant on self-disclosure, a desire to be helped and a willingness to undertake drug tests. Based on a 'privilege' system, there are a number of serious implications for those refusing or unwilling to take part. The operation of the 'non-privileged' units raises a number of serious concerns, not least the conditions that exist in the more austere regimes. It is also necessary to monitor the selection of prisoners for drug free units, given the high numbers of drug users in the system, and to consider how motivation to remain drug free is measured. As the resourcing situation in prisons is fluid, the issue is a central one. This chapter considers the availability of resources at the time this research was being carried out and the way in which they seem likely to develop. The effectiveness of existing resources as far as prison staff and prisoners are concerned is also analysed.

Throughout the research project, prison staff discussed the resources they were intending to, or would like to make available. Their provision often seemed an ad hoc process that could alter at any time. It was frequently the case that lack of accessible funding and clear direction, as well as resistance from staff, hampered progress. In general, available resources tended to reflect the recommendations laid out by HMPS (1991), consisting of individual or group counselling provided either by prison staff or outside agencies. Educational components usually took the form of information on drugs and their use, and some degree of discussion around harm-reduction. Several of the more general courses offered in women's prisons tackled issues such as self-esteem and personal hygiene, with many attempting to provide some elements appropriate to the needs of women, and offering some form of self-help where women could share and learn from each other's experiences. The lack of confidentiality inherent in penal regimes is a serious inhibition on the therapeutic environment supposedly created, as will be illustrated.

Although other courses on offer (such as personal awareness and education) may not have been specifically orientated to work with drug users, they too dealt with some of the related issues. Subjects around 'addiction' were also raised in various other settings, such as induction programmes and work with young offenders. This contributed significantly to the recognition by staff of the scale of the problems around drug use for many prisoners.

It became evident during the course of the research, that what is claimed to exist and what actually operates in individual prisons are often subject to wide variation. Although many institutions had mechanisms for running programmes for drug users, the operation of the penal regime regularly undermined this. Even when programmes were initiated it was common for classes to be cancelled due to lack of available rooms to accommodate them or due to staff shortages. The member of staff responsible for running a programme could be moved to another establishment with minimum notice, leaving no one competent to continue the course. Prisoners were often unable to attend groups on a regular basis due to court appearances, release dates and other commitments.

Availability of resources for drug users: attitudes and perceptions

Prison Medical Directorate Guidelines (HMPS, 1991, 2: 5), within the context of its multi-disciplinary approach, outlined the importance of involving prison officers in the provision of services for drug users:

> Prison officers have an increasing role to play with the development of the shared working in prison initiative. Prison officers are the people who have most daily contact with prisoners and are therefore best placed to provide informal welfare advice. This may simply be information on where to get help, but it is hoped that officers can be involved in providing advice and support themselves. This obviously happens informally all the time, particularly where there is a culture of trust between officers and prisoners, but will be increased by the provision of basic training to all officers, and perhaps identifying an officer on each wing or landing with an enhanced knowledge of drug issues.

This remained a priority in 2000, although services within prisons are increasingly being contracted out to local agencies.

Staff training

Of the prison officers interviewed across all institutions, 81 per cent stated that they had not received any training relating to the provision of care for drug users, despite the emphasis given to this in Prison Service guidelines. The content of the training received varied; some of which amounted to the provision of just very basic information:

> We had half an afternoon when [the police] came. They showed us different drugs, told us what they did, what hash smelt like, the value of the drug, what it does to you. They showed us pictures of folk that died of heroin overdoses. It was quite interesting. (Prison officer, HMP Two)

> We had a video one day that just shows you what drugs are what, what they look like and that. (Prison officer, HMP Four)

> A little bit at the college. I've also done a two-day drug awareness course here but that's about it - recognising the difference between drugs. (Prison officer, HMP One)

In some prisons, the training provided for staff working with drug users was more specifically directed at HIV and AIDS, such as counselling and listening skills. This was not universally the case and many officers reported that they had been unable to attend courses due to staff shortages. For most people, however, the knowledge they had received around drug use had been obtained 'on the job'. This applied to both discipline and medical staff:

> Whilst working on the drug rehabilitation unit. (Prison officer, HMP Five)

> Two years working on the hospital wing. (Prison officer, HMP Five)

> Most of my training about drugs has been in the prison setting, it's amazing what you pick up just sitting talking to prisoners. I have a great drug

vocabulary now. The majority has been from prisoners, very little from the actual nursing setting. (Nursing officer, HMP Two)

I did come across a few drug users when I did my training at a psychiatric hospital but they were very much a novelty. None at all as part of my prison training, it's basically been on the job training. I would like to have had more because you can only treat what you've seen, you're going into it blind. I think it's basically the same for the GPs as well. Certainly they couldn't go into any depth with rehabilitation or with the withdrawal regimes other than the standard one they use here. (Nursing officer, HMP Two)

Selection of staff to participate in drugs groups, or to become counsellors, was often ad hoc. It tended to be voluntary but those who were viewed by management as 'appropriate' candidates were encouraged to come forward. Generally, officers who had taken part in some form of counselling programme were likely to be advised to present themselves as counsellors or group workers.

Prisoners' views
Prisoners believed that most discipline and medical staff had a negative attitude to drug users that significantly influenced their responses. Much of this was attributed to the prisoner-guard relationship that also applied to medical staff. Prisoners also commented on the lack of training in relation to drug use and the subsequent failure of officers to understand or sympathise with the difficulties experienced by drug users in prison:

> That's why there is so much anger in here. They [the staff] don't know what they're talking about . . . They think because you inject that's it. But it makes their job harder when they put on all their airs and graces because the lassies aren't going to be humiliated in front of the other prisoners. (Prisoner, HMP Two)

> I think it's because they just don't understand, they really don't understand the first thing about addiction. In fairness, I don't think it's hostile remarks all the time, I think it's just that they don't understand, it's out of ignorance. Having said that - it is down to the people training prison officers to make them more aware. (Prisoner, HMP Five)

Many prisoners also recognised how the penal regime, with its emphasis on discipline/control and security, would inevitably preclude any understanding between themselves and officers. In particular, this complaint was directed at medical staff:

> I'm in the privilege unit: I don't get locked in, I'm a D category. One step out of line and forget it. They can do that to you. I'm meant to be a model prisoner but I'm a walking time bomb, especially at that health centre. I hate going up there because I just want to go mad at the nurses, they're so smarmy it's untrue. (Prisoner, HMP Two)

> The [drug] group officers have both been working here for ten to 15 years and they admitted themselves that when they arrived their attitude stank,

but they've become really mellow. I felt I could tell them anything, they weren't biased . . . Some of them here think it should still be a borstal and that you should be marching everywhere, their attitude still stinks. I think sometimes they forget you're a person, they just see us as prisoners. (Prisoner, HMP Two)

Confidentiality was a crucial issue. The provision of services by prison officers and other staff remains dependent on an atmosphere of confidentiality. This is unlikely to be achievable in an environment that relies on information and intelligence gathering as a form of regulation and control:

> I don't think I could trust anyone in here to talk to. I've said that I'd like to get counselled but that's all I've said. They've still got their uniforms, they're still prison officers . . . You can go and see the social workers but you've got to tell them [prison officers] on the block what you want to see the social worker for, and the doctor. It's not right. It's meant to be confidential but if you don't tell them you don't get to see the doctor. You can't win. (Prisoner, HMP Two)

> I don't think officers should be carrying it out [counselling], it's the uniform. Through various jobs in here I know that they do discuss inmates with each other. Even now I wouldn't go to an officer if something was really bothering me, I wouldn't go to a social worker in here. I don't want them to know anything about me. I don't think they can do anything in here because their hands are tied. (Prisoner, HMP Two)

Even when staff/prisoner relationships were tolerable, the problematic portrayals of drug use meant that prisoners were reluctant to discuss this with officers:

> She [my personal officer] is sound . . . I could tell her anything, but I don't tell her about the drugs 'cos that's one thing she'd go mad at . . . She'd freak, she just doesn't like drugs so I wouldn't tell her, I wouldn't risk my neck that much. (Prisoner, HMP One)

Women also experienced difficulty contacting personal officers and could easily be allocated to an officer with whom they found it difficult to communicate:

> If you could decide who you felt able to talk to and that person would be your personal officer that would be ok. But it's not like that . . . In theory it's good, in practice I don't know. Sometimes you have problems getting hold of your personal officer—some weeks she's on nights, then she's on leave . . . (Prisoner, HMP Five)

As noted in *Chapter 2*, the combination of roles - guard and counsellor - raises significant questions of compatibility as their objectives are often directly in contradiction. Prisoners are likely to have difficulty providing sensitive and confidential information about themselves to someone who is responsible for locking them up and who has the capacity to put them on report. This is not to suggest that individual staff are always unsympathetic and uncaring, but that their position and authority can preclude this in a wider context.

Giving up drugs

Women had varied previous experiences of trying to stop using drugs and 57 per cent of respondents had been in contact with a community drug agency prior to imprisonment, although this was often sporadic and for a limited period of time.[4] Several respondents had attended a residential rehabilitation programme and/or approached their GP for help. Most felt that they had been unsuccessful in giving up drugs either because they were not ready to stop or felt that the available support did not meet their needs:

> I've never gone to anybody for help, I've always tried to do it myself. There is help there probably, but I've never wanted to use it. (Prisoner, HMP Two)

> I kept saying I wouldn't go to a rehab. I wanted to come off on my own. They were going to fix me up with one from here but I refused. You just go in there and they isolate your problem - then you go back out into the real world. I'm thinking about going to one now though. I've tried everything else and nothing has worked. (Prisoner, HMP Four)

> The way I always look at it is that if you want to come off drugs you've got to do it yourself, nobody else can make you do it . . . but now I've got it into my head that I want to come off drugs . . . I look at other people, pals I went to school with and they've got good lives. They've got jobs, they can go on holidays and things like that. I haven't got that . . . this is the only holiday I know, coming in and out of here. (Prisoner, HMP Two)

> My drug counsellor still comes in to see me from outside. She's helped a lot but I'm still using in here. I do want to get off it though, I'm just not ready. Well I am ready, but it's hard. Sometimes it just takes one little thing and I start it off again. (Prisoner, HMP Three)

Availability of resources

Generally, prison staff were aware of the resources available within their individual institution, although they were often unaware and sometimes critical of the content of drug groups.

> I am aware of the user-friendly group and I'm aware of the pressure we put on them to try and make them go. If only because its time-out from the house, where they can talk and speak to other people and not be afraid to say what they want to because of the pressure from people in the house. (Prison officer, HMP Three)

> At least it provides the women with somewhere to come and talk about things - often it's the only time that someone has sat down and listened to them. (Education officer, HMP Four)

It frequently appeared that staff recognised the *lack* of facilities available:

> Basically they don't get any help, they don't get any medication, there's not much help for them. We tried to run a drugs group within the prison over two weeks but that's not going at the moment. (Prison officer, HMP Four)

> We used to have outside agencies coming in when the drugs group was on. But all the officers who were involved in the drugs group have now left and the teacher has left. (Prison officer, HMP Four)

> If they ask for help or we spot it we can usually arrange counselling for them. If they don't want to be helped there's not a lot we can do. We normally send them to the healthcare centre for it. (Prison officer, HMP One)

HMP Five had a range of services for drug users although there were waiting lists for programmes and classes were often cancelled due to staff shortages. However, staff who were aware that resources were available, despite their actual limitations, held the individual responsible for the uptake and success of these services:

> The onus is on the individual. If they wish to stop using we can provide all the help they require. If they have no intention of coming off drugs there is not a great deal prisons can do. (Prison officer, HMP Five)

> If someone genuinely wants to come off drugs I feel we should do all we can to support and encourage them with anything available. However, it should be realised that schemes are open to abuse and those suspected of 'using the system' should be prevented from doing so any further. (Prison officer, HMP Five)

This clearly reflects recurring attitudes within the penal system that the availability of rehabilitative resources provides individual prisoners with an opportunity to reform. It places the responsibility on the individual to succeed at this, despite the prevailing inadequacy of resources. Furthermore, prisoners who do not make the most of such opportunities are deemed legitimate targets for punishment and increased security measures.

Prisoners' views on the effectiveness of resources

The number of prisoners who were able to make use of available resources, where they existed, was limited. This was due to a number of factors already noted (resources were not always available, places were limited, many women did not wish to take up available services while in prison). However, 15 per cent of drug using respondents had contact with an outside drug agency while in prison and 33 per cent attended a drugs group run in the prison. But 64 per cent had *no* contact with any counselling or support group for drug users while in prison.

Those who had made use of prison resources had varied views on the effectiveness of available provisions. Prisoners' expectations and perceptions of their individual requirements influenced these views:

People just sit and discuss things [in the drugs group]. What I would want is help to rehabilitate myself outside, not just sitting in here and talking about it. (Prisoner, HMP Four)

I only went to get out of my work party. I wasn't really interested, it was only a skive. It didn't do me any good. I don't really know anyone in here that it's done any good. (Prisoner, HMP Two)

It was mainly visits from a lot of different agencies . . . what was particularly useful was when ex-users came in and told you how their lives had changed. When you saw them it made you think, 'If they can do it, well there is hope for me yet'. (Prisoner, HMP Two)

The group has made me look at myself in a new way. I feel confident that I can give staying off drugs a good try whereas before I didn't have much hope in myself. (Prisoner, HMP Five)

Women had mixed views on groups run by prison staff:

At first you feel a bit uneasy because you know they're screws, but at the end of the day they're just women, you know they care and they're trying to help you. So it didn't bother me. If I could relate to what they were saying then it was all right. If I couldn't relate to it then I wouldn't listen. (Prisoner, HMP Two)

The presence of drugs in the prison directly hampered the attempts made by some women:

The group is good. It helps a lot, but it doesn't stop you using. There's only you can do it - you've got to want to. I had stopped using but over the past few weeks I've been on it bad. (Prisoner, HMP Three)

It was also suggested that certain members of self-help groups were using the counselling meetings to bring drugs into the prison:

Basically I think they [an outside drug group] are a bunch of hypocrites. They come up preaching about getting people off drugs and the majority of them are sitting there pure full of it. The counsellors and the people that go to it. I don't think that's any way to go about counselling. I think if they come up here they should be straight. (Prisoner, HMP Two)

Staff involved in providing the resources regularly made connections between women's drug use and the position that many women found themselves in outside. In a discussion about the lack of resources in prison for women, a senior officer (working in HMP Two) remarked:

It's because you haven't got anyone on the roof here. Women turn it in on themselves. You get money and resources put into places like Shotts where you're housing a good number of sex offenders, and none into here where you're housing many of the victims of sex offenders.

Often, female staff addressed this issue in some way. Three female officers at HMP Four had set up a support and advice service for women who had been sexually abused. It operated on a personal basis and was intended to be confidential. The staff who offered the service believed there were many links between physical and/or sexual abuse and subsequent drug use. These issues often arose in more general group discussions:

> At one time I think we could have been a good divorce group, because basically a lot of them are in violent relationships. I'm not saying that is their reason [for drug use] but it's certainly one of them. We were advocating divorce, and that sounds terrible, to get them away from this situation. (Prison officer, HMP Two)

> We use our own experience. I was in a violent relationship for 20 years. I know you don't think, you *can't* think straight, when you're in that situation. You *must* get away from it . . . They think that things will get better as they get older. It doesn't get better . . . You can't take them out of it but it's to get them to address that it's not going to change, it's *never* going to change, unless they take control of their life and move on. (Prison officer, HMP Two)

The experience of male violence is probably similar to the experiences of many women both in prison and the community, but it seemed that when women came together in a group, such as the drugs groups, these issues played a prominent role in collective discussions. Undoubtedly this influenced the prominence given to issues of self-esteem and personal awareness, which tended to be incorporated into the content of many of the courses on offer. In many women's prisons, drug group workers invited groups such as Rape Crisis and Women's Aid into the institution to talk with the women. Prisoners stated:

> Some people take drugs for a deeper reason and I'd rather deal with that before I dealt with my drug problem. If I want to come off I will, if I don't I won't, simple as that and nobody talking to me is going to help me with that, only maybe with deeper problems . . . that's it really. (Prisoner, HMP One)

> When you're coming down off drugs it's not just coming down off drugs, it's about facing all the things that are in your mind all the time. So you're not just dealing with drugs in here, you're dealing with problems that you've got . . . They see my problems as drug-related and I know they're not. They stem a lot further back . . . (Prisoner, HMP Four)

Nevertheless there was widespread recognition that, in many ways, such resources could only deal with part of the problems faced by women, particularly outside the institution:

> We're very much treating them for today, treating them as they present without any thought for the future. We treat them in prison and release them back into society without any help, follow-up or referrals. We need to liaise with the community - drug counsellors, psychiatric hospitals, give the

girls advice on where they can go. (Nursing officer, HMP Two)

The problem is keeping off the drugs when they get out of prison. Although you can put across this positive aspect in here when they go out they go back to the same area, the same friends; they've always got their ties. We don't have an answer - I wish we did . . . If they go back to the same area, 90 per cent of the time they come back again, because they go back to the same friends and the same situations. They can talk positive in here; they can *see* what should happen. But actually *making* it happen, committing themselves - that's something totally different. (Prison officer, HMP Two)

They get on to this merry-go-round and the problems build up. A lot of them do the shoplifting because they need the money for drugs, that culminates in prison and so forth. That messes up families, they can't see a way of getting out of it and they do say that taking the drugs blocks out their problems but it's actually creating more and more. And they just can't see a way out of it and sometimes, I admit, neither can I. There's the environment they're going out to, the rehab and drug projects outside are totally inadequate. You've got a girl coming out of prison in the morning and if she's been into prostitution her pimp will be waiting there with a hit for her before she's even in a train or car. If they go out with a group who all use drugs, one person might think that they just want to go home but by the time they get to Glasgow or Edinburgh they'll go for a hit. (Prison officer, HMP Two)

The structural problems and lack of viable alternative lifestyles were obvious to the women themselves:

I'd like to give it up but it would have to be on my own terms. If I didn't use I would be bored. When you're on it you have to get up in the morning, go out shoplifting, get back and sell it, buy the gear . . . I went to college for a bit and I was racing about then, taking my kids to nursery and getting in for classes, but when that stopped I just went back on the gear again. (Prisoner, HMP Four)

It's difficult going back to the same town, same people, knowing who to get drugs from . . . A lot of people still on drugs seem to hate seeing an ex-user, they come up and tease you more, that's my experience anyway. (HMP Four)

Every time I get out I go back to the same circumstances, same house, same area, it's all around me - well that's my excuse anyway . . . I end up in here about nine months out of every year. (Prisoner, HMP Two)

In addition to the more structural problems that the women had to face in the community, there were various institutionally structured difficulties inside the prison:

The workshops have targets to meet and have to remain viable and cost-effective, so sometimes you can apply for a woman to come on a course but she can't be released from her work party. At the moment I'm faced with frustration when I want someone and they [prison officers] say, 'They're training on a machine'. I think, 'Well, they've only got 12 weeks left, they were abused and battered and they *need* my group'. It's very frustrating because they do *not* need to be making T-shirts do they? It's philosophy really. What is prison really about? What are we trying to address? Job skills in a world where there are no jobs anyway? If I thought it was just for containment I really couldn't work here. (Education officer, HMP One)

The problems of attempting to operate a therapeutic programme within a prison regime are easily identifiable. There are also differences in professional perspectives between the disciplines involved in operating penal regimes. For prison officers, even those who were designated drug counsellors, the importance of discipline and security was evident:

I do believe we're here to look after the people who have been put into custody. I rule with discipline because I believe if you care you've got control which is a form of discipline. I won't let the women feel they can just please themselves because I don't think that's good for them. I think when you're in a closed environment there's certain house rules, as I call them, that if we all conform to you won't get aggravation, because they know where they stand. I think it's good for them. (Prison officer, HMP One)

Often this caused frustration to individual workers:

We still have the security in mind and that's got to be first and foremost. Trying to get the girls to address this puts us into wearing two caps. We still have to remember the security but gain their confidence which probably makes our job harder . . . You can still have the discipline, you can still have the security but the attitude has to be different. (Prison officer, HMP Two)

Ultimately, the prison environment creates difficulties for the development of progressive, therapeutic initiatives. This is attributable to a number of factors: inter-disciplinary failure in communication; lack of resources for specific initiatives to be set up and maintained; the general organizational structure with its regimes and routines. A fundamental difficulty, however, is the emphasis on security and its frequent incompatibility with attempts to rehabilitate (Carlen, 1983; 1990; 1998; Dobash *et al.*, 1986; Sim, 1990).

It is clear that many individual workers in the different disciplines within prisons have attempted to overcome at least some of the obstacles presented by that environment in order that comprehensive resources for drug users can be provided. Inevitably, there are difficulties in effective delivery of these resources and in assessing their success. This is a significant cause of frustration for workers and often serves to render the services ineffective. For example, during the period of this research in one institution several of the innovative groups for drug users were abandoned as women were not taken onto the unit at the appropriate time or because a room was not available in which to hold the class. It would seem that such obstacles are not uncommon in the prison setting.[5]

Prisoners were aware of the limitations of resource provision within prisons and had direct experience of the structural difficulties presented by prison regimes. Many aspects of imprisonment hindered any existing resolve to stay free of drugs:

> The really sad thing about it is that you don't get any help to wean off . . . and then you're allowed an out of town visit once a month, and if you want to go for drugs you just go for drugs whereas if you were getting help on the inside you wouldn't want to go for them outside. (Prisoner, HMP One)

> I would need to go in a rehab, but prison's a bit like a rehab. I know I'd need to do it myself if I wanted to come off drugs and I do. But this isn't helping me in here. You need to get out just to get your head together. I've known it to happen that women who haven't touched drugs come in here and go out addicted. (Prisoner, HMP Four)

> A lot of people in here are always on about drugs, drugs, drugs; you get yourself worked up. They should have discussions or something. I've never met anyone who has had any help to stay off in here. But when you're outside, you've no job, boredom sets in and that's it. It would help if someone from outside came in. (Prisoner, HMP Four)

However, even when outside workers visited the prison the problematic issue of confidentiality often limited their effectiveness:

> An ex-officer who works with SAM [Scottish AIDS Monitor] came in and spoke to the girls. She was very good and always said if anyone wanted to talk about anything personal she would leave her number. But if the people in here saw you with her they would think you had the virus so people thought they couldn't speak to her. (Prisoner, HMP Two)

Doubts about the efficiency of resources and recognition of wider structural problems led to an often-pessimistic attitude about the long-term future. As prisoners recognised, the lack of material and practical (social and economic) resources created substantial obstacles. Additionally, they limited the effectiveness of any resources:

> I'll just go back to the same way, the way I was. Back on the methadone script. I'll just have to take it from there. (Prisoner, HMP Two)

> I always say I'll give it up, but I never do, I always go back to it. It's like a lifestyle isn't it? (Prisoner, HMP Four)

> Well I've nowhere to go when I get out so I don't know what I'll do. (Prisoner, HMP Two)

Changing existing resources

Staff were asked if they would like to see changes made to the available resources. Sixty per cent of all prison officers said they would. Individuals within this group held a variety of beliefs and attitudes relating to drug users and the best way to provide support/help, although some did not consider this to be a duty of discipline staff. Without doubt, officers' responses to prisoners are affected by the attitudes they hold about their lifestyle and the way in which they define drug use (i.e. as a 'criminal', 'medical' or 'social' problem). Those not wanting changes considered sufficient resources were already available:

> Facilities are there for users who wish to stop—there has to be the desire to change. (Prison officer, HMP Five)

> I don't think more groups would make a difference. I think a lot of them have a problem admitting it. They've got to want help and I think the help is there if they want it. Providing more groups wouldn't help. There is a group and we have a problem getting them to go and to take it seriously. Most of them enjoy drugs and have every intention of using again when they get out. They've got to want to change a lot. (Prison officer, HMP Three)

> I've never really been involved in it, but my own personal opinion is that unless they want to stop taking the drugs you won't make any difference no matter how much you try to talk to them. The majority don't want to, certainly the majority you speak to don't want to. You can try and educate them in here but they are still going back out to the same thing. Unless they move away from the area, the group that they're in, they'll never get out of it. (Prison officer, HMP Four)

Some staff considered lack of medication to be a major issue and felt more adequate medical help would be useful:

> The thing is that because a lot of them feel that what they're getting is inadequate, they are saying that they have an alcohol problem instead to get medication for that... Personally, the group conversation is that they would like a detox unit which would give them a higher amount and wean them down. (Prison officer, HMP Two)

It was generally felt, however, that this needed to be accompanied by other resources:

> I suppose prescribed medication would help and at least we'd get some measure of what they were using. But how would we know they weren't still using? I'd like to see counselling to show there's something else in life apart from drugs. (Prison officer, HMP Three)

Many of the respondents stated that they would like to see changes made in resource provision and identified a number of areas where they felt developments were required. These included: more education; counselling; outside agencies; a drug free unit; multi-disciplinary co-operation. The following comments were typical:

> More help for drug users on release from prison to prevent re-offending. (Prison officer, HMP Five)

> Drug free unit, voluntary for women with strict working rules. (Prison officer, HMP One)

> I think more help from outside agencies, because they are quite wary of prison officers. Plus the fact that we're not trained. (Prison officer, HMP Three)

These issues were reflected in the officers' additional comments. In particular, the idea of a drug free unit appealed to a number of staff, although they seemed cautiously optimistic about its potential effectiveness:

> I would like to see a drug free unit set up. One with a strict contract on behaviour and attending relevant meetings and discussions, so the unit cannot be abused by the minority. (Prison officer, HMP Five)

> I have worked in HMP Five for four years and from day one there has been continuous talk of a drug free unit; let's have a more constructive regime with more interesting activities, random drug testing, to help the women that find it more difficult than others to help themselves. HMP Five is by no means Utopia. When hierarchy realise HMP Five has an ultimate problem, or until there is a fatality due to drug abuse in the establishment it may seem apparent to outsiders and the media *we* chose to ignore it. (Prison officer, HMP Five)

Others identified changes that had an emphasis on security:

> A proper drug rehab with more staff (trained staff, medical staff experienced with drug addicts), dogs brought in more often, internal searches, cameras on visits, more staff on visits observing. Dogs in grounds, night patrols and searches of grounds. (Prison officer, HMP Two)

> Would like to see more regular searches with *dogs* to cut down the amount of drugs within HMP Five. *Then* maybe we can start helping the inmates. (Prison officer, HMP Five)

What prisoners wanted to see

> Personally I think there should be counselling for anyone who comes in and wants that. I think it should be done by someone from outside because things don't always stay confidential in prisons. (Prisoner, HMP Four)

> I think if you go on a course people should give samples. A drug free house would be good but saying that, you'd need to put drug free people on it. Random samples would stop people doing it, I think that's a good idea. (Prisoner, HMP Three)

> It would help if someone could sit down and talk to you. It's scary enough when you come in here for the first time never mind having to turkey on top of it. I think it would be better from someone outside. The prison officers are gossipers, I don't think any girl in here would trust a screw to tell them what's going on. (Prisoners, HMP Four)

Many women felt that it would be most effective to increase links with outside agencies to establish contact prior to release:

> More drugs groups, I think they're needed. Especially now when there's a lot of YOs [young offenders] coming in that have been full of it. I think if they can get them now before they go into the cons, you could do a lot with them. If they're willing to listen you can get people up from rehabs and

things, letting you know there is a life so you don't give up. (Prisoner, HMP Two)

The need for immediate action on release was a recurring concern among many women and the lengthy waiting time for acceptance into a rehabilitation programme caused many problems:

> I'm sitting here full of good intentions for when I get out but when you're sitting on the train and someone says they're going for a hit, that is it. That's the first feeding point for you. Nine times out of ten I always go home to see my [daughter] first because I don't want people saying I put drugs before her, but then it's planted in my head. (Prisoner, HMP Two)

Among staff and prisoners there was a comprehensive recognition of the limitations of what resources in prisons are able to offer, notwithstanding the very practical restrictions in what is available and the lack of priority given to therapeutic programmes. Recent emphasis is directed towards stopping drugs getting into, and being used in prison and attempts to achieve this are resulting in increasingly punitive measures being adopted. Simultaneously, the rhetoric of therapy and rehabilitation is presented to offset criticism. As illustrated, the very real limitations of providing this in the penal context have not been addressed. While individuals may benefit from the support made available, it is likely that the majority of prisoners will experience more punitive and intrusive measures (such as MDT) with few resultant benefits. Self-disclosure is becoming of greater importance and individuals are required to *prove* their enthusiasm and commitment to becoming and remaining drug free. The likely consequences of this in terms of quality of life for prisoners, while the Government and the Prison Service strive to achieve greater measures of security and control, require serious analysis.

CHAPTER 7 - CONCLUDING REMARKS

Resources for drug users in prison are clearly limited in their potential, both materially and ideologically. In some institutions, provisions are minimal and in others they are frequently hampered by the regime. The lack of confidentiality that operates in penal establishments, particularly where there is an emphasis on information gathering to control drug use, limits the potential of counselling. The failure to match resources in prison and in the community often leads to lack of continuity for prisoners or exclusion from services.

It is evident that the limited resources available in prison lead to specific procedures of assessment and categorisation. Clear distinctions were made between 'deserving' prisoners and 'undeserving' prisoners (see *Chapters 1, 3* and *4*). These procedures, which often operated informally, were based on the assumptions of prison staff that some women were likely to be amenable to treatment while others were unreformable. Those who did not express a desire to change (stop their drug use) were marginalised and monitored accordingly. Many prisoners had ideas as to how services could be improved, expressing a desire to see more input from outside agencies and better resourced provisions. However, given the paucity of existing resources and the emphasis on regulation and control, many women found the prison environment to be unsuitable and inappropriate for therapeutic initiatives.

ENDNOTES for *Chapter 7*

[1] See Pearce (1992) on HMP Edinburgh; Hindson (1992) on HMP Holloway.
[2] The Wolds has since been re-roled and now takes convicted prisoners also.
[3] The new initiative currently being introduced (CARATS) and the proposed developments in Scotland are supposedly based on additional government spending.
[4] This is similar to the findings from Louck's (1997) study.
[5] See Scraton, Sim and Skidmore (1991). They highlight the material and ideological obstacles that influence the formal and informal organization of prison regimes by researching the experiences of long-term male prisoners in Scotland. See also Carlen (1998) and Devlin (1998) for a discussion of women's prisons.

CHAPTER 8

Conclusion

The preceding chapters illustrate how images and ideologies come to influence policies and working practices. In particular, they show how social constructs around drug use and criminality - as they apply specifically to women - impact on social policy and institutional practice. By listening to the experiences of individuals within the prison system it is possible to consider how official discourse is translated into practice (by prison staff) and the consequences for people affected by policies and regimes (prisoners). It is evident that policies and operational practices are imbued with distinct priorities and objectives that reflect values and meaning throughout their implementation.

Against such a backdrop, this final chapter summarises the main findings of the research for *Women, Drugs and Custody* by focusing on certain key themes: the difficulties which female prisoners encounter as drug users; the practicalities of the day-to-day operation of prison regimes within an ideological context; and the limitations of therapeutic resources.

SUMMARY OF FINDINGS

An increasing number of individuals are coming into contact with the criminal justice system - directly or indirectly - through their use of drugs. This has resulted in growing numbers, particularly of women, being imprisoned. More and more female prisoners today are regular drug users. Various attempts have been made to do something (or *to be seen to be doing* something) for them. The discourse of official agencies highlights the importance of enabling prisoners to reduce or end their use of drugs in custody. This is often mere rhetoric. Yet attempts have been made, often by individual prison governors or members of staff, to provide some form of resources for users.

Image versus reality

Policy initiatives illustrate the emphasis placed by the Prison Services (both HMPS and SPS) on tackling both the supply and demand for drugs in prison. This involves a diversified strategy which aims to increase measures of security and control in order to prevent drug use and supply while also providing education and counselling in an effort to offset the demand. Clearly, the form these resources take depends on the opportunities available and the goodwill of management and staff within an individual establishment to enhance existing regimes. However, the stereotypes and images used to define drug users imply that they are unworthy of enhanced provisions – especially in a climate of competition for scarce resources. Yet this perception - and these images and stereotypes - have little basis in reality. The oft presented image of the 'junkie' bears little relevance to the women interviewed for this book.

Competing priorities
Ideological connotations associated with drug use and female criminality have serious consequences for prisoners and influence the implementation of policies and the operation of regimes. The Prison Services in both England and Wales and in Scotland have attempted to deal with drug users in prison by developing strategies that attempt to combine security and control with the provision of therapeutic and rehabilitative resources. It is envisaged that these measures will be put into operation by the same people: prison staff. However, when two distinct policy directions are intended to operate simultaneously it is likely that greater emphasis will be given to one element over another. The prioritisation of practices is undoubtedly influenced by ideological assumptions and personal and/or occupational culture. Many of the objectives that operate in relation to drug users are difficult to co-ordinate smoothly and are in most cases incompatible. Additionally, when resources are limited certain objectives will be prioritised at the expense of others. The emphasis accorded to discipline and security as a prime function of imprisonment is seen by many prison staff as their main objective. Other aims are often considered to be secondary and this is reflected in the organization and operation of penal regimes.

Regimes, resources and eligibility
The limited resources in prison and the emphasis on 'austere' regimes ensures that provisions in penal institutions do not exceed those available in the community. The issue of drug use illustrates the operation of this mechanism of 'less-eligibility' and again reflects the over-riding emphasis given to pursuing discipline and security. Condoms, needle exchanges and maintenance programmes are available in the community to maximise agency contact with drug users and to reduce the risk of infection from Hepatitis and HIV. This is not, or is only partially, the case in prisons, where condoms and syringes are not available and although medication is sometimes provided its recipients often view it as unsatisfactory (see *Chapter 5*).

Services in the community are limited in their capacity to solve the 'drugs problem' and defining success is itself a highly subjective pursuit. Many of the people interviewed for this book were aware of the resources available outside prison, but lengthy waiting lists and limited provisions often served to inhibit drug users' participation. The constraints on existing resources also meant that they were unable to meet the needs of all who made contact. This was true particularly for female drug users who had been incorporated into services designed more specifically for men. Many of them also acknowledged that while they were aware of outside resources they did not feel ready to stop taking drugs. Given the very real constraints that exist in prison *any* resources that are made available are likely to be limited in their effect.

The 'care' of drug users in custody

Three main areas of the research highlight the problems for penal institutions in their ability to 'care' for those in custody.

(i) Disclosure and withdrawal

The research illustrates the highly discretionary implementation of policies in relation to medical care and the provision of medication for drug users in prison. The importance of identifying drug users on entry into custody is emphasised in prison policies, with detoxification programmes intended to encourage disclosure. Guidelines (HMPS, 1987; 1991; 1995; 1998; SPS, 1994; Scottish Office, 1999) recommend that medication should be made available to all individuals who enter prison with a drug 'problem'. This should be provided on a short-term reducing basis and follows the recommendations made by the Advisory Council on the Misuse of Drugs, the Scottish Affairs Committee and Ministerial Drugs Task Force. This is substantiated by the findings of various research projects such as Turnbull et al. (1994); and Shewan et al. (1994). However, the length of time judged appropriate for withdrawal is disputed. The officially recommended period of seven days has been criticised by those working in the field (Ross et al., 1993) and by others who have carried out relevant research (Turnbull et al., 1994; Shewan et al., 1994; see also *Chapter 6*).

The limited medical support available and the frequent failure of establishments to provide adequate medication as part of a detoxification programme was problematic for many prisoners. This led women to conceal their drug use from the authorities, believing that it would not be in their interests to disclose this information when they did not perceive any benefits to be gained from doing so. Indeed, 31 per cent of drug users in this study did not inform the authorities of their drug use.

The clinical discretion of medical officers often meant that guidelines were not adhered to, thus some prisoners received less effective treatment than others did. Many women believed that medical officers should be able to use their discretion to develop individual programmes of care for them. However, discretionary decision-making becomes problematic when based on moralistic judgements and beliefs, which is often the case in relation to drug use, as the study shows. Additionally, the pressure on limited resources and time available to medical staff will also infringe on the opportunities available to design individualised programmes of care.

The location of drug dependent prisoners on entry to prison or during 'treatment' was problematic for many women (see *Chapter 5*). Most respondents did not wish to be placed on the hospital wing or on observation in a secure unit. Yet the disclosure of their drug use often necessitated reallocation as part of prison policy. While this enabled staff to monitor individual prisoners more closely, women considered the conditions of this accommodation - and the requirements of observation procedures - as punitive.

One establishment placed identified drug users on a hospital wing on reception where a reducing dose of an opiate substitute was administered over a five-day period. While this encouraged women to disclose their drug use, the procedure was heavily criticised by prisoners for its failure to counteract withdrawal symptoms effectively and for the speed of the reduction which many women found to be ineffective. In the other prisons, women were given a range of drugs intended to provide symptomatic relief from withdrawal symptoms. As their experiences illustrate, while many prisoners were grateful for at least some form of medical support, in general the treatment provided was considered to be of limited value and, again, many women continued to experience what were often severe withdrawal symptoms. As a result, 72 per cent of respondents who received medication were not satisfied with it. They believed the amount they had received was insufficient to meet their needs or to counter adequately the effects of the drugs they had taken outside and 66 per cent of this group continued to take illegal drugs while receiving prescribed medication.

The short-term courses (particularly of opiate substitutes) which were made available regularly failed to meet the requirements of many of the respondents. Where a standard course of treatment was provided, the severity of withdrawals experienced by women was directly related to the amount of drugs they had been using previously. So women who had been using drugs heavily prior to imprisonment experienced painful and often severe symptoms despite being given a short course of medication. This led many women to state that a major problem was the lack of appropriate individualised care.

The range of drugs available to counteract withdrawals included tranquillisers, anti-depressant drugs and sometimes hypnotics. These were administered for various periods of time, depending on the medical officer. As the research shows, in some cases women became addicted to them. The high rate of prescription drugs distributed in women's prisons has been criticised from a variety of directions. The research shows that the amount of drugs prescribed is closely related to the number of drug users who require medication on entry. However, for many women, the type of drug they were receiving (particularly Largactil) was inadequate or inappropriate. There was little continuity between prescribing practices in the community and those in prisons, where medical staff rarely contacted prisoners' GPs. Medical officers, on the other hand, felt that prisoners were often given excessive medication with much staff time being taken up administering drugs which, in their opinion, were not needed. They believed that this removed them from duties that they considered to be of greater priority.

Many of the women interviewed felt that medical staff were limited in their knowledge of drug use and issues around addiction. Not all doctors are trained in drug dependency/addiction and consequently the treatment they prescribe is heavily reliant on their views of drug users, is in line with present prison policies, or is founded on moral judgements. Overall, the level of medical care available in prison is highly problematic. Sim (1990) examines this in relation to prisoners in general; this work identifies the specifics of that problem as they relate to female drug users.

(ii) The use of illegal drugs within the prison system
Attempts to prevent access to drugs in prison seem doomed to fail. Stricter enforcement strategies lead to more covert responses by prisoners and to behaviour that poses even greater risks to health (such as shared injecting equipment). Clampdowns do little to recover drugs and are neither deterrent nor preventative. The emphasis given to measures of security and control highlights the punitive and controlling aspects of the system and enables categorisations to be made between 'treatable' and 'untreatable' prisoners.

The research emphasises the quite limited impact of targeting known drug users for scrutiny. As demonstrated in earlier chapters, not all drug users are known to the prison authorities, for a variety of reasons. Many did not disclose this information while others did not use drugs before entering prison. As a result of policies focusing on known users, problems associated with drug use in a controlled environment (such as bullying, intimidation and smuggling) were displaced onto those least likely to be suspected by staff.

The research also shows that sentencing women to prison to 'break their habit' - although occasionally effective - is generally misguided. For most of the women interviewed, detoxification was often enforced and uncomfortable. The prison environment and continual contact with other drug users led to a situation where drugs were regularly discussed and attempts to obtain them frequent. Consequently, the majority of women had access to drugs most of the time, but only limited access to resources and counselling when they felt the greatest need.

A significant number of respondents (69 per cent) who were drug users before coming into prison continued to use drugs while in prison. Others (ten per cent), who had not used drugs, began to do so while in custody and continued on release. Women experimented with different drugs in prison to those taken previously, depending on what was available and what was most popular at the time. Some respondents stated that they had been prescribed medication in prison that they had subsequently continued to use, either legally or illegally, on release. Certainly the study indicates that the experience of imprisonment is unlikely to persuade most women to end their use of drugs and, ironically, it often leads to drug use or experimentation. The continual emphasis on security and punishment does little to halt the supply and use of drugs in penal establishments. However it does serve to increase internal tensions, resulting in attempts by prisoners to resist clampdowns and controlling regimes.

(iii) Resources for drug users in prison
Policy guidelines emphasise the importance of providing resources directed towards reduction or cessation of drug use. These take the form of counselling programmes provided by multi-disciplinary teams within the prison, and programmes that help the individual to confront their drug use and work towards reducing or ending it. However, 64 per cent of the people interviewed for this book had no contact with any services for drug users while in prison. They often viewed the emphasis placed

Conclusion 145

on encouraging staff to take responsibility for developing and operating programmes for drug users as problematic. Most women believed counselling should be provided by trained counsellors/drug workers with no 'conflict of interest' from outside in the community and felt this to be essential because of the greater expertise of workers employed by drug agencies. Additionally, and more importantly for many prisoners, they felt that confidentiality was more likely to be maintained by workers who were not employed by the Prison Service. Indeed, they stated that they welcomed the chance to participate in the research as it gave them an opportunity to talk to someone from outside the Prison Service.

The difficulties which exist due to the distribution of power and status between prisoners and staff are unlikely to be easily overcome. The Prison Service is returning to the use of outside organizations in the provision of services to prisoners, although continuing to expand and develop the expertise of its own staff. While to an extent this approach is necessary, given the reduction of funding available to community organizations, it will deny appropriate and necessary access to services that were previously provided by goodwill. Yet funding for drug testing has been found and the financial considerations of this programme need to be placed against the denial of appropriate education and counselling programmes. Although individuals will doubtless obtain greater job satisfaction from a more diverse role, the use of internal prison staff ensures the prioritisation of an organizational emphasis on security and control.

There are additional problems in the organization of programmes for drug users. The Prison Service, in its resource provision, has failed to acknowledge the many different types of drug users. As noted earlier in this chapter, not everyone fits the heroin 'junkie' stereotype which informs many programmes and, as a result, several women did not believe that those resources which did exist could cater for their specific needs. This causes particular problems for prisoners who define themselves as 'recreational' users, and who are unable to identify with the dominant image of drug users. Yet their failure to participate (particularly if they have been charged with a drug offence) is viewed by the authorities as a failure to recognise or accept their 'problem', and a failure to seek solutions by changing their attitude. This leads to them being defined as appropriate targets for punishment. They are seen as 'untreatable'. This reflects an established principle of imprisonment whereby acknowledgement of 'wrongdoing' is a necessary pre-requisite for rehabilitation (as with prisoners seeking parole, sex offenders).

Prison may provide prisoners with an opportunity for access to information and advice around drug-related issues and harm-reduction. However, there are clear problems in terms of the provision of counselling and support. A number of difficulties ensue such as the lack of follow-up treatment during, as well as after, sentence. Care is required as to how information is presented, particularly in an environment where personal opinions and moral judgements often create further distortions.

Effective counselling relies on the proposition that the individual wants to end their drug use and is willing to work towards this.

Voluntarism and participation are essential factors in facilitating change. In the prison environment - where choice is clearly reduced or non-existent - these factors are unlikely to exist. As a result, people who fail to convince the authorities of their desire and motivation to end their drug use (by participating in counselling or programmes for drug users) will often become the focus for stricter security measures.

Providing services with a therapeutic emphasis is made more difficult by the prison environment with its lack of confidentiality and diminished opportunities for supportive counselling. Tackling the wider issues that relate to an individual's use of drugs becomes inherently problematic within this context. Despite the official rhetoric (which portrays the prison as enabling women to end their drug use) the reality is that prison denies the potential for developing a trusting/supportive environment. In contrast, prominence is given both materially and ideologically to security, control and punishment.

SOME IMPLICATIONS FOR PRACTICE

The findings illustrate how prisons magnify the problems experienced by drug users and how the regimes and physical conditions amplify the severity of the problematic aspects of drug use (such as withdrawal). Within this environment any support offered will be hard-pressed to overcome or counteract these structural obstacles.

The failure to address women's needs

Instead of prison being a reduction enhancing opportunity, prisoners have access to a range of drugs with some beginning their drug use while in custody. Sixty-nine per cent of respondents used drugs while in prison. There are commonly held assumptions, also widely reported in the media, that encourage sentencers to send people to prison as a form of detoxification. The belief that they are thus providing an opportunity for individuals to end their drug use is seriously flawed. It also neglects the punitive emphasis and context of imprisonment by presenting and reinforcing an image of therapy and rehabilitation which belies the reality as experienced by many women drug users. Yet with no viable alternatives developing in the community, this is unlikely to change. Throughout the investigations for this book, both prisoners and staff were well aware of the structural problems facing individual women and the distinct failure of prison, in most cases, to address their needs when released into the community.

A better approach to treatment and eligibility

The multiple problems associated with illicit drug use are amplified within the prison system. Drug users, staff and, often, non-drug using prisoners are faced with difficult situations resulting from the complex factors which provide the context of drug use in secure institutions. A significant conclusion is that prison serves to magnify the problems associated with drug use as a result of the operation of custodial regimes and the underlying objectives of imprisonment.

The effectiveness of resources provided within the penal environment must be questioned. There are major problems for those who require treatment for illness and their ability to receive adequate care is often doubtful in an environment based on austerity (Sim, 1990). This is worse for drug users, who are alternately depicted as mad or bad. As the Howard League (1990) argues, there is a need to develop *effective* resources for drug users in the community (see also Social Work Services and Prisons Inspectorate for Scotland, 1998), rather than to try and develop services in prison which will be limited in their effect but likely to lead to more women being sent there, ostensibly as a 'treatment'.

The notion of 'less-eligibility' influences the overall treatment of prisoners and is used to justify inadequate services in penal institutions. Sim (1990) has noted the simultaneous operation of the rhetoric of rehabilitation with that of a system based on less-eligibility. It is self-perpetuating. As Morgan (1992) notes, if improved conditions in prison do not reduce recidivism they cannot be justified. The notion of less-eligibility and the creation of a privilege system are inextricably linked to the development of order. Both predominate today, a clear continuation of policies developed by the Reform Movement.

The need to stop 'pathologising' and criminalising women

By examining the experiences of drug users in custody it is possible to illustrate how combinations of theoretical discourse around criminality and drug use are applied to women. Stereotypes and social constructs become part of official discourse and are used to define policies and procedures. Medical and legal discourses that operate to define drug users are also used to define 'deviant' women. Medicine and law have been fundamental in the construction of concepts of 'appropriate' and 'inappropriate' behaviour for women, thereby pathologising or criminalising those who do not conform to their designated role. Thus female drug users in prison are at the intersection of a range of intrusive discourses which are aimed at controlling behaviour and ensuring conformity. This does not mean that women as prisoners are ignored, as Zedner (1991) illustrates, but instead they become the focus for a wide range of normalising techniques. Measures introduced to monitor the activities of drug users soon become applied to all prisoners.

To lessen the effects of this process, opportunities are offered for conformity. The 'treatable' are categorised as distinct from the 'dangerous' or 'untreatable' - a system which operates both outside and inside the prison system (see Castel, 1991; Pitch, 1995) - with these categories often used to perpetuate their own reality. As Bordieu (1990: 137) notes: 'Social classifications . . . organize the perception of the social world and, in certain conditions, can really organize the world itself'.

Medical discourse concerned with women's imprisonment has, in the past, served to conceal the punitive aspects of regimes. The discourse specific to drug use serves much the same purpose. The language of therapy and rehabilitation/medication conceals the fact that those who fail to conform are punished. The study shows how social constructs and ideologies are used to create negative reputations around particular individuals and groups that then influence policies. For example, the depiction of drug users as 'problems' particularly as management problems, influences the attitudes and values of prison and medical officers. These are reinforced within the prison environment and come to define responses to women. Discretionary practices allow this, although they may also alleviate it, and institutional power and occupational culture come to legitimate it. This research shows how prisoners, at the receiving end, perceive and attempt to resist this.

The lessons of action and reaction
Resistance was manifested in challenges to the authority of individual staff, which often led to punishment, or the creation and sustenance of an alternative discourse. This took the form of support among the women themselves and a process of a redefinition of drug use. While staff attempted to halt the supply and use of drugs in prison, prisoners continually re-emphasised the pleasurable aspects of drugs, and networks for supply continued regardless of organizational practice. Attempts were often made to hinder programmes for drug users when they were not considered relevant although this had greater consequences for prisoners themselves than for staff. Prisoners attempted to challenge the stereotypes and depictions that came to define them, although this generally took place in an 'unofficial' forum. Occasionally, violence resulted.

THEORETICAL CONSIDERATIONS

Stereotypes and images associated with drugs (generally reminiscent of disease/death and crime/lawlessness) are implicit in the responses made to drug users, particularly those who are economically marginalised and who make up the greatest proportion of drug users in prison. Although drug use crosses all social barriers, and individuals from all social classes are imprisoned for drug offences, the majority of people in prison for *all* offences are young and working-class. Policing and prescribing policies as introduced in both prison and the community historically reflect an explicit *class* basis which relates to recreational drug use where the emphasis was on enforcement and regulation (McDermott, 1992; Kohn, 1992).

It almost goes without saying that the relationship between drug use and crime is particularly complex and remains inconclusive. Previous research has argued that drug use leads to crime or, alternatively, that crime leads to drug use. The women interviewed provided examples of both situations, and clearly the complexities which underlie the relationship between these factors - often also dependent on individual circumstances and random opportunity - required far greater exploration than can occur in a work of this kind. However, in very general terms, the economic circumstances of each woman tended to determine how her drug use was negotiated and financed. This affected her visibility in relation to the authorities.

Frequently, drug use has been associated with lawlessness, at the boundaries of social conventions and norms (see Kohn, 1992). Thus users have always been depicted as a threat which requires 'treatment' or eradication. They have become an appropriate, popular target for measures of social control. The marginalisation of individuals enables and perpetuates the creation of negative reputations which in turn influences a person's negotiation with the agencies of the state (see Scraton and Chadwick, 1987).

The research also shows how discourses around drugs are used to justify interventions into the affairs of other countries and the lives of individuals - ultimately their physical bodies, particularly with the introduction of MDT. This fits in with the operation of the penal establishment to intervene in a similar way to control or regulate individual bodies. Drugs foster images of crime *and* disease ('forces of disorder' Singer, 1993: 43) and drug users who end up in prison symbolise the edifices *of both*.

This book examines the rhetoric of rehabilitation and the intention of its operation to alter behaviour, to normalise people into 'acceptable' social behaviour, questioning the extent to which 'enforced' rehabilitation can ever be effective. By holding someone responsible for their actions and operating to change them rather than their circumstances, rehabilitation fails to address or challenge structures and their relations. As Sim (1994: 14) states, rehabilitation can remove attention from structural flaws to individuals whom it can 'scapegoat and pathologise'. Ryan (1976: 61) concludes:

> The victim blamers turn their attention to the victim in her post-victimised state. They want to bind up wounds, inject penicillin, administer morphine, and evacuate the wounded for rehabilitation. They explain what's wrong with the victim in terms of social experiences in the past, experiences that have left wounds, defects, paralysis and disability. And they take the cure of these wounds and the reduction of these disabilities as the first order of business. They want to make the victims less vulnerable, send them back into battle with better weapons, thicker armour, a higher level of morale.

For women drug users in particular, biology is identified as an influential factor in their actions, leading to a gender-specific application of rehabilitation. Thus, rehabilitation programmes focus on assertiveness training and programmes to enhance self-esteem. While these may be of benefit in some cases, they tend to operate from a theoretical basis which suggests the individual woman is in some way 'inadequate' and that this can be 'treated'. This form of counselling provides an alternative only when underwritten by a feminist analysis in which individuals' experiences are linked to wider structural issues. To achieve legitimacy the prison requires a display of humanity and benevolence that can be encapsulated in the notion of rehabilitation. Drug policy illustrates how this rhetoric can form part of a strategy to increase and rationalise the operation of legitimacy. For example, therapeutic programmes are used as preventative measures to reduce the demand for drugs, thereby providing a functional objective.

It has been suggested that imprisonment provides an important opportunity to 'change' the individual or to contain the unchangeable. This has particular relevance for drug users who, according to policy, have the ideal opportunity presented by imprisonment to reduce/end their use of drugs. Yet the likelihood of change is often mere rhetoric, given the limited resources available in prisons, where if no change is evident in the person, revenge can be exacted. Rehabilitation serves to categorise and normalise: the treatable versus the dangerous, thus defining the consequences in terms of treatment or punishment. Treatment requires that the individual denounces his or her drug use and professes a desire to change (like the confessional) or engages in the therapeutic discourse of the counsellor.

Therapy and rehabilitation operate conditionally. Earlier chapters show how this operates both in the community and the prison and how therapy and rehabilitation are reliant on a moralistic basis. Despite the emphasis given to rehabilitation as a means of altering the individual's behaviour and, more fundamentally, their moral values, in actuality a wide range of factors will influence whether or not they re-offend. As Coyle (1991) argues, the extent to which rehabilitation can be imposed externally is questionable. Wright (1982) points out if prisoners fail to 'make the most' of treatment and opportunities made available to them during their incarceration then they can be held responsible. But often these resources fail to significantly improve the prisoner's situation.

The findings challenge the orthodox analysis of penality and indicate some directions by which a feminist penology may be developed. Significantly, they demonstrate the need to understand women's experiences within a wider context, relating the circumstances of individuals to the structural relationships that revolve around and determine penality. This has particular relevance to the depictions of 'rehabilitation' and 'treatment' that are prevalent in women's prisons. The problem of medication was crucial for the majority of drug users. The lack of *appropriate* prescribing in prison resonated of policies of less-eligibility, and served to deny many women the care they needed. Indeed the failure of the prison system to meet the needs of many of the women interviewed was perceived as directly punitive.

While previous research, often from a feminist perspective, has criticised the high levels of drugs administered to women in prison, the research for this book challenges this view by indicating that *less* medication may not be the solution. What the majority of respondents wanted to see was more *adequate* and *appropriate* medication rather than more or less of it. Again, this illustrates the necessity to comprehend the experiences of women within a specific context that takes account of their needs and concerns (see also Loucks, 1997).

Finally, a number of assertions emerge from the research, which consolidate and extend findings from other studies:

- in women's prisons, informal and discretionary punitive practices are more likely to operate: 'subtle stratagems' (Zedner, 1991: 169). When the experiences of drug users are considered, these are often more pronounced;
- punitive ideologies remain to the fore in the female carceral system (use of strip and silent cells) despite the therapeutic language of rehabilitation that is often used to define women's imprisonment. The negative and stereotypical portrayals of drug users lead to an oscillation in the treatment they receive that moves between punishment and therapy;
- medical treatment, or the lack of it, and the processes of therapy often lend themselves to becoming strata in the operation of punishment. Despite the rhetoric of rehabilitation and policies which are apparently aimed at helping drug users, the emphasis on containment and regulation within the penal system allows little leeway for practices which are likely to be effective; and
- while small concessions may allow for individuals to reduce or end their use of drugs while in prison, the overall effects and classificatory processes that ensue have profound consequences for the majority of prisoners.

AREAS FOR SPECIAL ATTENTION

Since the research for *Women, Drugs and Custody* was completed, the Prison Services in Scotland, England and Wales, have increased the funding directed towards tackling the demand and supply of drugs in prison. With the introduction of CARATS in prisons in England and Wales, and similar strategy developments in Scotland (Scottish Office, 1999), increased provisions and resources have been directed at drug users. However, while these developments may alleviate some of the problems outlined in this book, they are unlikely to end the many problems which result directly from the prison environment. Such initiatives are required to operate within a system where security remains the priority.

Current developments, which have yet to be fully evaluated and are still in the process of implementation in some institutions, present a progressive attempt by the Prison Services to address drug problems in custody. More attention is now being given to encouraging drug users to identify themselves, to the development of Voluntary Testing Units and to establishing therapeutic communities within the penal estate. More coherent training strategies for prison officers are being introduced and community-based drug services provide a significant resource within prisons. Yet problems incurred by the prison environment will continue.

Many drug users will continue to conceal their drug use from the authorities for the reasons outlined in this book, the supply and use of drugs within prisons will continue, the failure of 'therapeutic' provisions to meet their objectives successfully is likely to remain problematic within the secure conditions of prisons. The problems affecting women in prison and the broader issues which have shaped their lives on the outside remain, in most cases, unaffected by such provisions, however innovative they may appear in presentation. Linking the distribution of resources to the Incentives and Earned Privileges Scheme is likely to reinforce the distinction outlined in this book between those who are willing to participate in services and those who are deemed deserving of further punishment.

Broader policies are continually changing: presently moving towards an expansion of penal institutions; increased numbers of prisoners serving longer sentences and more austere, security-conscious regimes. Given these developments, an ongoing examination and review of policies is required. At present, the lengthy sentences given for many drug offences, and the growing tendency to send users to prison, means that their numbers in custody will continue to increase, unless there is a sharp change in sentencing policy. As this book has illustrated, this has very particular consequences for women. Resources in the community must be developed to offer realistic alternatives to custody. Limited changes may improve certain aspects of penal regimes, however an overall commitment to re-evaluating the role of prisons - and particularly the imprisonment of women - is urgently required.

Bibliography

Abernethy R and Hammond N (1992), *Drug Couriers: A Role for the Probation Service*, Middlesex Area Probation Service.
Adams M (1993), 'How to Destroy the Market for Drugs?', *The Police Journal* (January), 42–46.
Adamson C (1984), 'Toward a Marxian Penology', *Social Problems*, 31(4), 435–458.
Adler I (1975), *Sisters in Crime*, New York: McGraw Hill.
Advisory Council on the Misuse of Drugs (1988), *Aids and Drug Misuse Part 1*, London: HMSO.
Advisory Council on the Misuse of Drugs (1989), *Aids and Drug Misuse Part 2*, London: HMSO.
Advisory Council on the Misuse of Drugs (1991), *Drug Misusers and the Criminal Justice System*, London: HMSO.
Advisory Council on the Misuse of Drugs (1993), *Aids and Drug Misuse Update*, London: HMSO.
Advisory Council on the Misuse of Drugs (1996), *Part III: Drug Misusers and the Prison System*, London: HMSO.
Allen H (1987), *Justice Unbalanced*, Milton Keynes and Philadelphia: The Open University Press.
Amariglio J (1988), 'The Body, Economic Discourse and Power', *History of Political Economy* 20(4), 583–13.
Armstrong D (1983), *Political Anatomy of the Body*, Cambridge: Cambridge University Press.
Arrowsmith P (1969), 'In Holloway', *New Society* (September 4), 349–350.
Auld J and South N (1985), 'Irregular Work, Irregular Pleasures' in Matthews R and Young J (eds.), *Confronting Crime*, London: Sage Publications.
Barrett M (1991), *The Politics of Truth*, Cambridge: Polity Press.
Barrett M and Phillips A (1992), *Destabilizing Theory: Contemporary Feminist Debates*, Cambridge: Polity Press.
Bartky S (1990), *Femininity and Domination*, New York and London: Routledge.
Becker H (1967), 'Whose Side Are We On?', *Social Problems*, 14, 239–247.
Becker H (1968), 'History, Culture and Subjective Experience: An Exploration of the Social Bases of Drug-Induced Experiences' in Becker H et al., *Institutions and the Person*, Chicago: Aldine Publishing Company.
Beier A (1985), *Masterless Men: The Vagrancy Problem in England 1560–1640*, London: Methuen.
Bell C and Newby H (1977) (eds.), *Doing Sociological Research*, New York: The Free Press.
Bennet G (1989) (ed.), *Treating Drug Abusers*, London and New York: Tavistock/Routledge.
Bennett T (1990), 'Links Between Drug Misuse and Crime', *British Journal of Addiction* 85, 833–835.
Berridge V (1991), 'Aids and British Drug Policy' in Whynes D and Bean P, *Policing and Prescribing: the British System of Drug Control*, London and Basingstoke: Macmillan.
Birke L (1992), 'Transforming Biology' in Crowley H and Himmelweit S (eds.), *Knowing Women*, Cambridge: Polity Press in association with the Open University.
Bishop N, Osborne A, Petterrson, T (1987), *The Drug Free Programme at the Hinseberg Prison for Women*, Report No. 3: National Prison and Probation Administration, Sweden.
Blount W, Danner T, Vega M and Silverman I (1991), 'The Influence of Substance Use Among Adult Inmates', *The Journal of Drug Issues*, 21(2), 449–467.
Boother M (1991), 'Drug Misusers: Rethinking Residential Rehabilitation', *Probation Journal*, 38(4), 181–185.
Boothroyd J (1989), 'Drugs: A Family Affair', *Police Review* (March 24), 603–605.
Bordo S (1992), 'Anorexia Nervosa: Psychopathology as the Crystallization of Culture' in Crowley H and Himmelweit S (eds.), *Knowing Women*, Cambridge: Polity Press in Association with the Open University.
Bourdieu P (1990), *In Other Words: Essays Toward a Reflexive Sociology*, Cambridge: Polity Press.
Box S (1987), *Recession, Crime and Punishment*, London and Basingstoke: Macmillan.
Boyd N and Lowman J (1991), 'The Politics of Prostitution and Drug Control' in Stenson K and Cowell D (eds.), *The Politics of Crime Control*, London: Sage Publications.
Brake M and Hale C (1992), *Public Order and Private Lives*, London and New York: Routledge.
Brazier M (1982), 'Prison Doctors and their Involuntary Patients', *Public Law* (Summer), 282–300.
British Medical Association (1997), *Prescribing of Condoms in Prisons: Survey Report*, British Medical Foundation for AIDS.
Briton C (1995), 'Mind Your Own Business', *Druglink* (January/February), 16–17.
Brophy J and Smart C (eds.) (1985), *Women in Law*, London: Routledge and Kegan Paul.
Buchanan J and Wyke G (1987), 'Drug Abuse, Probation Practice and the Specialist Worker', *Probation Journal* 34(4), 123–126.
Buchanan J, Collett S and McMullen P (1991), 'Challenging Practice of Challenging Women?', *Probation Journal*, 38(2), 56–62.
Burchell G, Gordon C and Miller P (eds.) (1991), *The Foucault Effect: Studies in Governmentality*, London: Harvester Wheatsheaf.

Cain M (1990a), 'Realist Philosophy and Standpoint Epistemologies or Feminist Criminology as a Successor Science', in Gelsthorpe L and Morris A (eds.), *Feminist Perspectives in Criminology*, Milton Keynes and Philadelphia: The Open University Press.
Cain M (1990b), 'Towards Transgression: New Directions in Feminist Criminology ', *International Journal of the Sociology of Law*, 18, 1–18.
Campbell J (1986), *Gate Fever: Voices from A Prison*, London: Weidenfeld and Nicolson.
Carlen P (1983), *Women's Imprisonment*, London: Routledge and Kegan Paul.
Carlen P (ed.) (1985), *Criminal Women*, Cambridge: Polity Press.
Carlen P (1990), *Alternatives to Women's Imprisonment*, Milton Keynes and Philadelphia: The Open University Press.
Carlen P (1994), 'Why Study Women's Imprisonment? Or Anyone Else's?', *British Journal of Criminology*, 34, 131–140.
Carlen P (1998), *Sledgehammer: Women's Imprisonment at the Millenium*, London: Macmillan Press.
Carter E and Watney S (eds.) (1989), *Taking Liberties: AIDS and Cultural Politics*, London: Serpent's Tail.
Carvell A and Hart G (1990), 'Risk Behaviours for HIV Infection Among Drug Users in Prison', *British Medical Journal*, 300(26), 1383–1384.
Casale S (1989), *Women Inside*, The Civil Liberties Trust.
Castel R (1991), 'From Dangerousness to Risk' in G Burchell *et al.* (eds.), *The Foucault Effect*, London: Harvester Wheatsheaf.
Chadwick K and Little C (1987), 'The Criminalisation of Women' in P Scraton (Ed.), *Law, Order and the Authoritarian State*, Milton Keynes and Philadelphia: The Open University Press.
Chambliss W (1994), 'Don't Confuse Me With Facts: Clinton "Just Says No"', *New Left Review*, 204, 113–126.
Christie B (1993), 'HIV Outbreak Investigated in Scottish Jail', *British Medical Journal*, 307 (July 17), 151–152.
Christie N (1994), *Crime Control As Industry*, London: Routledge.
Clark C (1995), 'The Drugs Problem: A Strategic Perspective', *The Police Journal*, (January), 17–21.
Cohen I (1989), *Structuration Theory*, London and Basingstoke: Macmillan.
Cohen S (1985), *Visions of Social Control*, Cambridge: Polity Press.
Cohen S and Taylor L (1977), 'Talking About Prison Blues' in Bell C and Newby H (eds.), *Doing Sociological Research*, New York: The Free Press.
Cohen S and Taylor L (1981), *Psychological Survival*, Second edition, London: Penguin Books.
Collison M (1991), 'Keeping Heroin Users out of Prison', *Probation Journal*, 38(1), 20–24.
Collison M (1993), 'Punishing Drugs', *British Journal of Criminology*, 33(3), 382–399.
Collison M (1994), 'Drug Offenders and Criminal Justice', *Crime, Law and Social Change*, 21, 49–71.
Connor S (1995), 'Prison Policies Put Inmates at Risk', *British Medical Journal*, 310 (February 4), 278.
Cooper B (1987), 'The "Short" Report on the Prison Medical Service', *Prison Service Journal*, 68 (October), 17–22.
Corbin A (1987), 'Commercial Sexuality in Nineteenth-Century France' in C Gallagher and T Laqueur (eds.), *The Making of the Modern Body*, Berkeley: University of California Press.
Coyle A (1991), *Inside: Rethinking Scotland's Prisons*, Scottish Child.
Coyle A (1994), *The Prisons We Deserve*, London: Harper Collins.
Dandeker C (1990), *Surveillance, Power and Modernity*, Cambridge: Polity Press.
Davis K and Oldersma J (1991), 'Introduction' in K Davis *et al.* (eds.), *The Gender of Power*, London: Sage.
De Haan W (1990), *The Politics of Redress*, London: Unwin Hyman.
Department of Health (1991), *Drug Misuse and Dependence*, London: HMSO.
Devlin A (1998), *Invisible Women*, Winchester: Waterside Press.
Dobash R and Gutteridge S (1986), *The Imprisonment of Women*, London: Basil Blackwell.
Dolan K, Donoghoe M and Stimson G (1990), 'Drug Injecting and Syringe Sharing in Custody and in the Community', *The Howard Journal*, 29(3), 177–186.
Donzelot J (1979), *The Policing of Families*, London: Hutchinson.
d'Orban P (1970), 'Heroin Dependency and Delinquency in Women', *British Journal of Addiction*, 65, 67–78.
Dorn N (1977), 'The Conservatism of the Cannabis Debate'. Revised version of a paper presented to the National Deviancy Conference, Sheffield.
Dorn N (1992), 'Clarifying Policy Options on Drug Trafficking' in O'Hare *et al.*, *The Reduction of Drug-Related Harm*, London and New York: Routledge.
Dorn N, James B and Lee M (1992), *Women, HIV, Drugs*, London: ISDD.
Dorn N, Murji K and South N (1992), *Traffickers*, London and New York: Routledge.
Dorn N and South N (1986), 'Criminology and Economics of Drug Distribution in Britain', *The Journal of Drug Issues*, 16(4), 523–535.
Dorn N and South N (1987), *A Land Fit for Heroin?* (eds.), London and Basingstoke: Macmillan Education.

Bibliography

Dorn N and South N (1990) 'Drug Markets and Law Enforcement', *British Journal of Criminology* 30(2), 171–188.
Dorn N and South N (1991a), 'Profits and Penalties' in D Whynes and P Bean (1991), *Policing and Prescribing*, London and Basingstoke: Macmillan.
Dorn N and South N (1991b), 'Drugs, Crime and Law Enforcement' in F Heidensohn and M Farrell (eds.) (1993), *Crime in Europe*, London and New York: Routledge.
Dorozynski A (1995), 'France: One in Five Prisoners Rejects Voluntary HIV Test', *British Medical Journal*, 310 (February 4), 281.
Duff A and Garland D (eds.), (1994), *A Reader On Punishment*, Oxford: Oxford University Press.
Edgar K and O'Donnell I (1998), 'Mandatory Drug Testing in Prisons: An Evaluation *Research Findings No. 75*': London: Home Office Research and Statistics Directorate.
Edwards G (1981), 'The Background' in G Edwards and C Busch (eds.), *Drug Problems in Britain*, London: Academic Press.
Edwards S (1989), *Women, the Law and the State*, London: Sage.
Ehrenreich B and English D (1978), *For Her Own Good*, London: Pluto Press.
Einstein Z (ed.) (1979), *Capitalist Patriarchy and the Case for Socialism*, London and New York: Monthly Review Press.
Eisenstein H (1984), *Contemporary Feminist Thought*, London and Sydney: Unwin Paperbacks.
Enright S (1994), 'Tackling the Drugs Problem', *New Law Journal* (April 15), 492–494.
Epstein Jayaratne T (1993), 'The Value of Quantitative Methodology for Feminist Practice' in M Hammersley (ed.), *Social Research*, London: Sage Publications in association with the Open University Press.
Ettorre E (1992), *Women and Substance Use*, London and Basingstoke: Macmillan.
Ettorre E and Riska E (1995), *Gendered Moods: Psychotropics and Society*, London and New York: Routledge.
Expenditure Committee (1978–9), *Women and the Penal System*, London: HMSO.
Faulk-Whynes J (1991), 'Drug Issues in Health Education' in Whynes D and Bean K, *Policing and Prescribing*, London and Basingstoke: Macmillan.
Farrington D and Morris A (1983), 'Sex, Sentencing and Reconviction', *British Journal of Criminology*, 23(3), 229–248.
Fazey C (1991a), 'The Consequences of Illegal Drug Use' in Whynes D and Bean P, *Policing and Prescribing*, London and Basingstoke: Macmillan.
Fazey C (1991b), 'An Empirical Study of the Relationship between Heroin Addiction, Crime and Medical Treatment' in O'Hare P. et al. (1992), *The Reduction of Drug-Related Harm*, London and New York: Routledge.
Featherstone M, Hepworth M and Turner B (eds.) (1991), *The Body: Social Process and Cultural Theory*, London: Sage Publications.
Feinberg J (1970), 'The Expressive Function of Punishment' in Duff A and Garland D (1994) (eds.), *A Reader On Punishment*, Oxford: Oxford University Press.
Feinman C (1994), *Women in the Criminal Justice System*, Third edition, Westport: Praeger.
Finch J (1984), 'It's Great to have Someone to Talk to', in Hammersley M (ed.) (1993), *Social Research*, London: Sage Publications in association with The Open University Press.
Fitzgerald M (1977), *Prisoners in Revolt*, England: Penguin Books.
Forsythe B (1993), 'Women Prisoners and Women Penal Officials, 1840–1921', *British Journal of Criminology* 33(4), 525–540.
Foucault M (1967), *Madness and Civilisation* London: Tavistock.
Foucault M (1973), *The Birth of the Clinic*, London: Tavistock.
Foucault M (1976), 'Sexuality and Solitude' in M Blonsky, *On Signs*, London: Blackwell.
Foucault M (1977), *Discipline and Punish*, London: Penguin Books.
Fraser A and George M (1992), 'The Role of the Police in Harm Reduction' in O'Hare P et al., *The Reduction of Drug-Related Harm*, London and New York: Routledge.
Fraser J (1994), 'An Investigation into Women Prisoners' Attitudes towards a Proposed Drug Free Zone at Holloway', Psychology Department, HMP Holloway.
Fraser N (1989), *Unruly Practices*, Cambridge: Polity Press.
Freeman M (1984), *The State, the Law and the Family*, London and New York: Tavistock Publications.
Gans H (1968), 'The Participant Observer as a Human Being', in Becker H et al. (eds.), *Institutions and The Person*, Chicago: Aldire Publishing Company.
Garland D (1990), *Punishment and Modern Society*, Oxford: Clarendon Press.
Garland D and Young P (eds.) (1983), *The Power to Punish*, London: Heinemann Educational Press; New Jersey: Humanities Press.
Gelsthorpe L (1990), 'Feminist Methodologies in Criminology' in L Gelsthorpe and A Morris (eds.), *Feminist Perspectives in Criminology*, Milton Keynes and Philadelphia: The Open University Press.
German L (1981), 'Theories of Patriarchy', *International Socialism*, 2(12) , 33–51.
Giallombardo R (1966), *Society of Women: A Study of a Women's Prison*, New York: Wiley.

Giddens A (1979), *Central Problems in Social Theory*, London and Basingstoke: Macmillan Press.
Giddens A (1984), *The Constitution of Society*, Cambridge: Polity Press.
Giggs J (1991), 'Epidemiology of Contemporary Drug Abuse' in Whynes D and Bean P, *Policing and Prescribing*, London and Basingstoke: Macmillan.
Gilman M and Pearson G (1991), 'Lifestyles and Law Enforcement' in Whynes D and Bean P, *Policing and Prescribing*, London and Basingstoke: Macmillan.
Glaser B and Strauss A (1967), *The Discovery of Grounded Theory*, New York: Aldine Publishing Company.
Gomme A (1992), 'The Management of HIV Disease in the Correctional Setting', *Prison Service Journal*, 87, 54-73.
Gordon C (1980) (ed.), *Power/Knowledge: Selected Interviews and other Writings*, New York: Pantheon Books.
Gore S and Bird A (1983), 'No Escape: HIV Transmission in Jail, '*British Medical Journal*, 307 (July 17).
Gore S et al. (1995), 'Drug Injection and HIV Prevalence in Inmates of Glenochil Prison', *British Medical Journal*, 310 (February 4), 293-296.
Gould L, Walker A, Crane L and Lidz C (1974), *Connections: Notes from the Heroin World*, New Haven and London: Yale University Press.
Gramsci A (1971), *Selections from the Prison Notebooks*, Edited and translated by Q Hoare and G Nowell-Smith. London: Lawrence and Wishart.
Green P (1990), *The Enemy Without*, Milton Keynes and Philadelphia: The Open University Press.
Green P (1991), *Drug Couriers*, The Howard League for Penal Reform.
Green P (1998), *Drugs, Trafficking and Criminal Policy: The Scapegoat Strategy*, Winchester: Waterside Press.
Griffin S, Peters A and Reid M (1993), 'Drug Misusers in Lothian: Changes in Injecting Habits 1988-90', *British Medical Journal*, 306(13), 693.
Gruer L, Cameron J and Elliott L (1993), 'Building a City Wide Service for Exchanging Needles and Syringes', *British Medical Journal*, 306 (22 May), 1394-1397.
Gunn J, Maden T and Swinton M (1990), *Mentally Disordered Prisoners*, London: Home Office. Revised 1991.
Gunn J, Maden T and Swinton M (1991), 'How Many Prisoners Should be in Hospital?', *Research Bulletin*, 31, 9-15.
Hagan F (1993), *Research Methods in Criminal Justice and Criminology*, Third edition, New York: Macmillan Publishing Company; Canada: Maxwell Macmillan.
Hall P (1993), 'Medicine and UK Prisons', *The Lancet*, 342 (July 3), 43.
Hall S et al. (1978), *Policing the Crisis*, London and Basingstoke: Macmillan.
Hamlin M and Hammersley D (1989), 'Managing Benzodiazepine Withdrawal' in Bennet G (ed.), *Treating Drug Abusers*, London and New York: Tavistock/Routledge.
Hammersley M (1992), 'On Feminist Methodology', *Sociology* 26(2), 187-211.
Harvey L et al. (1992), 'Gender Difference in Criminal Justice', *British Journal of Criminology*, 32(2), 208-217.
Harwood V et al. (eds.) (1993), *Pleasure Principles*, London: Lawrence and Wishart.
Hawkins G (1976), *The Prison: Policy and Practice*, Chicago and London: The University of Chicago Press.
Hayes P (1992), 'Requirements as to Treatment for Drug or Alcohol Dependency', *Probation Journal*, 39(2), 82-86.
Heidensohn F (1981), 'Women and the Penal System' in Morris A and Gelsthorpe L (eds.), *Women and Crime*, Greenwood Conference Series 13, University of Cambridge.
Heidensohn F (1986), 'Models of Justice: Portia or Persephone?', *International Journal of the Sociology of Law*, 14, 287-298.
Heidensohn F (1996), *Women and Crime*, Second edition, The Open University Press and Macmillan.
Henderson S (ed.) (1990), *Women, HIV, Drugs*, London: ISDD.
Henderson S (1992a), 'HIV and Drugs: Handy Hints for Women' in P O'Hare et al., *The Reduction of Drug-Related Har*, London and New York: Routledge.
Henderson S (1992b), *Women, HIV, Drugs*, London: ISDD.
Hester M (1992), *Lewd Women and Wicked Witches*, London and New York: Routledge.
Hill D (1991), 'The Prisoner Within', *The Guardian: Weekend* (November 30).
Hillyard P (1993), *Suspect Community*, London: Pluto Press in association with Liberty.
Hillyard P and Percy-Smith J (1988), *The Coercive State*, London: Fontana/Collins.
Hindler C et al. (1995), 'Drug Users' Views on General Practitioners', *British Medical Journal*, 310 (February 4), 302.
Hindson N (1992), 'Treatment Experiences from Holloway' in West Midlands Regional Health Authority, *Drug Users in Prison*, Conference Proceedings (June 17).
Hinton J (1983), *Dangerousness: Problems of Assessment and Prediction*, London: George Allen and Unwin.
Hirst P (1986), 'The Concept of Punishment' in Duff A and Garland D (1994) (eds.), *A Reader On Punishment*, Oxford: Oxford University Press.
HM Chief Inspector of Prisons (1992a), *Report of a Short Inspection: HM Prison Risley*, London: Home Office.

Bibliography

HM Chief Inspector of Prisons (1992b), *Report of an Unannounced Short Inspection: HM Prison and YOI Styal*, London: Home Office.
HM Chief Inspector of Prisons (1994), *HM Prison and YOI Styal*, London: Home Office.
HM Chief Inspector of Prisons (1997), *Women in Prison: A Thematic Review*, London: Home Office.
HM Prison Service (1987), *Policy Statement on Throughcare of Drug Misusers in the Prison Service*, London: HMSO.
HM Prison Service (1991), *Caring for Drug Users*, London: HMSO.
HM Prison Service (1992), *Caring for Prisoners at Risk of Suicide*, London: HMSO.
HM Prison Service (1995), *Drug Misuse in Prison*, London: HMSO.
HM Prison Service (1998), *Tackling Drugs in Prison: The Prison Service Drug Strategy*, London: HMSO.
Hoigard C and Finstad L (1992), *Backstreets: Prostitution, Money and Love*, Cambridge: Polity Press.
Home Affairs Committee (1986), *Misuse of Drugs*, London: HMSO.
Home Office (1968), *Prison Policy: Women and Girls*, PD4 Study 1, London: HMSO.
Home Office (1977), *Prisons and the Prisoner*, London: HMSO.
Home Office (1991), *Regimes for Women*, London: HMSO.
Home Office (1992), *Gender and the Criminal Justice System*, London: HMSO.
Home Office (1994), 'Statistics of Drug Addicts Notified to The Home Office', *Statistical Bulletin*, 10/94.
Home Office (1995a), 'Projection of Long Term Trends in the Prison Population', *Statistical Bulletin*, 4/95.
Home Office (1995b), 'The Prison Population', *Statistical Bulletin*, 8/95.
Home Office (1995c), 'Statistics of Drug Addicts Notified to the Home Office', *Statistical Bulletin*, 17/95.
Home Office (1995), *Tackling Drugs Together*, London: HMSO.
Home Office (1998), *Tackling Drugs to Build a Better Britain*, London: HMSO.
Hornsby–Smith M, 'Gaining Access' in Gilbert N (ed.) (1993), *Researching Social Life*, London: Sage.
Howard League for Penal Reform (1990), *Prison Medical Service*.
Howe A (1994), *Punish and Critique*, London and New York: Routledge.
Hudson B (1993), *Penal Policy and Social Justice*, London and Basingstoke: Macmillan.
Husak D (1992), *Drugs and Rights*, Cambridge: Cambridge University Press.
Hutter B and Williams G (eds.) (1989), *Controlling Women: The Normal and the Deviant*, London: Croom Helm in association with the Oxford University Women's Studies Committee.
Ignatieff M (1978), *A Just Measure of Pain*, England: Penguin Books.
Ignatieff M (1983), 'State, Civil Society and Total Institutions' in Cohen S and Scull A, *Social Control and the State*, Oxford: Martin Robertson.
Ingrey–Senn R, 'Prison Medicine' Report of a conference held (1979) by the King's Fund Centre and Howard League for Penal Reform: London.
ISDD (1983), 'Rolleston: The Defence of the Right to Prescribe', *Druglink* (January/February), 12–14.
ISDD (1995), 'New Prison Policy Promises Treatment as well as Drug Testing', *Druglink* (May/June), 4.
Jarvis G and Parker H (1989), 'Young Heroin Users and Crime', *British Journal of Criminology*, 29(2), 175–185.
Jarvis G and Parker H (1990), 'Can Medical Treatment Reduce Crime Amongst Young Heroin Users?', *Research Bulletin*, 28, 29–32.
Jefferson T and Shapland J (1994), 'Criminal Justice and the Production of Order and Control', *British Journal of Criminology*, 34(3), 265–290.
Johnson R and Toch H (eds.) (1982), *The Pains of Imprisonment*, Beverly Hills: Sage Publications.
Joint Prison Service and NHS Executive Working Group (1999), *The Future Organization of Prison Healthcare*, Department of Health.
Keene J (1997), 'Drug Misuse in Prison: Views from Inside', *The Howard Journal*, 36 (1), 28–41.
Kelly, L. (1990), 'Journeying in Reverse' in Gelsthorpe L and Morris A (eds.), *Feminist Perspectives in Criminology*, Milton Keynes and Philadelphia: The Open University Press.
Kelly L and Radford J (1987), 'The Problem of Men' in Scraton P (ed.), *Law, Order and the Authoritarian State*, Milton Keynes and Philadelphia: The Open University Press.
Kennedy D et al. (1991), 'Drug Misuse and Sharing of Needles in Scottish Prisons', *British Medical Journal*, 302, 1507.
Kennedy H (1992), *Eve was Framed: Women and British Justice*, London: Vintage.
King L (1986), 'Drug Education for Youth', *Police Review* (February 21), 400–402.
King R and McDermott K (1990), 'My Geranium is Subversive', *British Journal of Sociology*, 41(4), 445–471.
Kinnell H (1989), 'Prostitutes, Their Clients and Risks of HIV Infection in Birmingham', Department of Public Health Medicine, Occasional Paper.
Klare H (1973), *People in Prison*, Pitman Publishing.
Kohn M (1992), *Dope Girls: The Birth of the British Drug Underground*, London: Lawrence and Wishart.
Lee M and Mainwaring S (1995), 'No Big Deal: Court–Ordered Treatment in Practice', *Druglink* (January/February), 14–15.
Lidz C and Walker A (1980), *Heroin, Deviance and Morality*, Beverly Hills and London: Sage Publications.
Lloyd A (1995), *Doubly Deviant, Doubly Damned*, Penguin Books.

158 Women, Drugs and Custody

Lombroso C and Ferrero W (1895), *The Female Offender* cited in F Heidensohn (1996), *Women and Crime*, The Open University Press and Macmillan.
Lonsdale K *et al.* (1943), *Some Account of Life in Holloway Prison for Women*, The Medical Reform Council.
Loucks N (1997), 'Research into HMI Cornton Vale', *Scottish Prison Service Occasional Papers*, No 1/98.
McAlley B (1988), 'Immigration Control and the Prison Service', *Prison Service Journal*, 69 (January).
McConville M, Sanders A and Leng R (1991), *The Case for the Prosecution*, London and New York: Routledge.
McDermott P (1992), 'Representations of Drug Users' in O'Hare P *et al.* (eds.), *The Reduction of Drug-Related Harm*, London and New York: Routledge.
McDonald M (ed.) (1994), *Gender, Drink and Drugs*, Oxford: Berg; USA: Providence.
McGrath R (1993), 'Health Education and Authority', in V Harwood *et al.*, *Pleasure Principles*, London: Lawrence and Wishart.
MacGregor S (ed.) (1989), *Drugs and British Society*, London and New York: Routledge.
MacGregor S and Ettorre B (1987), 'From Treatment to Rehabilitation' in Dorn N and South N (eds.), *A Land Fit for Heroin?*, Macmillan Education.
McKeganey N *et al.* (1992), 'Female Streetworking Prostitution and HIV Infection in Glasgow', *British Medical Journal*, 305 (October 3).
McMahon M (1990), '"Net-Widening": Vagaries in the Use of a Concept', *British Journal of Criminology*, 30(2), 121–149.
McNay L (1992), *Foucault and Feminism*, Cambridge: Polity Press.
Maden A, Swinton M and Gunn J (1990), 'Women in Prison and Use of Illicit Drugs before Arrest', *British Medical Journal*, 301 (November 17), 1133.
Maden, A, Swinton M and Gunn J (1991), 'Drug Dependence in Prisoners', *British Medical Journal*, 302 (April 13), 880.
Maden A, Swinton M and Gunn J (1992), 'A Survey of Pre-Arrest Drug Use in Sentenced Prisoners', *British Journal of Addiction*, 87, 27–33.
Maden A, Swinton M and Gunn J (1994), 'A Criminological and Psychiatric Survey of Women Serving a Prison Sentence', *British Journal of Criminology*, 34(2), 172–191.
Malloch M (1999), 'Drug Use, Prison and the Social Construction of Femininity', *Women's Studies International Forum*, (22) 3, 349–358.
Mandaraka-Sheppard A (1986), *The Dynamics of Aggression in Women's Prisons in England*, Gower.
Marks J (1994), 'Deaths from Methadone and Heroin', *The Lancet*, 343 (April 16), 976.
Mason D, Birmingham L and Grubin D (1997), 'Substance Use in Remand Prisoners', *British Medical Journal*, 315, 18–20.
Mathieson T (1990), *Prison on Trial*, London: Sage Publications. Second English edition (2000), Winchester: Waterside Press.
Matthews R and Young J (eds.) (1986), *Confronting Crime*, London: Sage Publications.
Matza D (1969), *Becoming Deviant*, London: Prentice Hall.
Melossi D (1990), *The State of Social Control*, Polity Press.
Melossi D and Pavarini M (1981), *The Prison and The Factory*, London and Basingstoke: The Macmillan Press.
Mies M (1993), 'Towards a Methodology for Feminist Research' in Hammersley M (ed.), *Social Research*, London: Sage Publications in association with The Open University.
Mills H, Bennetto J and Williams R (1994), 'The Real Cost to Society: Special Report, *The Independent* (March 2).
Ministerial Drugs Task Force (1994), *Drugs in Scotland: Meeting The Challenge*, Scottish Office Home and Health Department.
Moore R (1977), 'Becoming A Sociologist in Seabrook' in Bell C and Newby H (eds.), *Doing Sociological Research*, New York: The Free Press.
Morgan R (1992), 'Not Just Prisons', *Policy Studies*, 13(2).
Morris L (1994), *Dangerous Classes*, London and New York: Routledge.
Morrissey E (1986), 'Power and Control Through Discourse', *Contemporary Crises*, 10, 157–179.
Mort F (1987), *Dangerous Sexualities*, London and New York: Routledge and Kegan Paul.
Mott J (1986), 'Estimating the Prevalence of Drug Misuse', *Research Bulletin*, 21, 57–60.
Mott J (1989) 'Reducing Heroin Related Crime', *Research Bulletin*, 26, 30–33.
Mott J (1991), 'Crime and Heroin Use' in Whynes D and Bean P, *Policing and Prescribing*, Macmillan.
Muncie J and Sparks R (eds.) (1991), *Imprisonment: European Perspectives*, New York: Harvester Wheatsheaf in association with The Open University.
NACRO (1991), 'Offences Against Discipline in Women's Prisons', *Briefing Paper* No. 8.
NACRO (1992), *A Fresh Start for Women Prisoners*, London: NACRO.
Nadelmann E (1988), 'The Case for Legalisation', *The Public Interest*, 92, 3–31.
Naffine N (1987), *Female Crime*, Sydney: Allen and Unwin.
National Addiction Centre (1998), *An Analysis of the Mandatory Drug Testing Programme*, NAC.

Bibliography 159

Newcombe R (1995), 'Methadone Mortality', Conference paper, John Moores University, Liverpool (June).
Newman F (1993), 'The Drug Traffic in the Punjab', *The Police Journal* (January), 76–86.
Nielsen J (ed.) (1990), *Feminist Research Methods*, San Francisco and London: Westview Press.
Oakley A (1981), 'Interviewing Women: a Contradiction in Terms' in Roberts H (ed.), *Doing Feminist Research*, London and New York: Routledge.
Oakley A (1992), *Social Support and Motherhood*, Oxford, UK and Cambridge, USA: Blackwell.
O'Connor J (1993), 'Out of Control', *Police Review* (15 January), 18–20.
O' Hare P et al. (1992), *The Reduction of Drug-Related Harm*, London and New York: Routledge.
Padel U (1987), 'Double Dealing in Drugs', *Prison Report* 1.
Parker H (1986), 'Heroin: A Solution with a Problem', *Social Studies Review* 2(2), 2–6.
Parker H, Bakx K and Newcombe R (1988), *Living With Heroin*, MiltonKeynes and Philadelphia: The Open University Press.
Parry A (1995), 'UK Methadone Programmes: A Public Health Disaster?', Conference paper, John Moores University, Liverpool (June).
Patton C (1985), *Sex and Germs*, Boston: South End Press.
Pearce J (1992), 'Alcohol and Drug Problems in Prisons' in Plant M, Ritson B and Robertson R (eds.), *Alcohol and Drugs: The Scottish Experience*, Edinburgh: Edinburgh University Press.
Pearson G (1987), *The New Heroin Users*, Basil Blackwell.
Pearson G (1992), 'Drugs and Criminal Justice' in O'Hare P et al., *The Reduction of Drug-Related Harm*, London and New York: Routledge.
Perry L (1991), *Women and Drug Use: An Unfeminine Dependency*, ISDD.
Pitch T (1995), *Limited Responsibilities*, London and New York: Routledge.
Plant M (1990) (ed.), *Aids, Drugs and Prostitution*, London and New York: Routledge.
Pollak O (1950), *The Criminality of Women*, New York: Barnes Perpetua.
Poovey M (1987), 'Scenes of an Indelicate Character' in Gallagher C and Laqueur T (eds.), *The Making of the Modern Body*, Berkeley: University of California Press.
Porter R (1987), *A Social History of Madness*, London: Weidenfeld and Nicolson.
Poulantzas N (1975), *Political Power and Social Classes*, London: Verso.
Poulantzas N (1978), *State, Power, Socialism*, London: NLB.
Power K et al. (1991), 'Sexual Behaviour in Scottish Prisons', *British Medical Journal*, 302 (June 22), 1507–1508.
Power K et al. (1992a), 'Comparison of Sexual Behaviour and Risk of HIV Transmission of Scottish Inmates', *Aids Care*, 4, 53–67.
Power K et al. (1992b), 'Intravenous Drug Use and HIV Transmission Amongst Inmates in Scottish Prisons', *British Journal of Addiction*, 87, 35–45.
Pringle R and Watson S (1992), 'Women's Interests and the Post-Structuralist State' in Barrett M and Phillips A (eds.), *Destabilizing Theory*, Polity Press.
Quinn P (1989), *The Law and Penology of Prison Discipline* (Unpublished work), University of Durham.
Quinney R (1980), *Class, State, Crime*, Second edition, New York: Longman.
Rabinow P (1984) (ed.), *The Foucault Reader*, New York: Pantheon Books.
Rafter N (1990), *Partial Justice*, Second edition, New Brunswick and London: Transaction Publishers.
Ramazanoglu C (1989), *Feminism and the Contradictions of Oppression*, London and New York: Routledge.
Ramazanoglu C (1992), 'On Feminist Methodology', *Sociology* 26(2), 207–212.
Ransome P (1992), *Antonio Gramsci: A New Introduction*, New York: Harvester Wheatsheaf.
Reading H (1976), *A Dictionary of the Social Sciences*, London: Routledge and Kegan Paul.
Regan C (1995), 'Judges, Drug Policy and Drug Sentencing', *Justicia* (June).
Reinharz S (1993), 'The Principles of Feminist Research' in Kramarae C and Spender D (eds.), *The Knowledge Explosion*, New York: Harvester Wheatsheaf.
Rose J (1980), *Elizabeth Fry: A Biography*, London and Basingstoke: Macmillan.
Rose N (1985), *The Psychological Complex*, London: Routledge and Kegan Paul.
Ross M et al. (1994), 'Prison: Shield from Threat or Threat to Survival?', *British Medical Journal*, 308, 1092–1095.
Rotman E (1990), 'Beyond Punishment' in Duff A and Garland D (eds.) (1994), *A Reader On Punishment*, Oxford University Press.
Ruggiero V and Vass A (1992), 'Heroin Use and the Formal Economy', *British Journal of Criminology*, 32(3), 273–291.
Ruggiero V, Ryan M and Sim J (1995), *Western European Penal Systems*, London: Sage Publications.
Rushton R (1993), 'Changing the Drug Culture at Holloway Prison', Paper presented to Prison Service Psychology Conference (October).
Ryan W (1976), *Blaming the Victim*, Vintage Books.
Scott J (1990), *Domination and the Arts of Resistance*, New Haven and London: Yale University Press.
Scottish Affairs Committee (1994), *Drug Abuse in Scotland*, First Report London: HMSO.
Scottish Office (1999), *Tackling Drugs in Scotland: Action in Partnership*, The Stationery Office.

160 Women, Drugs and Custody

Scottish Prison Service (1994), *Guidance on the Management of Prisoners Who Misuse Drugs*, SPS.
Scraton P (ed.) (1987), *Law, Order and the Authoritarian State*, MiltonKeynes and Philadelphia: The Open University Press.
Scraton P (1990), 'Scientific Knowledge or Masculine Discourses?' in Gelsthorpe L and Morris A (eds.), *Feminist Perspectives in Criminology*, Milton Keynes and Philadelphia: The Open University Press.
Scraton P (1991), 'Recent Development in Criminology: A Critical Overview', Paper for the Centre for Studies in Crime and Social Justice.
Scraton P and Chadwick K (1986), *In the Arms of the Law*, Pluto Press.
Scraton P and Chadwick K (1987), 'Speaking Ill of the Dead' in Scraton P (ed.), *Law, Order and the Authoritarian State*, Milton Keynes and Philadelphia: The Open University Press.
Scraton P, Sim J and Skidmore P (1991), *Prisons Under Protest*, Milton Keynes and Philadelphia: The Open University Press.
Scull A (1983), 'Community Corrections' in Garland D and Young P (eds.), *The Power to Punish*, London: Heinemann Educational Books; New Jersey: Humanities Press.
Scull A (1984), *Decarceration*, Second edition, Polity Press.
Seear N and Player E (1986), *Women in the Penal System*, Howard League for Penal Reform.
Sen S (1992), 'Heroin Trafficking in the Golden Crescent', *Police Journal* (July), 251–256.
Shaffir W and Stebbins R (eds.) (1991), *Experiencing Fieldwork*, Newbury Park: Sage Publications.
Shaw M (1975), *Marxism and Social Science*, Pluto.
Shaw M (1992), 'Issues of Power and Control', *British Journal of Criminology*, 32(4), 438–453.
Shewan D, Gemmell M and Davies J (1994), *Drug Use and Scottish Prisons*, SPS Occasional Papers, No.6.
Showalter E (1985), *The Female Malady*, Virago.
Sim J (1987), 'Working for the Clampdown' in Scraton P (ed.), *Law, Order and the Authoritarian State*, Milton Keynes and Philadelphia: The Open University Press.
Sim J (1990), *Medical Power in Prisons*, Milton Keynes and Philadelphia: The Open University Press.
Sim J (1991), 'When You Ain't Got Nothing You Got Nothin' to Lose', Paper presented at the British Criminology Conference, University of York.
Sim J (1993), 'Reforming the Penal Wasteland?' in Player E and Jenkins M (eds.), *Prisons After Woolf*, London: Routledge.
Sim J (1994), 'Prison Medicine and Social Justice', Perrie Lecture.
Singer L (1993), *Erotic Welfare*, New York and London: Routledge.
Sivanandan A (1990), *Communities of Resistance*, Verso.
Skeggs B (1992), 'Confessions of a Feminist Researcher', *Sociology Review* (September), 14–18.
Smart B (1983), 'On Discipline and Regulation' in Garland D and Young P (eds.), *The Power to Punish*, London: Heinemann Educational Books; New Jersey: Humanities Press.
Smart C (1976), *Women, Crime and Criminology*, London: Routledge & Kegan Paul.
Smart C (1989), *Feminism and the Power of Law*, London and New York: Routledge.
Smart C (1992), *Regulating Womanhood*, London and New York: Routledge.
Smith D (1990), *Texts, Facts and Femininity*, London and New York: Routledge.
Smith K (1989), *Inside Time*, London: Harrap.
Social Work Services and Prisons Inspectorates for Scotland (1998), *Women Offenders: A Safer Way*, The Scottish Office.
Sontag S (1989), *Aids and its Metaphors*, Penguin Books.
South N (1994), 'Drugs: Control, Crime and Criminological Studies' in Maguire M *et al.* (eds.), *The Oxford Handbook of Criminological Research*, Oxford: Clarendon Press.
Sparks R (1994), 'Can Prisons be Legitimate?', *British Journal of Criminology*, 34, 14–28.
Sparks J and Bottoms A (1995), 'Legitimacy and Order in Prisons', *British Journal of Sociology*, 46(1), 45–62.
Stanley L (ed.) (1990), *Feminist Praxis*, London and New York: Routledge.
Stanley L and Wise S (1990), 'Method, Methodology and Epistemology in Feminist Research Processes' in Stanley L (ed.), *Feminist Praxis*, London and New York: Routledge.
Stanley L and Wise S (1993), *Breaking Out Again*, London and New York: Routledge.
Stimson G (1987), 'The War On Heroin' in South N and Dorn N (eds.), *A Land Fit for Heroin*, Macmillan Education.
Stimson G *et al.* (1988), 'Syringe Exchange Schemes for Drug Users in England and Scotland', *British Medical Journal*, 296 (18 June), 1717–1719.
Strausbaugh J and Blaise D (eds.) (1991), *The Drug User*, New York: Blast Books; Baltimore: Dolphin–Moon Press.
Sumner C (1990a), 'Foucault, Gender and the Censure of Deviance' in Gelsthorpe L and Morris A (eds.), *Feminist Perspectives in Criminology*, Milton Keynes and Philadelphia: The Open University Press.
Sumner C (ed.) (1990b), *Censure, Politics and Criminal Justice*, Milton Keynes and Philadelphia: The Open University Press.
Swann R and James P (1998), 'The Effect of the Prison Environment Upon Inmate Drug Taking Behaviour', *The Howard Journal*, (37) 3, 252–265.
Synnott A (1992), 'Tomb, Temple, Machine and Self', *British Journal of Sociology* 43(1), 79–110.

Bibliography 161

Szasz T (1974), *Ceremonial Chemistry: The Ritual Persecution of Drugs, Addicts and Pushers*, London: Routledge and Kegan Paul.
Taylor A (1993), *Women Drug Users*, Oxford: Clarendon Press.
Taylor A *et al.* (1995), 'Outbreak of HIV Infection in a Scottish Prison', *British Medical Journal*, 310 (February 4), 289–292.
Taylor I (1991), 'Big Crime: The International Drug Trade', *Social Studies Review*, 6(3), 121–124.
Taylor S (1991), 'Leaving the Field' in Shaffir W and Stebbins R (eds.), *Experiencing Fieldwork*, Newbury Park: Sage Publications.
Thomas W (1923), *The Unadjusted Girl*, Boston: Little Brown.
Tippell S (1989), 'Drug Users and the Prison System' in MacGregor S (ed.), *Drugs and British Society*, London and New York: Routledge.
Trace M (1990), 'HIV and Drugs in British Prisons', *Druglink* (January/February), 12–15.
Turnbull P (1992), 'Drug Use: Injecting Before, During and After Imprisonment', Conference paper, West Midlands Regional Health Authority (June 17).
Turnbull P, Dolan K and Stimson G (1991), *Prisons, HIV and AIDS*, AVERT.
Turnbull P, Dolan K and Stimson G (1992) 'Prevalence of HIV Infection among Ex-Prisoners in England' *British Medical Journal* 304 (11 January), 90–91.
Turnbull P, Dolan K and Stimson G (1993) 'HIV Testing and the Care and Treatment of HIV Positive People in English Prisons', *AIDS Care*, 5(2), 199–206.
Turnbull P, Stimson G and Stillwell G (1994), *Drug Use in Prison*, AVERT.
Turner B (1984), *The Body and Society*, Basil Blackwell.
Turner B (1992), *Regulating Bodies*, London and New York: Routledge.
Usher J (1989), *The Psychology of the Female Body*, London and New York: Routledge.
Van Maanen L (1991), 'Playing Back the Tape' in Shaffir W and Stebbins R (eds.), (1991), *Experiencing Fieldwork*, Newbury Park: Sage Publications.
Walby S (1992), 'Post-Post Modernism?' in Barrett M and Phillips A (eds.), *Destabilizing Theory*, Polity Press.
Walker N (1980), *Punishment, Danger and Stigma*, Oxford: Basil Blackwell.
Walkowitz J (1980), *Prostitution and Victorian Society*, Cambridge: Cambridge University Press.
Walkowitz J (1982), 'Male Vice and Feminist Virtue', *History Workshop*, 13, 79–93.
Wallis R (1977), 'The Moral Career of a Research Project' in Bell C and Newby H (eds.), *Doing Sociological Research*, New York: The Free Press.
Weber M (1930), *The Protestant Ethic and the Spirit of Capitalism*, London: Unwin University Books.
Weeks J (1989), 'Aids, Altruism and the New Right' in Carter E and Watney S (eds.), *Taking Liberties*, Serpent's Tail.
Weil A (1972), *The Natural Mind*, Penguin Books.
Wever L (1992), 'Drug Policy Changes in Europe and the USA', *International Journal on Drug Policy* 3(4), 176–181.
White P, Park I and Butler P (1999), *Prison Population Briefing: England and Wales*, London: Home Office.
Whynes D (1991), 'Drug Problems: Drug Policies' in Whynes D and Bean P (1991), *Policing and Prescribing*, Macmillan.
Wilson J and Leasure R (1991), 'Cruel and Unusual Punishment', *Nurse Practitioner*, 16(2), 36–39.
Woolf, Lord Justice and Tumin, Sir Stephen (1991), *Prison Disturbances*, London: HMSO.
Worrall A (1990), *Offending Women*, London and New York: Routledge.
Wright M (1982), *Making Good*, Burnett Books.
Wright Mills C (1956), *The Power Elite*, London: Oxford University Press.
Wright Mills C (1959), *The Sociological Imagination*, Penguin Books.
Young J (1971), 'The Role of the Police as Amplifiers of Deviance' in Cohen S (ed.), *Images of Deviance*, Penguin Books.
Young M (1994) 'The Police, Gender and the Culture of Drug Use and Addiction' in McDonald M (ed.), *Gender, Drink and Drugs*, Oxford: Berg; USA: Providence.
Young P (1983), 'Sociology, the State and Penal Relations' in Garland D and Young P (eds.), *The Power to Punish*, London: Heinemann Educational Books; New Jersey: Humanities Press.
Zackon F (1988), *Heroin: The Street Narcotic*, London: Burke Publishing Company.
Zakuta L (1968), 'We Distinguish—They Discriminate' in Becker H *et al.*, *Institutions and the Person*, Chicago: Aldine Publishing Company.
Zedner L (1991), *Women, Crime and Custody in Victorian England*, Oxford: Clarendon Press.

Index

abstinence 51 64 80
access, for research 16
addicts/addiction 49 50 53 54 57 66 113 125 143
Advisory Council on the Misuse of Drugs 51 64 *et seq.* 102 120 142
AIDS etc. 48 51 58 60 64 67 72 102 103 120
AIDS and Drug Misuse 51 52 102
Scotland 105
alcoholism 93 99 119
alienation 57
alternatives to custody 52 66 73 120 151
amphetamines 108 121
anti-social behaviour 53
anxiety 94
asylum(s) 28 29 30
'attention seeking' 96
benzodiazapenes 77 79 94 95 103
black women in prison 33
bifurcation 43 *et seq.* 50 *et seq.*
biology 30 58 149
bleach 107
body 60
    search 116 and see *strip search*
boredom 104 110
Brain Committee 50
Bullying 103 114 115
cannabis 44 46 89 103 105 *et seq.* 108
CARATS 70 72 151
Caring for Drug Users 66 70 76 121
CCTV (Scotland) 71
cell wrecking 31
children 56 57 66
class 47 148
cleanliness 27 28
clinical judgement/management 66 77 80 142
clitoridectomy 31
cocaine/crack 44 46 89 108 114
'cold turkey' 95 99 111
community aspects 48 64 72 120 132 141 151
community safety 52 53
condoms 65 72
confidentiality 67 77 78 101 128 144
contagion 27 29 48
Contagious Diseases Acts 1864, 1866, 1869 30
continuity/lack of 138

control
    drugs, control of women prisoners by 91
    drugs, of 53 and see *Dangerous Drugs Acts etc.*
    issues 113 144
    prison, in 101 144 and see *security*
    sexual control 31
    social/women 21 30 35 40 53 58 60 147
convulsions 94 95
Cookham Wood, HMP 102
co-ordinated approach 76
Cornton Vale, HM Institution 7 34 107 108
counselling 9 66 67 69 105 119 128 144
Counselling, Assessment, Referral, Advice and Throughcare Services, see *CARATS*
crime
    control/prevention 51 52 53
    drug related/links 53 54 (cost of) 69 148
    fear of 69
    prevention 64
criminalisation 11 46 49 58 120
critical theory 14
cultural/sub-cultural aspects 43 44 52 54 55 59 103
custody 61
    care and treatment in 64 (and see *treatment*)
    and see *prison*
Dangerous Drugs Acts (various) 44 *et seq.* 49 54
dangerousness 46 48 54 59 72 149
day release 108
dealing 54 55
    and see *supply*
deaths
    custody, in 7 34
    drug related 52 67
debauchery 37
decay 45
degradation 117
demand 66 68 69 70 103 107 119 149
dependence 56
depression 94 97
'deviant'
    drugs 43
    women 11 29 31 37 43 55 56 147

detoxification
 programmes/services/arrangements 67 68 77 90 122 142 146
Diazepam 94
disciplinary offences 36
discipline issues 113 134
disclosure 76 *et seq.* 84 *et seq.* 142 *et seq.*
 prisoners' views 88 *et seq.*
 prison officers' views 85 *et seq.*
discretion see *clinical judgement etc.*
discrimination 24
disease model 11 27 45 47 48 49 58 148
'disruptive' behaviour 96
disturbed women 58
dogs 107 116 137
domesticity 28 29 31
drug detection/finds 71 103
drug free units 124 137
Drug Misusers and the Criminal Justice System, Part 1 66
Drug Misuse in Prison 69 124
drugs
 classification etc. 44
 currency as 102 104
 'giving up' 129
 prostitution 58
 and see *'deviant' drugs, drug use, prison*
Drugs Czar 45
Drug Strategy Co-ordination Group/Co-ordinator (SPS) 70
drug tests 69
 random 69
 and see *MDT*
drug trafficking 33 46
drug treatment and testing order 120
drug use
 coping mechanism, as 57
 drunkenness and 119 and see *alchoholism*
 funding habit 33
 growth in Scotland 103
 identification of users 65 66 77
 illegal/illicit 102 *et seq.* (and see *drug users in prison*)
 impact of prison on 106 *et seq.*
 problems associated with 102 *et seq.*
 social construction of 43 *et seq.*
drug users in prisons etc. 76 *et seq.*
 attitudes 126 *et seq.*
 disclosure 8 9
 fear of identification as 9
 groups 129 *et seq.*

hard drugs 76
hospital wing 77 80 87
illegal/illicit use 8 76 *et seq.* 102 *et seq.* 143
increase in 8
management of 113
numbers 88 89 90
perceptions of 126 *et seq.*
resources for 8 9 12
targeting 70 107 116 144
use of illegal drugs in prison 9 103
Durham, HMP 80
economy of prison 54 103 116
 and see *drugs (currency), illegal etc. drugs in prison*
ecstasy 46
education 9 46 48 67 70 119 *et seq.*
 prison, in 64 67 102
eligibility/less-eligibility 12 71 91 141 147
emotion 19 30 39 57
empowerment 58
England and Wales 7
 number of women in prison 33
Eugenisist theories 31
Expenditure Committee (1978) 102
family 59
Faulk, Dr Malcolm 7 107
femininity/unfemininity 43 55
feminist aspects 10 11 14 23
fighting 115
fitting 94 96
Fresh Start for Women Prisoners etc. (NACRO) 34
Fry, Elizabeth 28 31
funding of drug agencies 72
gender 21 28 40 47 55
Glenochil, HMP 67 68 105
Guidance on the Management of Prisoners Who Use Drugs (Scotland) 68
guidelines, see *policies/guidance*
gynaecological
 examination/explanations 30 31
hallucination 94 99
hallucinogens 108
hard drugs 76 107 121
 MDT, and 107
harm
 harmful behaviour 102
 minimisation (in prison) 64
 reduction 51 66
health/health risks/healthcare 37 46 60 69 71
Healthcare Service for Prisoners 71

164 Women, Drugs and Custody

hedonism 56 61
Hepatitis B 105
heroin 46 52 54 55 108
HIV see *AIDs etc.*
HM Inspectorates
    (England and Scotland) 7 33 34 105 106 122
holistic approach 67
Holloway, HMP 34 39 106 123
home leave 108 115
Home Office 16 102
    Addicts Index 66 77
Hornsby, Phil 103
hospital wing 80 142
Howard, John 28
Howard League 119 146
hygiene 27 28 30 32
hypnotic drugs 38
hysteria 31
ideology 10 12 21 25 32 40 43 55 61 140 *et seq.*
illegal drugs in prison 8 76 *et seq.* 102 *et seq.* 143
images, see *stereotyping etc.*
imprisonment
    opportunity presented by 8
    incentives and earned privileges 70
indignity 116
informants 69
injecting 67 68 79 100 102 103 104 *et seq.* 112 *et seq.* 121
    Scotland 105
    and see *sterilisation tablets*
insanity 31
    and see *asylum(s)*
Institute for the Study of Drug Dependency (ISDD) 54
institutionalisation 73 100
    approaches 43
    discourses, of 100
    ideology 13 40
intelligence analysts 71
inter-disciplinary approaches, see *multi-agency aspects*
intimidation 114 116
    and see *bullying*
isolation, sense of 97
labelling 47, and see *stereotyping etc.*
Ladies Association 28
Largactil 39 81 90 94 143
legitimate/illegitimate use of drugs 8 52 76 *et seq.* 102 *et seq.* 143
less-eligibility, see *eligibility*
linguistic aspects 35

Loucks, Nancy 107 108
LSD 103
maintenance 67 68
    discouraged 100
maintaining order, see *control, discipline, security*
male dominated arrangements 34
mandatory drug testing, see *MDT*
marginalisation 11 47 57 61 71 118 148
MDT 69 70 71 107 116 123 145 148 151
media 7
medical officers 66 68 76 77 107
medication 78 87 89 90 136 143
medicine/medical model/aspects 27 31 37 *et seq.* 46 56 59 76 90 142 *et seq.* 150
mental aspects 39
    and see *asylums, insanity*
methadone 64 66 67 68 79 80 94 106
methodology 10 14
Millbank Penitentiary 29
Milton bleach 107 113
Ministerial Drugs Task Force (Scotland) 67
Misuse of Drugs Act 1971 50 54 64
Mogadon 80 *et seq.*
monitoring 35 36 101
moral
    aspects 27 28 30 45 49 53 55 142
    judgements by medics/staff 78 99 143
    'moral panic' 45 59
motherhood 56
multi-agency/disciplinary aspects 67 76 119 122 144
multi-dimensional approaches 70
needle exchange/sharing/supply 51 64 67 68 72 102 104 107 121
negative images 11
neurotic women 58
observation 87 96 101
    and see *surveillance*
official discourse 13
opium/opiates 44 76 *et seq.* 89 90 108 143
overdose 56 103
pain 73
Parole Release Scheme 120
paternalism 28
patriarchy 21 30 55 57
'personal influence' 30
Physeptone 90

policing 46
policies/guidance 8 64 67 (Scotland) 76 (Scotland) 126 142 144
prescribing/prescription 46 49 51 65 90 91 101 143 150
  accumulating prescribed drugs 111
  control of 70
  over-prescribing 38 91
  refusal to prescribe 38
  substitute 67 78 and see *methadone*
preventative policies/strategies 60 107 *et seq.*
  and see *crime prevention*
prison
  development of 25
  identification of drug users 65 66
  officer roll and training 126
  and see *medical officers*
Prison Officers Association (POA) 102 103
  Survey (1984) 102
Prison Service 64
  Corporate Plan
  Medical Directorate 66 76 80 126
  policy 76
prostitution 60 119 133
psychological aspects/support 67 94 101
psychotic episodes 94
psychotropic drugs 38 39
punishment 11 25 40 43 48 52 72 147 150
  guilt, and 56
  prison, in 69 70 76 98 99
  treatment, versus 71 73
  racist aspects 44 47
  and see *black women in prison*
randon urine tests 123
  and see *MDT*
reception process 77 80
reform 12
Reform Movement 27 28 147
refuges 29
regime aspects 10 21 28 29 30 31 33 *et seq.* 76 118 134 140 *et seq.*
  Regimes for Women 34 36
regulation 21 43
rehabilitation 9 12 31 34 43 48 53 71 73 74 111 122 134 145 149
  residential 68
relationships
  staff/prisoners 32 98 107 117 128
release 122 138
remand prisoners 109

remission 29
  loss of 37
Report of Drug Dependants etc. 120
resources 12 72 119 *et seq.* 126 *et seq.* 129 144
Risley, HMP 7
robbery 114
Rolleston Committee 49
safer practices, directing prisoners towards 80
Scotland 7
  drug related deaths 52
  number of women in prison 33
  policy guidance 67 76
Scottish Affairs Committee 67 68 142
Scottish Office 67
secure wing 87
searches 69 71 107 116
  cells 107
  forcible by prisoners 7 114
security 67 68 69 71 87 101 103 113 134 144
self-disclosure 66
self-mutilation 31 40
sex
  safe sex 59
  sexuality 30 31 59
sleeplessness 93 97
sleeping pills 102
'sick' 46 53 57 58
silent cells 37
situational context 45
smuggling 68 103
  food into prison 103
  visits, during 108 122
social
  construction 55 147
  'problem' 56 64 67 76
stereotyping constructs/images 11 13 40 55 85 98 141 147 148
sterilisation tablets 68
  and see *injecting, needle etc. exchange, syringes*
stigma 87 104
stress 57 110
suicide, threats of 40
Styal, HMP/ YOI 7 107 122
strategy 67 69
strip
  cells/conditions 37 79 96 97 101 103
  search 37 103 107 116
suffragettes 31 32
suicide, thoughts of 97

supply 12 43 66 69 107
support 9 69 70 101 122 145
surveillance 35 36 43 46 66 87 107 123
increased 70 71 78
syringes 64 104
and see *injecting, needle etc. exchange, syringes*
Tackling Drugs in Prison 70
Tackling Drugs in Scotland: Action in Partnership 71
Tackling Drugs to Build a Better Britain 52 53 70
Tackling Drugs Together 8 51 59 69
testing, see under *drugs*
therapuetic aspects 9 35 48 53 71 111 119 *et seq.* 133 140 *et seq.*
throughcare 70 76
tolerance/non-tolerance 68 69 104
tranquillisers 78 89 102 108
treatment 43 47 52 58 64 67 69 70 102 119 *et seq.*
facilities/lack of 66
probation order, under 120
punishment versus 71 *et seq.*
treatability/untreatability 10 11 48 54 72 100 144 145

trust /distrust 67 77 137
turkey, see *'cold turkey'*
vaginal examination 30 31
Valium 80 *et seq.*
venereal disease 32
vice 29 30
violence 36 46 113 117
visits/visitors 68 69 103 (drugs in food) 107 108 116

withdrawal 37 50 61 65 76 *et seq.* 90 93 142 *et seq.*
psychological support 94
Wolds, HMP The 123
women
'deviant' 11 29 55 56
drugs, and 55
imprisonment of 21 28 *et seq.* 33 (numbers)
Women and the Penal System 102
Women in Prison 7 34
Women Offenders—A Safer Way 7 34
women's prisons 7
Woolf report 34 72
work 98 134

'From the very heart of government'

Crime, State and Citizen

A FIELD FULL OF FOLK

David Faulkner

Crime, State and Citizen is a wide-ranging and authoritative appraisal of the factors which sustain the fragile balance between effective government and individual rights and obligations in modern-day Britain. It is about: how Britain governs itself today; the rights and responsibilities of its citizens; the character of its public services and their relations with the state.

Writing at a time when issues such as the Rule of Law, human rights and cultural and human diversity are to the fore, David Faulkner examines these and similar questions by focusing on the politics and policies, and the professional standards and day-to-day arrangements, for dealing with crime and criminal justice - thereby touching on issues of immediate concern to Parliament, the Government, the courts, the other criminal justice services and individuals. He also explores the underlying aims and principles of justice, social inclusion, public safety (including matters of concern to victims of crime), accountability and legitimacy before suggesting how they should be applied and inescapable conflicts resolved.

David Faulkner is Senior Research Associate at the University of Oxford Centre for Criminological Research, where he writes about and teaches criminal justice, penology and government and public administration. He is Chair of the Howard League. In *Crime, State and Citizen* he also draws on a 30-year career working at the very heart of government – which included periods as Deputy Secretary of State in charge of the Criminal, Research and Statistical Departments of the Home Office, as Private Secretary to one Home Secretary (James Callaghan) and senior adviser to eight others, and in the Cabinet Office. Over a period of 20 years he held direct responsibility for key aspects of the workings of criminal justice in the United Kingdom. He has contributed chapters to other works and published countless articles, but this is his first book. 360 pages. ISBN 1 872 870 98 8. £22.50 plus £2 p&p

With a Foreword by Lord Windlesham

01962 855567
www.watersidepress.co.uk

Another key text from
Waterside Press

Also from Waterside Press

Drug Treatment In Prison

An Evaluation of the RApt Treatment Programme

Carol Martin and Elaine Player

The findings of a two-year study into the effectiveness of the RApt Drug Treatment Programme which enables male prisoners with self-confessed problems of substance misuse to lead a drug and alcohol-free life in prison and in the community after release.

The report also assesses whether completion of the programme is associated with a reduction in the likelihood of reconviction post-release.

A unique and highly significant collection of information and data.

ISBN 1 872 870 26 0 £10 plus £2 p&p (Europe £3; Rest of the World £6).

Drugs, Trafficking and Criminal Policy
Penny Green

A survey of drugs policy which focuses on drug trafficking and drug traffickers and in which the author demonstrates that the vast majority of people arrested, convicted and imprisoned for such offences are low-level players - causing her to argue that scapegoating has played a central role in shaping drugs policy, as part of a drugs war. It is people at the bottom end of the drugs trade who give substance to its ideology and reality. Penny Green argues that unless drug control moves beyond its present emphasis - beyond criminal policy and law enforcement into the arena of geo-political analysis, international poverty, Third World debt and domestic welfare - there can be no resolution to the human tragedy which this phoney war on drugs has come to embody.

1998 ISBN 1 872 870 33 3. £18 plus £2 p&p (Europe £3; Rest of the World £6).

Please send to WATERSIDE PRESS • DOMUM ROAD • WINCHESTER • SO23 9NN
Full catalogue /Orders ☎ Tel/fax 01962 855567 E-mail: watersidepress@compuserve.com
Or visit www.watersidepress.co.uk for latest legal news and where you can order via the Internet in secure conditions – and view over 100 Waterside publications on criminal justice and penal affairs.

Women, Drugs and Custody – From the publishers of *The Prisons Handbook*